One Writer's Garden

EUDORA WELTY'S HOME PLACE

Susan Haltom and Jane Roy Brown

Photographs by Langdon Clay

UNIVERSITY PRESS OF MISSISSIPPI   JACKSON

www.upress.state.ms.us

The development and publication of this book were made possible
through the generous support of Evelyn and Michael Jefcoat.

The University Press of Mississippi is a member of the Association of American University Presses.
All color photographs are by Langdon Clay unless otherwise credited.
Excerpts from *Eudora Welty: A Biography* copyright © 2005 by Suzanne Marrs,
reprinted by permission of Houghton Mifflin Harcourt Publishing Company.

Library of Congress Cataloging-in-Publication Data
Haltom, Susan.
  One writer's garden : Eudora Welty's home place / Susan Haltom and Jane Roy Brown ; photo-
graphs by Langdon Clay.
    p. cm.
  Includes bibliographical references and index.
  ISBN 978-1-61703-119-9 (cloth : alk. paper) — ISBN 978-1-61703-120-5 (ebook) 1. Welty, Eudora,
1909–2001—Homes and haunts—Mississippi—Jackson. 2. Authors, American—Homes and
haunts—Mississippi—Jackson. 3. Gardens, American—Mississippi—Jackson—History—20th
century. 4. Gardens—Conservation and restoration—Mississippi—Jackson. I. Brown, Jane Roy. II.
Clay, Langdon, 1949– III. Title.
  SB466.U65J334 2011
  712'.609760904—dc22   2011000701

British Library Cataloging-in-Publication Data available

For Evelyn and Michael Jefcoat

Literary gardeners of Laurel, Mississippi,
patrons of American gardens,
supporters of garden restoration,
and champions of this book

"'Etoile de Hollande' is the standard of excellence."
—from *How to Grow Roses*,
J. Horace McFarland and Robert Pyle, 1937

CONTENTS

Preface ix
Acknowledgments xv
Introduction xix

PART I—Spring, 1920s

Chapter 1. Chestina 3

Chapter 2. "When the Garden Was New" 21

Chapter 3. Progressive Women and Their Roots in Gardening 43

PART II—Summer, 1930s

Chapter 4. "Meeting Death Head On" 63

Chapter 5. "Medicine to the Soul" 75

Chapter 6. "You and Me, Here" 101

PART III—Fall, 1940s

Chapter 7. "The Subject Was Flowers" 123

Chapter 8. "In the Fall I Will Miss You Then" 139

Chapter 9. "Flowers Are Older Than War" 155

Chapter 10. "Happy and Thankful for Much" 173

PART IV—Winter, Postwar and Beyond

Chapter 11.   "Not a Garden Any More, but What It Is"   195

Epilogue: "It Would Be Like Hell to Do"   213

Appendices

Appendix I: Decades of Welty Plants   235

Appendix II: Original Plant List for 1119 Pinehurst Street   237

Appendix III: Annuals in the Welty Garden   238

Appendix IV: Roses in the Welty Garden   240

Appendix V: Partial List of Plants in Welty Prose   242

Appendix VI: Resources for Historic Landscape Preservation   244

Appendix VII: Discussion Questions for Book Clubs   245

Notes 246
Bibliography 256
Credits 261
Index 262

PREFACE

This is the story of a garden at the home of a famous American writer, Eudora Welty (1909–2001). Although the house and garden at 1119 Pinehurst Street in Jackson, Mississippi, are attractive, comfortable, and well made, it is fair to say that neither is noteworthy solely as a work of art. Their association with Welty is the main reason they have been preserved for the public.

Henry Mitchell, a fellow southerner and long-running garden columnist at the *Washington Post*, once described Welty as "Rose-Gardener, Realist, Storyteller of the South." Welty is best known as a short-story writer, and the garden has a compelling story of its own. Welty gave Susan Haltom permission to tell it after their conversations, in the last decade of Welty's life, revealed a nearly lost garden. Without her blessing, this book would not exist. By this time, most of the other people who would have remembered the garden had passed away. Very few of Welty's younger friends and acquaintances knew that she had been a gardener, and literary scholars had no reason to associate the abundant references to flowers and gardens in Welty's writing with her own hands-on experience. On the few occasions when Welty spoke about the garden in her later years, she usually called it "my mother's garden."

Eudora's mother, Chestina Welty (1883–1966) did, in fact, create and design the garden, in 1925. Her choices of plants, colors, forms, and architectural details displayed her personal preferences. They also echoed the prevailing style and taste of her generation and her social circumstances, which in turn mirrored wider trends and influences: Progressive-era optimism, a rising middle class, prosperity, new technology, women's clubs, garden clubs, streetcar suburbs, civic beautification, conservation, plant introductions, and garden writing. Most of the middle-class gardens of this period, extraordinary or not, have been lost to changing taste and ownership. The scarcity of similar gardens makes this small garden even more significant.

Several years after Welty died, in 2001, her papers became available to the public. Her correspondence revealed more of the garden's story, including its profound role in this writer's life. By the time she reached her late twenties, Welty had become a capable gardener in her own right. Tutored by her mother, she had grown both knowledgeable and passionate about flowers, and, like her mother, she had established a private, deep connection to the garden and to gardening.

Eudora stated that it was in the garden that "I first set myself at a storyteller's remove." References to flowers and gardens colored her fiction and correspondence. Their consistent presence in her writing reveals that the flower garden lay at the heart of her inner world, sustaining her creativity and stirring her imagination. Gardening also linked her to a network of fellow laborers in the soil—yardmen (as garden workers are called in the South), garden-club women, nurserymen, and the farm women who sold plants through the *Mississippi Market Bulletin* to which Welty subscribed. Welty, a lifelong student of humankind, never lost her fascination with her fellow gardeners, a colorful and opinionated tribe whose members cropped up in her writing. In her last decade, Welty told Haltom, "I think that people have lost the working garden. We used to get down on our hands and knees. The absolute contact between the hand and the earth, the intimacy of it, that is the instinct of a gardener."

"One place comprehended can make us understand other places better," Welty observed in her essay "Place in Fiction." We hope that this book inspires readers to explore what their gardens mean to them and how they serve as touchstones that awaken a connection to the larger natural world.

WRITING PROCESS

Curious friends and colleagues have asked how we have collaborated: Who did what? How did we combine our individual contributions—research, structuring, writing—to arrive at a unified voice and point of view? The fact that one of us lives in Mississippi and the other in Massachusetts only fans the curiosity.

Our collaborative process was mysterious, even to us. The only clear individual role is the one Haltom played before the book began. After talking with Eudora Welty about the garden, Haltom excavated the garden's remains, conducted extensive site research, wrote a cultural landscape report to guide the garden's rehabilitation, and oversaw the rehabilitation, investing hundreds of hours of physical labor. We agreed that she needed to tell this story in the first person, under her by-line, in the epilogue. For several years Haltom also had been giving lectures on the garden, drawing connections to the imagery of flowers and gardens in Welty's writing. Haltom met Brown in 2004, when Brown, a landscape historian and journalist, visited the garden to report on it for *The Christian Science Monitor*.

Geographical distance called on us to divide the labor pragmatically, based on personal preferences, skills, and proximity to resources. Haltom proved adept at combing the archives, but also at big-picture thinking and organizing ideas and material. Brown explored societal movements and national landscape-design trends in relation to this garden. As we wrote the drafts, identifiable contributions melded into a truly coauthored manuscript. We revised the first and final versions side by side at our laptops, from the first paragraph to the last endnote.

SOURCES

The garden's rehabilitation over a period of ten years yielded more clues about its physical structure. When the important primary documents—Chestina's garden records and Eudora's photographs and correspondence—became available at the Mississippi Department of Archives and History, they verified what Welty had told Haltom in their discussions about the garden. We chose to focus on Welty's correspondence with her agent and friend, Diarmuid Russell, and with John Robinson, with whom she was in a romantic relationship between the late 1930s and the early 1950s. Both men were sophisticated gardeners. Welty's letters to both were generally rich in accounts of the garden she tended with her mother, and, depending on which man she was writing to, they also revealed different experiences and insights. More sources exist, and we hope other scholars will explore them.

The scholarship of Suzanne Marrs, Eudora Welty's biographer, has provided the essential chronology for, and much of the interpretation of, the selected biographical events in this book. We have confined our story to Welty's life in relation to the garden, which means that her rich relationships with her brothers, her father, and most of her many friends are not chronicled in these pages. Welty's life spanned most of the twentieth century, and only between 1925 and 1945—the rehabilitated garden's official period of significance—was the garden intact as Chestina Welty envisioned it. During the next ten years Eudora began to be less and less involved, and Chestina's health declined.

We have also drawn on interviews with Eudora Welty and analysis of her writing by scholars Peggy Prenshaw, Patti Carr Black, and Michael Kreyling, whose book *Author and Agent* was another well-thumbed resource. For the history of middle-class home gardens and landscapes we have probed books and magazines featuring American garden writers of the 1920s through the 1940s: Louisa Yeomans (Mrs. Francis) King, Helena Rutherfurd Ely, Julia Lester Dillon, Elizabeth Lawrence, and others. Among the more recent books documenting this period we have repeatedly returned to Christopher Grampp's *From Yard to Garden: The Domestication of America's Home Grounds*; Virginia Tuttle Clayton's *The Once and Future Gardener: Garden Writing from the Golden Age of Magazines, 1900–1940*; and Denise Wiles Adams's *Restoring American Gardens: An Encyclopedia of Heirloom Ornamental Plants, 1640–1940*.

Where we have drawn relationships between garden imagery from Welty's correspondence and her fiction, we have tried to limit the discussion to the garden on the ground. While we do assert connections between her garden experience and the images and scenes that appear in her fiction, we deliberately stop short of interpreting those images and scenes from the standpoint of literary analysis. Because our main focus is on this garden and the two women who tended it, we explored the local and regional context first, and if trends exhibited in the garden extended beyond that, we touched upon them.

The book's structure parallels the seasons of central Mississippi. The creation and emergence of the garden, its pinnacle, its downturn, and finally, its decline, suggested the progression of seasonal change.

Readers of this book need not have read Eudora Welty's stories or novels to appreciate this story. That said, we sincerely hope that at least some readers will be inspired to acquaint or reacquaint themselves with the work of this author, whose extraordinary art and humanity have influenced two generations of American writers.

Susan Haltom and *Jane Roy Brown*

ACKNOWLEDGMENTS

We welcome the opportunity to recognize those whose generosity, of so many kinds, helped us along the way. This book originated in 1997, when Eudora Welty granted Susan permission to tell the story of her mother's garden so that others could learn from it. The enthusiastic support of her nieces, Mary Alice Welty White and Elizabeth Welty Thompson, who shared their memories as well as important family documents, allowed the fulfillment of that vision.

This long project required our husbands, Jim Haltom and Bill Regan, to make do with less attention and companionship, even as we called on them for more support. They understood our passion for this project and urged us to follow it. All women should be so fortunate. Susan also deeply appreciates the support of her sons, David, John, and Scott, who are proud of their mom.

In the close circle surrounding Eudora Welty, her friends Patti Carr Black and Hunter Cole were especially generous with guidance and encouragement. Suzanne Marrs, another close friend of Eudora's, wrote the biography and other scholarly sourcebooks that have informed our understanding of Welty's life and literature. She also willingly gave her time to answer our specific questions about Welty's life and work.

Elbert Hilliard and Hank Holmes, past and present directors, respectively, of the Mississippi Department of Archives and History, introduced Susan to Eudora Welty, opening a new chapter in Susan's life and work. The staff of the Mississippi State Archives and Records Services Division staff, whose knowledge of their material is matched by their initiative and enthusiasm, made the research for this book a true pleasure. In particular, Forrest Galey in Special Collections shared her expert guidance with unwavering grace and generosity. Alanna Patrick, Betty Uzman, Anne Webster, Clinton Bagley, Grady Howell, Joyce Dixon-Lawson, Judy Hocking, Ellen McWilliams, and Susan Johnson, among others, also helped cheerfully.

Many scholars graciously shared their knowledge and research: Jenny Rose Carey at the Ambler Arboretum of Temple University; Elizabeth Lawrence biographer Emily Herring Wilson; Welty literary scholars Peggy Prenshaw, Michael Kreyling, and Pearl Amelia McHaney; and landscape historian Judith B. Tankard. Experts on American gardens and horticulture with whom we consulted include Anne Myers, Garden Club of America historian; Kathleen Stradar and Hebe Splane, co-vice chairmen of the GCA Garden History and Design Committee; David Ellis and Katy Moss Warner of the American Horticultural Society; and Joyce Connolly at the Smithsonian Archives of American Gardens. Lois Cleland, Eudora Welty's cousin, and Michael Robinson, a nephew of Eudora's friend John Robinson, lent memories and documents.

Photographer Langdon Clay responded to a phone call from out of the blue and quickly signed on as principal photographer, throwing himself wholeheartedly into the project. He perched backward at the top of a ladder, stalked a snowstorm at six a.m., and sweated through the midday humidity of August to capture the Welty garden in every season.

Leila Salisbury, director of the University Press of Mississippi, championed this project from the beginning, and Anne Stascavage, Valerie Jones, and Shane Gong smoothed the learning curve for these first-time authors. Art director John Langston brought a collaborative spirit and heartfelt enthusiasm to the design and layout. Our copy editor, Carol Cox, expertly polished the manuscript.

Family members and friends offered encouragement, refuge, and support, especially Jeanine Gay, Elizabeth and Paul Fugate, Bob and Glenn Haltom, Marit Cranmer and Efrem Marder, Ruah Donnelly, Emmy Meador, Julianne Summerford, Julie Wilson, Sherrie Semmes, Karin Giger, Nancy Bierman, and Robin Kibler.

Without those who restored and supported the Welty garden, this particular book would not exist. Evelyn and Michael Jefcoat immediately recognized the garden's significance, and, with one sentence, became the garden's primary benefactors: "Whatever you need, consider it done."

Their trust, passion, and inspiration were as important to the garden's restoration as the funding they continue to provide. They were equally magnanimous in supporting this book.

Bill Noble at the Garden Conservancy and the members and directors of the Southern Garden History Society guided the historical research for the garden restoration. Lucy Allen, director of the Museums Division of MDAH, and her predecessor, Donna Dye, were among the restoration's original supporters. The Eudora Welty Foundation makes improvements possible by enfolding the garden into its goals.

In her role as the founding director of the Eudora Welty House, Mary Alice White continually supported the garden restoration and delighted in it. She responded to the prospect of this book with immediate enthusiasm, and she and the staff of the Welty House placed all of their resources at our disposal. Karen Redhead, who succeeded White as director of the Welty House, has taken a personal interest in the garden, allowing it to progress and prosper. Staff members Amy Steadman, Meemie Jackson, Elaine Blaine, and Katie Hamm, along with the docents and other volunteers, embraced the story of the garden and brought it to thousands of Welty House visitors. Robert Parker Adams, the Welty House restoration architect, and his late wife, Mary, lent their love of history and literature to the garden's preservation.

Many people share the maintenance of the Welty garden. The Cereus Weeders do more than weed—they plant, they harvest seeds, they laugh, and they support both the garden and one another. For this they deserve unbounded thanks: Lee Threadgill, Elaine Chatham, Emily Dunbar-Smith, Mary Ann Fontaine, Leigh Eley, Darian Gibson, and Marsha Cannon. The Welty rose garden owes its resurrection entirely to the "Rose Ladies" of the Garden Club of Jackson: Paula James, Libby Kendall, June Stone, and Miriam Ethridge. Master gardener Cecile Wardlaw, who works with historic gardens, helps by providing horticultural expertise.

Landscape contractors Eric Hays and Andrew Bell show special sensitivity and care in working with this historic environment. Ed Nichols of Elephant Valley Nursery searches for specific heirloom plants and grows them especially for this garden. Nurserymen and horticulturists were generous with both expertise and plant donations. These included Mike Shoup of the Antique Rose Emporium, Scott Kunst of Old House Gardens, heirloom daffodil specialist Celia Jones, the American Daffodil Society, Bobby Green of Green Nurseries, George and Carole Sawada of Overlook Nursery, Tom Johnson and the American Camellia Society, and other camellia experts who helped identify and preserve the varieties in the Welty garden. Jon L. Peter at the New York Botanical Garden assisted in identifying heirloom daylilies. Anner Whitehead of the Historic Iris Preservation Society reintroduced heirloom tall bearded irises. Bill Welch of Texas A&M and Greg Grant of Stephen F. Austin University provided generous horticultural guidance. Jonelle Primos shared valuable books from the Mynelle Gardens library. The Garden Club of Jackson, a member club of the Garden Club of America, continues to give both time and monetary support.

Thank you all.

INTRODUCTION

"It was my mother who emotionally and imaginatively supported me in my wish to become a writer," Eudora Welty wrote in her memoir, *One Writer's Beginnings* (1984).[1] Her mother, Chestina Andrews Welty, also created the garden at the family home at 1119 Pinehurst Street, in Jackson, Mississippi. For both reasons, it seems fitting to start this story with an event that marked Chestina's early life and demonstrated her character. For today's readers it may be hard to imagine the courage she had to summon within herself as a young girl alone on a difficult journey from her native West Virginia to a strange city. But in her day other women and girls were called upon to shoulder similar responsibilities with equally high stakes. Life and geography demanded it.

When she married a young Ohio man, Christian Welty, Chestina brought these qualities and other experiences to her new life in Mississippi, where the Weltys were regarded as unconventional—starting with Chestina's and Eudora's unusual names. "Eudora," derived from the Greek "honored gift" or "gift without limits," was passed down from Chestina's mother, Eudora (Carden) Andrews, who in turn had been named for her mother, Eudora Ayres. As for the "unlikely name Chestina," Eudora once told her *New Yorker* editor, William Maxwell, "where it came from I have often wondered. A corruption of Justina? A feminine form of Chester? When the Chesapeake and Ohio RR began using the name 'Chessie'"— the name Chestina's family called her—"and applied it to a cat [as an emblem], my mother wasn't too well pleased about the cat part."[2]

Suzanne Marrs observes in *Eudora Welty: A Biography* that Chestina "was more direct and outspoken than most Jackson women, and she encouraged her daughter to excel in academics when other Jackson ladies might speak dismissively of girls who were 'brains.'"[3] All accounts of Chestina attest that she, too, had an able, insatiable, independent mind. As a girl, she read the collected works of Charles Dickens. She later worked her way through teachers' college, where she was fascinated by botany.

By Eudora's own account, both parents showered her with books when she was a young child and enjoyed reading them aloud to her. Her parents brought their own preferences to the literary realm. Not surprisingly, her insurance executive father was wary of fiction because "it was forever inferior to fact," Eudora recalled in *One Writer's Beginnings*, adding that Chestina, on the other hand, "sank as a hedonist into novels." Chestina's passion for learning gave her an appreciation for all books, however. During World War II, she heard a report that some Chinese scholars, "fearing their great library would be destroyed, took the books up in their hands and put them onto their backs and carried all of them, on foot, over long mountain paths, away to safety. Mother cried for them, and for their books."[4]

Chestina Welty was proud of her daughter's profession and of her success. After all, Eudora Welty's writing earned her what most writers dream about but few attain: popularity with readers and literary acclaim, both during her lifetime. Among the honors she reaped were the Pulitzer Prize, the French Legion of Honor, the Howells Medal for Fiction, the Gold Medal for Fiction, the National Book Foundation Medal for Distinguished Contribution to American Letters, the National Medal of Freedom, and the National Medal of the Arts. She also was the first living writer to be published in the Library of America series.

Welty, a cosmopolitan woman, traveled widely and remained active in the intellectual and literary circles of the twentieth century. She lived and wrote in the comfortable house her parents built, surrounded by her mother's garden. It is only fitting that she would draw some of her greatest inspiration from her daily experiences and memories of her home place.

PART I

Spring—1920s

CHAPTER ONE

Chestina

My mother thought it was ill-becoming to brag about your courage; the nearest she came was to say, "Yes, I expect I was pretty venturesome."[1]

—Eudora Welty, *One Writer's Beginnings*

In March 1899, in the mountains of central West Virginia, a thirty-seven-year-old man named Ned Andrews writhed under a pile of quilts in a rural farmhouse, pain knifing through his abdomen. The farm was near Maysel, a pin dot on the map forty miles east of Charleston, the state capital.[2] Ned's wife and six children clustered around the bed, helpless to relieve his suffering, knowing that if he did not get to a doctor, he would die. The roads down the steep mountainsides were impassable, so a neighbor offered to ferry the afflicted man on a raft across the Elk River to a spot where he could flag the train to Baltimore. But Ned was too ill to travel alone—someone must flag the train, ride with him to Baltimore, get him to a hospital. Who would go? Chestina, called Chessie, the eldest child and only girl, was fifteen and plucky. The next-eldest was only thirteen. Their mother, Eudora Carden Andrews, had to stay and take care of the younger boys.

More than eighty years after these events, Eudora Welty described the journey that forever marked her mother's life: "Leaving her mother and the five little brothers at home, Chessie went with him. Her father lay on the raft, on which a fire had been lit to warm him, Chessie beside him. The neighbor managed to pole the raft through the icy river and eventu-

Chestina Carden Andrews in the early 1900s, probably taken by her suitor, Christian W. Welty, in West Virginia. © Eudora Welty LLC; Eudora Welty Collection, Mississippi Department of Archives and History (MDAH).

ally across it to a railroad. They flagged the train...."[3] Chessie managed to get them to Baltimore and navigate the unfamiliar city to Johns Hopkins hospital, where Ned underwent an emergency appendectomy. But it was too late; he died on the operating table, and Chessie rode the train home alone, her father's body in a coffin.

Ned Andrews had been a lawyer, but not a wealthy one, and his death left his family in straitened circumstances. At seventeen, Chessie "piled up her hair and went out to teach in a one-room school,"[4] scraping enough money together to take summer teacher-training courses at Marshall College (now Marshall University) in Huntington. She later told Eudora, her only daughter and eldest child, that botany had been her favorite subject.

Why Chestina was drawn to the science of plants is hard to say. Among the Welty family photographs is a picture of her as a young woman, wearing a wide-brimmed hat and propped on an elbow in front of a rosebush and other flowers. It was likely taken in West Virginia, but no one is left to identify its exact location. The Andrews farmhouse is gone, and with it any evidence of whether Chestina's mother kept such a flower garden in her country dooryard. When Eudora was a child, she noticed "the bright flowers in the yards of my aunts" during the Weltys' visits to West Virginia. "The Victorian flower beds were like bites in the grass," she said, revealing the source of an image she used in her story "Old Mr. Marblehall."[5]

The picture of Chestina in the garden was probably taken by her fiancé, Christian Webb Welty. The two met in 1903, when Chestina was still a schoolteacher. Christian was "a young man from Ohio, who had come to work that summer in the office of a lumber company in the vicinity," Eudora wrote. Like Chestina, he had grown up on a farm, taught school, and lost a parent in childhood. (His mother died when he was seven, leaving him a note of one sentence: "My dearest Webbie: I want you to be a good boy and to meet me in heaven. Your loving Mother.") Engaging and bright, Christian dreamed of starting a new life in a different part of the country. Like many other young people of the Progressive era, his eyes were fixed on the future, with its promise of technological marvels that would lead to unprecedented human progress, a vision that he never abandoned.[6]

In October 1904, the two young people were married in the Andrews farmhouse. The newlyweds boarded a train for the World's Fair (formally known as the Louisiana Purchase Centennial Exposition) in St. Louis, then the nation's fourth-largest city.[7] Chestina's leaving home this time— by choice—may have been even more difficult than her wrenching trip to Baltimore years earlier. Hers was a close-knit clan, and one of her young

Chestina Andrews and Christian Welty courting in West Virginia, 1903. © Eudora Welty LLC; Eudora Welty Collection, MDAH.

brothers was so distraught at her departure that he flung himself on the ground; but Chestina was leaving behind more than the people she loved—she was leaving the mountains.

The mountains of West Virginia formed the bedrock of Chestina's being, or so her daughter believed. "I think when my mother came to Jackson she brought West Virginia with her," Welty mused in *One Writer's Beginnings*. When, as a child, Eudora visited her mother's family and their mountaintop farm, she once took a frightening spill down a slope, and it left a lasting impression: "It seems likely to me now that the very element in my character that took possession of me there on top of the mountain, the fierce independence that was suddenly mine, to remain inside me no matter how it scared me when I tumbled, was an inheritance. Indeed, it was my chief inheritance from my mother, who was braver. . . . It is what we shared, it made the strongest bond between us and the strongest tension. To grow up is to fight for it, to grow old is to lose it after having possessed it. For her, too, it was most deeply connected to the mountains."[8]

Chestina probably needed every scrap of this fierce independence to carry her through the painful parting. By Eudora's account, her father was not a person to dwell upon the past, and, as their train rolled west, he may have comforted his wife by extolling their dreams of a shared future in a place that they had chosen together. When they arrived in St. Louis, the World's Fair, with its myriad exhibits celebrating progress in all its material forms, would have affirmed Christian's forward-leaning outlook. X-ray machines, electric typewriters, and wireless telegraphs were among the new inventions on display, along with the latest innovations in plumbing, heating, and lighting for the home. Transportation was one of the fair's major themes, and displays showcased the latest modes of travel—one, called "Under and Over the Sea" depicted a trip to Paris "by submarine boat and return by airship." The Palace of Transportation devoted 80,000 square feet to 140 foreign and domestic automobiles, which were just coming into mass production.[9]

Christian, a keen amateur photographer, must have found his way to the latest photography equipment on view in the Palace of Liberal Arts.

With her botanical interest, Chestina probably strolled through the Palace of Horticulture, where a conservatory exhibited hundreds of floral specimens. Perhaps even more inspiring were the fifty acres of elaborate outdoor gardens on Agriculture Hill, which showcased roses, bulbs, perennials, and aquatic plants available from the nursery owners in attendance. Other outdoor exhibits employed floral spectacle as a communication medium: A "Great Floral Clock" featured a dial a hundred feet wide with numerals fifteen feet high, made entirely of flowers; and a five-acre "Living Map" of the United States was composed of 819 plant species representing the agricultural products of each state.[10]

To modern eyes, such gaudy flourishes—along with the fair's ornate neoclassical architecture and prolific Victorian carpet bedding—may seem out of step with the fair's futuristic theme. Was Chestina puzzled or enthralled by the curlicued parterres and giant water lilies? Was Christian, who in a few years would oversee the construction of the first skyscraper in his adopted city, disappointed not to see examples of highrise buildings? Perhaps, being country people, the newlyweds equated

the fair's sheer spectacle with a dazzling modernity. The answers to these questions may always remain a mystery. Regardless, what they did next was entirely modern: they boarded another train to make their home in a city that was new to them both—Jackson, Mississippi.[11]

Eudora once asked her mother, "Why here?" Chestina replied that during the couple's engagement, Christian had researched up-and-coming places that would be affordable on a starting salary. Having narrowed the locations to Jackson, Mississippi, and the Thousand Islands region in upstate New York, he left the final choice to Chestina. She chose Jackson. The fact that her parents both came from Virginia families who had migrated to West Virginia in the Civil War era may have led Chestina to prefer the location in the South. She had a "very strong Virginia tie which she kept all her life," Eudora said.[12]

Chestina's relatives in the mountains, however, did not equate Virginia with Mississippi. They warned her "against catching malaria and dying immediately," Eudora once recounted. "They couldn't imagine anybody coming down into the swamps—that's what they thought of the place. So my parents were quite brave to come down and very adventurous—romantic, really—to start out that way."[13]

Long after both parents were dead, Eudora discovered some old photographs in their house. They showed scenes of faraway places—Niagara Falls among them—some with an earnest young Christian Welty posing in the foreground. With the photos were a railway timetable with ferry schedules and excursion prices from Halifax, Nova Scotia, for the month of August 1903, the year before her parents married. "I could see now that of course he would have gone up there to look over the Thousand Islands and ridden the train or sailed the St. Lawrence from Ontario to Halifax, stopping off for Niagara Falls, and taken those pictures to bring her, before he'd say a rash thing like that to Chessie Andrews," Eudora wrote. "And here they were, the [pictures of the] choice she didn't take. . . ."[14]

Christian Welty seemed particularly inspired by the physical forces of change—technology, science, and industry—that were reshaping the

Souvenir booklet from the Thousand Islands resort region straddling New York and Canada, bought by Christian Welty in the summer before he married. His fiancée, Chestina Andrews, chose Jackson, Mississippi, over the Thousand Islands as the place to settle. Courtesy of Eudora Welty LLC.

world at a previously unimaginable pace, and in the Jackson of 1904, progress was unfolding in these tangible forms. "My father . . . saw [progress] as an almost visible thing," Eudora once told an interviewer. "He thought that Jackson could be made progressive, and they could make the most of things even without money. . . ."[15]

After being burned by General Sherman during the Civil War, Jackson had become a vast construction site as it underwent a transformation from town to city, riding a boom in the region's cotton and lumber industries. The air rang with hammer blows, the clang of pickaxes, and the whine of enormous saw blades. Work crews laid down sewer lines and paved streets and sidewalks for the new neighborhoods that doubled the city's area during the century's first decade, when the Weltys joined an influx of nearly 13,500 new residents. Jackson boasted electric street-lights and an electric trolley line. New enterprises—gristmills, fertilizer factories, a foundry—sprang up as the state's railroad network expanded, opening new markets.[16]

Baby Eudora Welty, summer 1909. © Eudora Welty LLC.

In 1906, Christian found a job with Lamar Life Insurance, a new company in a growing industry.[17] That same year, Chestina gave birth to their first child, a son, named after his father; but the boy died at fifteen months of age. At Lamar Life, Christian rose rapidly through the ranks, and in 1908 the couple was able to build a two-story house on North Congress Street. Eudora was born here in 1909, followed by her brothers—Edward, in 1912, and Walter, in 1915.[18] Family photos taken by Christian Welty show an interior decorated with fashionable Mission-style furniture and a porch with a climbing rose, but the shallow front yard was an unadorned strip of lawn bordering the sidewalk. (Later photographs show the slender trunks of young street trees there.) Out back, at least in these early years, a Jersey cow and chickens shared a fenced yard.

It was common in the early 1900s for people to keep farm animals in urban backyards, not to mention laundry lines, trash bins, coal or firewood, cisterns, and privies—all the utilities that cities eventually provided.[19] Given the advanced state of Jackson's services, the Weltys' backyard probably didn't contain a privy, but it may have held a washtub and a clothesline, trash bins, and perhaps a small kitchen garden, especially during World War I, when Americans were urged to plant victory gardens.

Over time, as the Weltys grew more affluent and the city's amenities improved, the rustic working yard may have been gradually transformed into a hospitable place of grass and trees where the children could play. Decades later, Eudora recalled a sycamore tree there, on which she and her brothers had nailed boards to reach its wide-spreading branches.[20]

Eudora in the backyard at North Congress Street, where Chestina kept a cow and chickens, as was customary at the time, even in cities. Eudora Welty LLC; Eudora Welty Collection, MDAH.

The Welty children at their grandfather Jefferson Welty's farm near Logan, Ohio, c. 1917. Canna and cosmos grow nearby. © Eudora Welty LLC; Eudora Welty Collection, MDAH.

What the backyard probably did not contain, at least in the years when Chestina was raising three young children, was an elaborate flower garden. She found ways to soften the home with plants, as Welty suggested in her short story "The Winds": "[The girl] hung from and circled in order the four round posts, warm and filled with weight, on the porch. Green arched ferns, like great exhalations, spread from the stands. The porch was deep and wide and painted white with a blue ceiling, and the swing, like three sides of a box, was white too under its long quiet chains. She ran and jumped, secure that the house was theirs and identical with them—the pale smooth house seeming not to yield to any happening, with the dreamlike arch of the roof over the entrance like the curve of their upper lips."[21]

In her works of nonfiction too, Welty captured the sensory experience of her childhood in Jackson, a place where the seasons produced not only flowers, but also roots and fruits, purveyed by a cast of colorful "familiars":

> The blackberry lady and the watermelon man, the scissors grinder, the monkey man whose organ you could hear coming from a block away, would all appear at their appointed time. The sassafras man at his appointed time (the first sign of spring) would take his place on the steps of the downtown Post Office, decorated like a general, belted and sashed and hung about with cartridges of orange sassafras root he'd cut in the woods and tied on. They were to make tea with to purify your blood. . . ."[22]

Chestina Welty with Eudora and brother Edward admiring roses at North Congress Street. Eudora Welty LLC; Eudora Welty Collection, MDAH.

The Jackson of Welty's childhood was a city in which trees were reliable companions, as well-respected as the city's human residents: "Trees you were growing up with remained where they were and you knew them in all their seasons. They just got bigger, still lining the same streets where you walked. In those days, the sidewalks yielded to the trees and went around them. The big tree in front of Carnegie Library at Mississippi and Congress took over the prime parking place in the street itself, and the curb ran out in a big half-moon to take care of the roots."[23]

In making room for the natural world, the city, though intimate in scale, created an expansive sense of place where young bodies and imaginations enjoyed unbounded exploration. "Our play was unscheduled, unorga-

nized and incessant—in our backyards, our friends' backyards, in the public parks and especially in the summertime, we ran free," Welty recalled.[24] And in "The Winds," she conjured a palpable sense of those pleasures: "She went along chewing nasturtium stems and sucking the honey from four-o'clock flowers, out for whatever figs and pomegranates came to hand. She floated a rose petal dry in her mouth, and sucked on the spirals of honeysuckle and the knobs of purple clover. She wore crowns. She added flower necklaces as the morning passed, then bracelets. . . ."[25]

Jackson's green spaces may have nourished Chestina Welty in similar ways during the fifteen years the family lived at 741 North Congress Street. After 1923, the Weltys would occupy two rented homes before moving into the house they eventually built at 1119 Pinehurst Street, but Eudora believed that her parents had probably envisioned the new house while they were still living in her childhood home: "I think all this time we were planning [the new house], which was then out in the country with rural free delivery, a gravel road and a little wooden bridge over that creek down there."[26] Likewise, Chestina's garden at Pinehurst Street probably grew for years in her thoughts and dreams before it found physical form.

Sept, 1925

What to Wear and Wield in the Garden

In early twentieth-century America, many horticultural books and articles written by and for women addressed proper attire for working in the garden—no small matter in the days when street-length skirts trailed in the mud, caught branches and brambles, and tangled with toes going up or down slopes. Writers also dispensed common-sense advice on stocking a tool shed. Helena Rutherfurd Ely, in *A Woman's Hardy Garden* (1903), wrote that a tool room (or a closet with shelves) should contain not only tools, but a scrapbook that logged blooming dates, fertilizer requirements, plant orders, and other details of garden maintentance, as well as a pair of old suede gloves and a sunbonnet ("pink ones are not so bad"). "Retired behind its friendly shelter, you are somewhat deaf to the world; and at the distant house, people may shout to you and bells be rung at you, and, if your occupation be engrossing, the excuse 'no one can hear through a sun-bonnet,' must be accepted."

That same year, another writer, Ida D. Bennett, observed that beginners typically buy too much equipment, "but later one realizes that it is brains and not tools that make the successful gardener. A hotbed, a cold-frame or two, a work-table in some convenient place, a trowel, wheel-barrow, spade, pitchfork, rake, hoe, a few yards of stout cord, a hatchet to sharpen stakes, a watering-pot, rubber sprinkler, rubber gloves, a good supply of pots and wire-netting, and a couple of good mole-traps cover the real necessities. Incidentals, such as wire-sieves, lath-screens, trellises, and the like, may be made as they are required."

On the subject of clothing, Bennett advised, "Easy, broad, solid shoes—not any old run-down pair—should be considered as essential as a spade, or rake, and skirts that clear the instep, and hang comfortably. . . . Skirts of blue denim, made Princess style, and ankle length, with comfortable shirt-waists—denim for cool days, calico for warm—make a thoroughly comfortable outfit."

Equally if not more important, women got advice about what *not* to wear, such as "a mannish costume, with manners and customs to correspond," mentioned by Elsie Varley in a popular magazine of 1911. It was not until the 1940s that women could shun skirts for more practical trousers or breeches without social repercussions.

Long skirts presented hazards in the garden. From *The Flower Garden: A Handbook of Practical Garden Lore*, Ida D. Bennett, 1903.

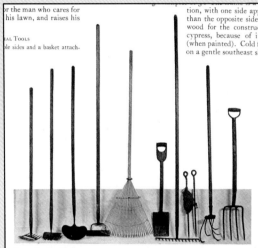

Large Garden Tools

The tools shown above from left to right are a small rake, a hoe, an edger, a scuffle-hoe, a bamboo rake, a spade, a large iron rake, iron stakes with garden line, a cultivator and a fork

Small Garden Tools

The tools shown above from left to right are pruning shears, a weeder, a hand fork, a child's rake, a basket for various purposes, a combination rake and spade, a trowel, a claw foot and a curved trowel with a forked point

[94]

From *The House Beautiful Gardening Manual*, 1926.

A sunbonnet for turn-of-the-century gardeners. From *The Flower Garden: A Handbook of Practical Garden Lore*, Ida D. Bennett, 1903.

CHAPTER TWO

"When the Garden Was New"

To get the best effects we should have complete pictures in our minds at least, but better on paper—before even one house is built. Thus the house and garden and landscape blend as one.

—Chestina Welty's garden journal, undated entry[1]

Miss [Eudora] Welty, the gifted daughter of Mr. and Mrs. C. W. Welty, entertained very delightfully on Wednesday afternoon at five: thirty o'clock when she had her friends of the 1925 Graduating Class of the Central High School, of which she is a member, to share her hospitality. The affair was in the nature of an al fresco party given on the lawn about the new home of the Weltys now being constructed on Pinehurst Place. . . . A massive punch bowl rested in a bed of flowers and was gracefully presided over by Miss Jane Percy Slack, and this bower proved very popular.

—Jackson newspaper clipping[2]

Wednesday afternoon Eudora had her garden party and it was just adorable. She had the lawn divided into "Babyland" and "The Land of the Grown Ups." If anybody acted dignified or grown up, he was put into the "Land of the Grown Ups" and could get out only by doing a stunt. Everybody else stayed in "Babyland" and played kid games. . . . [O]f course Eudora's party would be clever and original.

—From the scrapbook of Eudora Welty's classmate
Mary Doris Comley about their graduation from Jackson High School, 1925[3]

Chestina Andrews Welty and Christian Webb Welty / Jackson / 1927. Photograph by Eudora Welty. © Eudora Welty LLC.

"The house was on a slight hill (my mother never could see the hill) covered with its original forest pines, on a gravel road then a little out from town," Welty wrote in *One Writer's Beginnings*. Recalling the early years in the house on Pinehurst Street often prompted her to remember the tall pines that grew on the property before the house was built, and how her father had instructed the architect to preserve the seven mature specimens that enclosed the house site. Even before construction started, she recalled her mother saying that the house would be healthy, because of the "salubrious pines" growing there, adding, "She liked to use big words." Eudora took pleasure in recalling the pines' aroma— "They did smell good," she said,[4] as though she were at that moment catching a whiff of their clean, resinous scent—and she enjoyed telling people that at age twelve, she had celebrated the magical qualities of pine in a prize-winning jingle—her first published work.[5]

The lot that Christian and Chestina Welty chose for their new home was directly across the street from Belhaven College in Jackson's first suburb, made possible by the extension of a trolley line north of the city center. As in other American cities at the time, the development was carved out of farmland at the edge of the expanding city. Having owned an automobile for several years, the Weltys were not dependent on the trolley for transportation, but the line made the prospect of real-estate development a lucrative one, placing the benefits of a rural atmosphere—salubrious pines included—within convenient reach of the city. Jackson's first streetcar suburb came to be called Belhaven.[6]

In the early 1920s, Jackson's population had grown to twenty-two thousand, and a surge in prosperity after World War I triggered a building boom. Eclectic housing styles, reflecting romantic notions about the architecture of various European periods and countries, were fashionable throughout America in the mid-to-late 1920s. A typical assortment lined

Downtown Jackson, historic postcard, c. 1908. Courtesy of Steve Colston Photography.

Facing page:

1119 Pinehurst Street, Eudora sitting in window on left. "Nearly ready for occupancy, July, 1925." © Eudora Welty LLC; Eudora Welty Collection, MDAH.

Belhaven's streets, including the Weltys' two-story, Tudor Revival house, which featured that style's characteristic steep roofs, cross gables, massive chimneys, and tall, narrow windows. Decorative half-timbering accent-

ed walls of stucco and brick. A matching single-car garage sat slightly behind the house. Originally, Christian Welty wanted to route the driveway to the garage from another side street, but Chestina "wouldn't let him have it," Eudora said, presumably because that scheme would have split the backyard in half. (Perhaps Chestina shared the opinion of her contemporary, the garden writer Mrs. Francis [Louisa Yeomans] King, who wrote, "[T]he waste of good ground underneath the garage, and the fearful ugliness of its bulk on the small lot, are things which all gardeners of the better sort must feel and deplore.") So the driveway entered from Pine-hurst Street, along the property's western boundary. The

The driveway at the Welty house was located to allow maximum space for gardening. Photograph by Susan Haltom.

Easter 1925, 1119 Pinehurst Street. From the beginning, the Weltys used their yard for photographs on special occasions. © Eudora Welty LLC; Eudora Welty Collection, MDAH.

house lot, about three-quarters of an acre, was irregularly shaped, 140 feet wide at the street and a little more than twice as deep. The house and garage would occupy only a fraction of this area. Chestina would use all parts of the surrounding yard for her gardens.[7]

The architect of the Weltys' house, Wyatt C. Hedrick (1888–1964), was based in Fort Worth, Texas, and he had designed the Lamar Life headquarters building on Capitol Street, also completed in 1925.[8] The corporate tower was proclaimed to be "Jackson's first skyscraper." For Christian Welty—then a company vice president—who oversaw every phase of its design and construction, it likely symbolized his contribution to progress in his adopted city. During the building's construction, Christian made regular Sunday morning visits to the site, often with Chestina and the children in tow. The finished structure was "a delicately imposing Gothic building of white marble, thirteen stories high with a clock tower at the top. . . . The architect pleased him with his gargoyles: the stone decorations of the main entrance took the form of alligators, which related it . . . to Mississippi," Eudora later observed.[9]

Eudora, age sixteen or seventeen, atop the new Lamar Life building. © Eudora Welty LLC.

In comparison to this symbol of urban progress, the Welty residence was understated, nestled among the pines. The dark trunks formed a loose enclosure, and their branches shaded the roof and walls. Except for a water oak in the front—which Chestina also forbade to be cut—no deciduous trees stood near the building. In most ways, the house was conventional for its time and place. "The idea was proportion and nothing irregular in its design," Eudora noted. During her many years of living here, she had reason to appreciate the thought Hedrick had given to

Chestina Welty among the "salubrious pines" at Pinehurst Street, c. 1927. © Eudora Welty LLC.

April 1927. The Weltys' porch faced the side yard, a popular spot for family games and photographs. © Eudora Welty LLC.

cross-ventilation, provided by the building's spacious stairwell, intersecting upstairs hallways, and an attic fan. French doors and high ceilings also helped to draw the heat up and out. "[T]here was so much good shade around the house due to the trees, and there wasn't very much pavement around to reflect the heat. . . . So there was coolness everywhere. And space everywhere," Welty said.[10]

The house faced north, to Pinehurst Street. The front door and its matching copper screen were designed in the form of a Tudor arch, set in a projecting gable. The door opened into a foyer, a small space between the outside door and an inner door, designed to trap cold winter air. Although a common feature of northern houses, the foyer must have baffled southern natives. ("I always thought it was because my father was a Yankee and knew that double doors in the north of a house make it warmer," Eudora mused.) After the foyer, a spacious front hallway opened to rooms on either side and to the staircase. On the main floor a sitting room and the living room faced Pinehurst Street and took in views of the front yard and Belhaven College. The living room connected to the dining room, where three more windows overlooked the side yard. Eudora, who said many times how grateful she was that her parents surrounded their children with books, observed that "any room in our house, at any time of day, was there to read in." Certainly the large windows in all the rooms of the house provided ample light for reading. Two French doors in the living room opened to the porch.[11]

In a neighborhood where many houses featured front porches, the Weltys' porch faced their side yard. For most of their neighbors, the front porch was a social space overlooking a very public front yard. People would sit out on the porch and watch passers-by, perhaps beckoning a friend up to enjoy a glass of iced tea and conversation. The Weltys used their porch and the adjacent side yard—a grassy space enclosed by trees and shrubs, and later, floral borders—as more private spaces that functioned as outdoor rooms. Here the family enjoyed games—golf and croquet, as well as cards and word games. The side yard also was where the children and their parents posed for photographs to commemorate graduations,

View from the kitchen window at the Eudora Welty House, showing a restored rose arbor in the Upper Garden, 2010.

anniversaries, and other family occasions. Chestina, an accomplished bridge player, taught and played bridge on the porch. At the end of a hot summer day, family members would retreat to the coolness there.[12]

The kitchen was on the southeast corner. Below, the ground sloped downhill, and the house, built into the slope, stood almost a full story above ground, giving the kitchen windows a sweeping overview of the backyard. A breakfast room, a library, and a small bathroom rounded out the south end of the first floor.

Upstairs, Eudora's bedroom was the largest, extending from the front of the house to the back. It provided both northern and southern exposures, and the pines near the windows gave the room the feeling of a tree house. Across the hall was a smaller bedroom and, adjacent to it, an enclosed sleeping porch that overlooked the backyard.[13]

A GARDEN IN THE MAKING

"[T]he receiving line, it was *al fresco*, we stood out under the trees, and had a punch bowl. . . . [I]t was sort of my mother's idea, of something adventurous, and it was," Eudora recalled about her high-school graduation party in 1925. What made it adventurous, even a little eccentric for the times, was that Chestina Welty staged it on the lot of the new house, before construction was finished; it was as if she was so excited about the garden she envisioned that she could not wait to use it. "That was a happy time, when the garden was new," Eudora recalled near the end of her life.[14]

Very little evidence has surfaced to reveal what Chestina planted during the first two years. Family snapshots show glimpses of a privet hedge and a deodar cedar in the side yard, which do not appear in later photographs. From later documentation it is obvious that Chestina understood the difference between landscape-scale design and individual flower gardens. Gardeners of her generation traded Victorian "bites in the grass" flowerbeds for floral borders enclosed by hedges, fences, arbors, and trellises. Following the advice of such popular garden writers as Mrs. Francis King and Helena Rutherfurd Ely, gardeners of the early twentieth century also began planting shrubs around the foundation, which related house and garden.[15] Within the interconnected spaces, masses of perennials were organized in sweeps of color. This planting style was promoted by the English garden designer Gertrude Jekyll, who greatly influenced King and other American garden writers.[16]

Eudora at sixteen, in her high school yearbook photo, 1925. © Eudora Welty LLC.

Chestina and Christian Welty and friend enjoying the front yard, late 1920s. © Eudora Welty LLC.

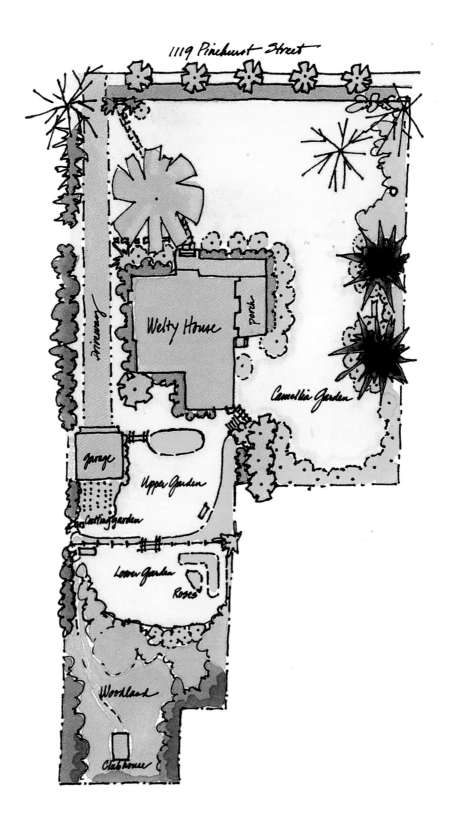

General garden layout, 1925–1935. This also reflects the arrangement of the restored garden today. Drawing by Susan Haltom, 2010.

1119 Pinehurst Street

Welty House

Porch

Camellia Garden

Garage

Upper Garden

Cutting Garden

Lower Garden

Roses

Woodland

Clubhouse

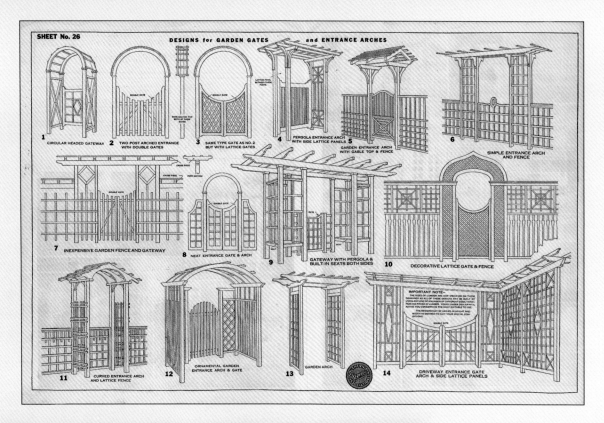

Gardeners of the 1920s could choose from a dazzling selection of garden architecture and furniture. From *Beautifying the Home Grounds*, booklet published by the Southern Pine Association of New Orleans, Louisiana, 1920s, collection of Susan Haltom.

Undated photo of the arbor dividing Chestina Welty's Upper Garden and Lower Garden, probably taken by Eudora. © Eudora Welty LLC.

A number of influences converged in American home gardens of the early twentieth century: the Arts and Crafts movement, the Colonial Revival movement, wild gardens, and English cottage gardens. Most of these were born of nostalgia for an imagined, simplified past—a reaction to the burgeoning industry that was fueling the growth of cities, attracting thousands of newly arrived immigrants, and overwhelming the social order.[17]

Women of Chestina's generation learned from garden writers that exposure to outdoor scenery would improve physical health and lift spirits in this period of mind-boggling change. "According to garden writings of the day," observes Virginia Tuttle Clayton, "an intimate, 'livable' garden designed with old-fashioned charm and simplicity, or one that incorporated native plants to emulate the effects of the natural American landscape, would provide the type of soothing domestic space that could counteract the ill effects of contemporary, frenzied life and restore unnerved Americans to a wholesome, contented state of mind and body. In fact any garden would serve—although simple, old-fashioned gardens and wild gardens, with their favored associations, might prove especially effective."[18]

Or, in the blunt words of one such writer, Helena Rutherfurd Ely, "If the rich and fashionable women of this country took more interest and spent more time in their gardens, and less in frivolity, fewer would suffer from nervous prostration, and the necessity for the multitude of sanitariums would be avoided."[19]

Chestina set about designing her home landscape with an equal measure of deliberation and passion. To define her three main outdoor rooms, she combined trees and shrubs with romantic arbors and trellis fencing, a popular, inexpensive alternative to costly walls and trees. ("The trellis . . . may be the loveliest garden accessory possible, or it may cheapen the garden beyond description . . . ," cautioned King, who advised beginning gardeners not to set up a trellis around the entire garden.[20]) The side yard was loosely outlined by flowering shrubs and shaded by pines and scattered oaks. Chestina planted an eastern red cedar on each side of the bench. Beyond the porch, an arbor framed the passage down a shallow

flight of steps into the Upper Garden, as Chestina called it. The steps marked the top of a gradual downhill slope that extended through the end of the garden.

The Upper Garden was enclosed by the house, the garage, a trellis, and a straight privet hedge, which screened out views of neighboring houses.

A contemporary over-
head view of the gar-
den spaces, 2009.

clockwise from left:

The more utilitarian Lower Garden with flowering fruit trees and cold frame, late 1920s. © Eudora Welty LLC.

Chestina and a friend pick flowers in the Upper Garden, late 1920s. © Eudora Welty LLC; Eudora Welty Collection, MDAH.

Eudora in the arbor between the Upper Garden and Lower Garden, undated. © Eudora Welty LLC.

Chestina with her sons and a friend in the cutting garden, April 1927. © Eudora Welty LLC.

Chestina also planted flowers along the edges. This was her primary garden, where she tried out design ideas and occasionally entertained friends.[21] Another arbor, this one with two facing benches, formed a passage through a trellis fence to the Lower Garden. The benches became a favorite setting for family photographs and a shady place to rest. The arbor also created a transition between the designed garden and the garden of work; for not only did the Lower Garden contain Chestina's rose beds and fruit trees, but also a cold frame and a compost pile. Along the far southern edge of the grass was a row of white flag irises (*Iris albicans*), locally called "cemetery whites" because they often decorated gravesites. Beyond lay the woodland garden, a wilder area where Chestina planted roadside flowers and her sons built a clubhouse.

These two private garden rooms composed the view from the kitchen, breakfast room, and library downstairs, and upstairs, the sleeping porch. In the kitchen, two large windows framed a view of two arbors. These pleasing details attest to Chestina Welty's attention to the design of the overall landscape. In 1921 King instructed, "Since the garden (and now we shall consider under that name only that part of the lot back of the house) is . . . an out-of-door room, we must first look upon it in its connection with the house. The main axis of the whole plan at the back should be determined upon before anything else is thought of; an important doorway or other opening at the back of the house is usually the point to determine this; and upon the straight line from this doorway to the far end of the property the whole thing must hinge. . . ." Chestina later noted in her garden journal that the "gardener must . . . consider his garden design as viewed from his house—working outward from this to insure continuity between house and garden." But it is obvious that she knew this in 1925.[22]

Behind the garage was a modest cutting garden, where Chestina grew flowers such as larkspur, ragged robins, daisies, and zinnias. In the South, women grew cut flowers for home arrangements and to share at weddings, funerals, and other special occasions. Flowers grown at home added personal meaning. "The home-grown flowers came early, and the florist flowers late," Welty wrote in her short story "The Wanderers," describing a

Eudora's brothers, Walter (left) and Edward, at work on a construction project, probably in the late 1920s. © Eudora Welty LLC; Eudora Welty Collection, MDAH.

But gardener must at same time consider his garden design as viewed from his house - working outward from this to insure continuity between house & garden. — Must work down from landscaping and up from garden design, and do this so well that the two meet and mingle without revealing that they are two.

An undated passage from Chestina Welty's garden journal, late 1930s, shows that she was sophisticated about design at the landscape scale. © Eudora Welty LLC.

facing page:

A slightly off-center vantage point accentuates the subtle grade change between the Upper Garden and Lower Garden and the repeated form of the trellises, 2009.

home funeral. "[A]ll the other flowers . . . [were] now steadily being made into wreaths on the back porch."[23] While bereaved family members were occupied inside the house, friends and neighbors gathered on the back porch to weave wreaths from the homegrown bouquets. This was so customary that it happened without prompting or invitation.

Women also presented small bouquets, or nosegays, from their cutting gardens when they visited friends or received visitors. In Eudora's story "Kin," for example, the character Kate says, "You know Aunt Beck—she never let us leave . . . without picking us our nosegay on the way down this walk, every little thing she grew that smelled nice, pinks, four-o'clocks, verbena, heliotrope, bits of nicotiana—she grew all such little things, just for that, Di. And she wound their stems, round and round and round, with a black or white thread she would take from a needle in her collar, and set it all inside a rose-geranium leaf, and presented it to you at the gate—right here. That was Aunt Beck," said Kate's positive voice. "She wouldn't *let* you leave without it."[24]

While such traditions were passed down from mother to daughter, much of Chestina's knowledge about gardening, and, especially, about garden design, was also acquired deliberately, through study. Like any good teacher, Chestina was a perpetual student. And in the Progressive era, when women without extensive formal educations needed information, they turned not only to books, but also to each other.

Maligned Magenta:
"Let's Not Go Down That Street"

"**M**other wouldn't have magenta in her garden," Eudora Welty said, adding that once, on a drive through Jackson, her mother instructed her, "Let's not go down that street, they have all that thrift."

Thrift (*Phlox subulata*), though a lighter shade than true magenta, was close enough to rouse Chestina's aversion. She was not alone; magenta was at the center of a raging controversy in the early twentieth century. Taste arbiters of the day including Gertrude Jekyll, the British painter, garden writer, and garden designer known for her sophisticated orchestration of color, led the charge against "malignant magenta." E. A. Bowles, another British garden writer, called it "that awful form of original sin." American disciples took up the cause, including the writers Mrs. Francis (Louisa Yeomans) King, Louise Beebe Wilder, and Alice Morse Earle. In her book *Colour in My Garden*, Wilder remarked "that even the word magenta, seen often among the pages of [Earle's] charming book, 'makes the black and white look cheap,' and again 'if I could turn all magenta flowers pink or purple, I should never think further about garden harmony, all other colours would adjust themselves.'"

The reasons for the controversy involved more than fashion. One insightful historian, Susan Lan-

Butterfly bush (*Buddleia davidii*). Photograph by Susan Haltom.

man, untangled magenta's noxious associations in an article in the *Garden History Society Journal* (Vol. 28, No. 2, Winter 2000) called "Colour in the Garden: 'Malignant Magenta.'" She points out that arsenic was commonly used in pesticides, giving crops a magenta color that indicated that the lethal poison had been applied. Jekyll and others distressed by the effects of industrialization eschewed it for such associations with pollution, and its manufacture from aniline dyes, which themselves were derived from the coal whose smoke blackened England's skies. Lanman concludes, "The nuanced responses of designers and patrons who chose to ban magenta from their borders are understandable once the detailed meaning of 'malignant magenta' is teased out, and one is reminded of the rich social and cultural complexities embedded in gardens."

Chestina Welty's Original Plant List

One of the few surviving artifacts from Chestina's garden planning is a plant list found in the attic of the Welty house after Eudora died. Dated January 6, 1926, and typed on legal-sized sheets, the document lists 805 plants in 35 groups, at prices ranging from $2.50 (blackberries) to $78.25 (banana shrub, eleagnus, glossy privet). Each price group contained from one to four species, mostly trees and shrubs. The cost totals $890.45—equivalent to more than $10,700 today. Though its source remains a mystery, it may have come from the Texas architectural office that designed the house, or perhaps a local nursery. Notes on the back in Chestina's hand suggest that she narrowed the plant list to fourteen trees and shrubs, including yaupon (*Ilex vomitoria*), gardenia (*Gardenia jasminoides*), spireas (*Spirea* sp.), cherry laurel (*Prunus laurocerasus*), eastern red cedar (*Juniperus virginiana*), winter honeysuckle (*Lonicera fragrantissima*), philadelphus (*Philadelphus coronarius*), and vitex (*Vitex agnus-castus*), all popular in southern gardens of the day. The complete list appears in Appendix II.

Double-flowering peaches. Wayside Gardens catalogue, 1944. Collection of Susan Haltom.

CHAPTER THREE

Progressive Women and Their Roots in Gardening

Although the club movement was late in reaching the Southern States, it is nowhere stronger today, and Southern club women are among the most earnest and effective workers.

—Helen M. Winslow, *The Delineator*, 1903[1]

Go make thy garden fair as thou canst
    Thou workest never alone:
Perhaps he whose plot is next to thine
    Will see it and mend his own.

—Garden Lovers Group Motto,
The Woman's Club, Jackson, Mississippi[2]

T he women who flooded into America's booming cities at the turn of the twentieth century had reason to miss their mothers and sisters back on the farm. At least there, women could work together, or with their husbands and children, as they moved among diverse laborious tasks. In the cities and new sub-urbs, with limited opportunities for higher education and jobs outside the home, many women felt isolated and socially starved.[3] Whether they

The Ox Woman

On an East Indian farm, a woman drives a wooden plow, another woman pulls—and a black ox pulls beside her.

Washing, cleaning, and pumping water are tasks which electricity does for the farm woman. But electric light, the electric iron, electric milkers and separators, and a dozen other devices make life easier on the farm. Ask your electric power company for the G-E Farm Book, which tells what electricity can do for you.

The American farm has many conveniences. But the farm woman often toils at the washtub, at the churn, and carries water. In some communities electricity is now doing these tasks at small cost and in half the time.

GENERAL ELECTRIC

An advertisement promotes labor-saving devices as a mark of American progress, in *Better Homes and Gardens*, October 1926. Collection of Susan Haltom.

dug ditches or balanced the books in a large company, men in city jobs left their wives at home during business hours. Although the conventional wisdom holds that the parade of new, time-saving domestic appliances reduced housework and freed more time for leisure pursuits like gardening, one history of the period points out that as vacuum cleaners and electric washers got cleaning done faster, they also raised the standard of cleanliness, so that what the housewife "gained with the washing machine, she lost with bigger washes and the departure of the laundress." The result was that the number of hours spent doing housework was probably the same in 1920 as it had been in 1900. Moreover, the increasingly marked division of labor between the sexes, plus the commercial availability of packaged food and other goods, took away from women as much as they gave, "moving production of clothing and many foods out of the home, depriving them of household help, and taking their husbands away throughout the day."[4]

That said, automobiles and telephones were also bringing these same women into contact with a wider world—by World War I, many middle-class women were running their household errands in cars. But a society that anointed women as its moral custodians still confined their sphere of influence to the home. Out of their desire to learn, socialize, and get out of the house, women formed clubs that focused on the study of literature and culture as a "direct means" of intellectual and moral self-improvement. "One would imagine that society had no ailment, spiritual or moral, that could not be relieved by a good strong dose of culture, administered in a book capsule . . . ," declared a 1906 novel about woman's clubs. The staggering number of such clubs spoke to the hunger for a bigger role in public life. As the club movement snowballed at the turn of the twentieth century, members abandoned their cultural focus to tackle social reforms—preferring "Doing to Dante, Being to Browning," as one writer quipped.[5]

Garden clubs were natural offshoots of woman's clubs—as was the case in Jackson, Mississippi—because the home grounds fell squarely into the female realm, morally and physically. New streetcar suburbs like Belhaven spurred the transition from utilitarian house yards, like the one behind the Weltys' house on North Congress Street, to the artful outdoor rooms Chestina designed at 1119 Pinehurst Street. In such beautified surroundings, every member of the middle-class family could enjoy the outdoors. Enjoyment, however, was not entirely the point; according to the pundits of the day, natural beauty had the power to boost physical health, rejuvenate the spirit, and raise morals.[6]

"We seek to preach freedom from the very housetops," crowed one writer and publisher, "to induce worthy citizens to cultivate their health as well as their gardens and, in so doing, to do their duty by their children through . . . surroundings which will make them sturdy, self-reliant and observant, and best fit them for their own battle of life. Fundamentally, there is no excuse for weaklings among those raised in the country and the out-of-doors." These ideas gave reformers a new weapon with which to fend off a host of social ills caused, they believed, by the galloping growth of cities and industry. As a member of the Baltimore Women's Civic League declared, "[S]ocial and civic workers are only beginning to realize that gardens will automatically prevent many of the evils they labor . . . to correct."[7]

An advertisement for garden tools was aimed at women, one clad in progressive boots and jodhpurs, in *The Garden Magazine*, May 1923. Collection of Susan Haltom.

Such convictions spurred an intense focus on home gardening between about 1900 and World War II, triggering a groundswell of garden writing in books and magazines, domestic gardening, and, beginning in the 1880s, the formation of garden clubs—trends that fueled one another.[8] In addition to local clubs, a national association was gaining ground. In 1913, when horticultural and plant societies were few, the Garden Club of Philadelphia invited eleven other garden clubs to join in the creation of a national garden club. The new organization, the Garden Club of America (GCA), aimed "to stimulate the knowledge and love of gardening among amateurs, to share the advantages of association through conference and correspondence in this country and abroad, to aid in the protection of native plants and birds, and to encourage civic planting." Two years later, a GCA president reflected on these goals more poetically: "We . . . are beginning to realize that we have come together on an irresistible wave of desire for the beauty of gardens. Our object is to 'garden finely' and to induce others to join us in this neglected art."[9]

The early GCA members faced a daunting challenge at a time when, to most Americans, vegetables were more important than flowers. In England, popular garden designers including Jekyll and William Robinson had inspired gardeners at both large estate properties and small cottage plots; but in America, the great surge of gardening was just beginning. The conservation movement was still in its infancy, and people who were interested in native wildflowers were often considered eccentric. "Yet, even if latent, there must have been an urge to garden, for when garden clubs were started, they spread and proliferated in every direction," a 1976 GCA booklet stated. "Members came to meetings on foot, in carriages, or by train. Automobiles were rare and it was an event to see ladies arrive in an open car, their large hats swathed in pale voluminous chiffon veils against the dust of unpaved roads."[10]

Their object of inspiring the public to "garden finely" and to form clubs around this mission succeeded—so well that by 1919 the president of the GCA reported, "It sometimes seemed that 'club' outranked 'garden'. Does it and should it? Gardening is a lonely sport, but in association we have found sympathetic souls (or fellow cranks) and 'garden' should mean more to us, not less."[11] Their success in linking individual clubs with each other and with the central organization has continued to the present day.

Similar ideas to those which spurred the growth of garden clubs had also propelled the spread of late-nineteenth-century Village Improvement Societies, which pushed for cleaner, more orderly, and more scenic public landscapes in rural villages. On their heels came the City Beautiful movement—an informal nationwide campaign inspired by the "White City" at the 1893 Columbian Exposition (World's Fair) in Chicago and promoted by civic leaders throughout the country. Though advocates of the City Beautiful included city officials, business leaders, landscape architects, and city planners, in many cases women led the charge to beautify the public landscape. In addition to creating more parks, cities including Jackson lined their streets with trees with the help of women unafraid to wield a shovel. Clubwomen planted flowers and shrubs in median strips and exhorted homeowners to keep attractive front yards, which, in the prevailing view, composed part of the public landscape.[12]

With the emphasis on greenery as a cure for social problems of every ilk, it was only a matter of time before reform-minded women formed organizations dedicated to gardening and gardens—and to enlarging women's role in this important civic arena. In 1914, a year after the Garden Club of America was founded, King founded the Woman's National Farm and Garden Association "to stimulate interest in the conservation of our natural resources and an appreciation for country life," as well as to

A Residence Street, Jackson, Miss.—17

Inspired by the City Beautiful movement, street trees and landscaped front yards formed a new public landscape in the early twentieth century. Historic postcard, undated. Courtesy of Steve Colston Photography.

Horticulture and landscape design allowed women to expand their professional opportunities and opened new avenues for social change. Advertisement in *The Garden Magazine*, May 1923. Collection of Susan Haltom.

support the new School of Horticulture for Women (founded in 1910) at Ambler, Pennsylvania. Women's education in landscape architecture also was making inroads in the Northeast, at the Lowthorpe School of Landscape Architecture for Women (1903) and the Cambridge School of Architecture and Landscape Architecture for Women (1916), both in Massachusetts.[13]

THE
WOMAN'S LAND ARMY
of AMERICA

TRAINING   SCHOOL
UNIVERSITY of VIRGINIA
JUNE 15 TO SEPTEMBER 15 • COURSES TWO WEEKS
TUITION FREE • BOARD $5.00 PER WEEK
Apply WOMAN'S LAND ARMY, U. S. EMPLOYMENT SERVICE, 910 E. Main Street, RICHMOND, VA.

The Woman's Land Army, modeled on a similar British organization, took advantage of female labor and advanced the acceptance of women in the work force. Poster by Herbert Andrew Paus, c. 1918. Courtesy of Library of Congress.

In many fields, this steady advance of professional education and the rise of more organized amateur activities for women ran parallel with trends in male society. But in the realm of gardens, landscapes, and conservation, colleges and clubs promoted women from keepers of the home grounds—still a respectable and ever more sophisticated pursuit—to stewards of the civic landscape. Not until World War I, however, did women find a chance to visibly prove themselves where it really counted—in the working world. When thousands of men exchanged farm fields for battlefields, the Woman's Land Army filled the shortage. Clad in men's farm overalls or in their official uniform of "breeches," shirt, and broad-brimmed straw hat, the WLA "farmerettes," or "soil sisters," were trained to help out at farms in any way needed.[14] The work—picking fruit on high ladders, hauling lumber, milking cows, and driving tractors—was far more diverse than traditional female farming tasks.

The farmerettes' clothing signified the radical innovations of the program. Pants for women were decades away from being socially acceptable—this was one factor that may have kept the WLA from catching on in Mississippi—but the ankle-length skirts of the day put their wearers at risk, and the design of female work "breeches" required careful study. "The two most necessary points to embody in suitable breeches are length in the seat to admit of bending over freely, and freedom in the knee, so as not to constrict the leg muscles and fatigue the worker," reported the director of the WLA's Wellesley College Training Camp, in Massachusetts.[15]

Twenty years before the Fair Labor Standards Act and forty-five years ahead of the Equal Pay Act, the farmerettes demanded and got an eight-hour workday and wages equal to those of male farm workers. In filling men's boots to feed the nation, they challenged conventional female roles, dress, and behavior—all before being able to vote.[16]

Even after 1920, when they finally won suffrage, women continued to work through the clubs that had achieved reforms in every area of public life. But the advance of the women's club movement and the focus of individual clubs varied regionally and locally. Repairing their ravaged cities and farms in the aftermath of the Civil War, in particular, gave women in the South plenty to do without casting about for ways to improve themselves. Although in the club movement they soon caught up with their sisters in other parts of the country, clubs in the South lingered in the literary phase after those in other parts of the country had plunged into Progressive social causes.[17]

Chestina Welty, a passionate reader since childhood (Eudora once quipped that her mother "read Dickens in the spirit in which she would have eloped with him"), typified the clubwoman of this literary stripe. She had grown up when the zeal for self-improvement was sweeping the land, and long after her years in the one-room schoolhouse, she continued to see herself both as a teacher and a lifelong student of gardening and horticulture as well as literature. "My mother liked the direct experience of a garden. She liked learning about plants and their origins and how they developed," Eudora said. Like many of her contemporaries, Chestina valued gardening as a way to gain insights that could be applied to life in a broader sense. "[A] garden is a grand teacher. It teaches patience and careful watchfulness; it teaches industry and thrift; above all, it teaches entire trust," opined Jekyll.[18]

Chestina's inquisitive mind and strong work ethic served as important leadership qualities that bloomed in club life. "Mrs. Welty is a charter member of the Woman's Club," noted a 1928 Jackson newspaper article. "She served two years as chairman of service, under the old organization, when our departments were, Health, Knowledge, Service, and Spirit. She con-

Chestina in the Upper Garden, undated.
© Eudora Welty LLC.

"IT'S NOT A HOME UNTIL IT'S PLANTED"

The Vogue for the
Outdoor Living Room

Advertisement in *Holland's,*
the Magazine of the South,
November 1930. Collec-
tion of Susan Haltom.

ceived the idea of a Garden Lover's group, and assisted by others who had the same vision, launched this work in the second year of her chairmanship. In that sense, she is the mother of this group and well-beloved as such."[19]

Founded in 1922, the Woman's Club in Jackson counted more than two hundred members by the end of the decade. In structure and development, it paralleled hundreds of similar clubs throughout the country, with committees and departments devoted to literature, American citizenship, civics, legislation, fine arts, the American home, applied education, music and art appreciation, and parenthood and psychology. Chestina was active chiefly in departments related to gardening and conservation, but she also served in others over time. In addition to home gardening, she envisioned a "glorious highway, planted on either side with colorful Crepe Myrtles, the Club flower."[20]

Before this grand vision came humble beginnings. Lacking a site for a shared teaching garden, the members of the Garden Lovers group, eager to begin their education, concocted an imaginary one:

> For this year [1928–29], the group planned to design a home and garden "to be located here in Jackson under the exact conditions existing at this time, with all the advantages and all the handicaps enjoyed or endured by every garden maker who plants a seed or culls a flower.
>
> The Garden Lovers will landscape the grounds, plant shrubbery and a perennial border, provide a rose garden and answer to the best of their ability all questions of soil, water, labor, drouth, pests, plant food and other problems which arise in the garden. A careful record of this garden will be presented to the club at each meeting and preserved as a permanent help to home gardeners.
>
> Though the Garden Lovers must use their imaginations to visualize this garden, the accounts that are given will be the result of experience and actual information about the subjects discussed.[21]

Chestina toiled as Head Gardener in this fertile landscape of the mind, which served up the topics for the club's monthly programs that year, beginning with "Locating the House—Its Relation to the Garden." Subsequent programs plunged them into the hypothetical dirt—soils, planting, feeding, dividing and transplanting, cuttings, pruning, picking out desirable perennials and bulbs, and successive bloom—before returning to the topic of design. The imaginary garden even spawned imaginary regrets: the final program was given over to "Things I Wish We Had Done in Our Garden; Our Dream Garden Visualized—Plans [f]or Another Year."[22]

At her own home, Chestina clearly had more resources at her disposal, although she remained keenly aware that she, like most of her peers, depended on her husband for these: "Mother said it took a man to make a garden because women didn't have any money. If a man said '*do it!*,' it got done," Eudora once remarked. In her home garden, Chestina applied the lessons from the imaginary garden in a very real way, as a 1928 prize and an accompanying newspaper article made clear. Out of twenty-five homes throughout Jackson, the "home of Mr. and Mrs. C. W. Welty on Pinehurst won the decision of the judges for the best entire place," the article reported. "The garden, which lies at the back of the house and is entered through an arched gateway, is so much a part of the natural beauty of the place that one scarcely notices the transition from lawn to garden. This is a garden to be lived in; with its protecting circle of trees, and restful stretches of sod bordered with flowers. The blue of Larkspur and the exquisite pink of Shirley poppies made it particularly lovely at the time of the judges' visit. . . ."[23]

This description shares the genteel tone of society writing, but Chestina did not strive to attract her neighbors' adulation. On the contrary, her core independence and courage freed her from fretting about what her neighbors thought. As her later garden notebooks reveal, Chestina's

Larkspur blooms in April in the Welty garden. Photograph by Susan Haltom.

garden was a crucible for horticultural experiments and a personal artistic expression as much as a contribution to a beautiful streetscape.

Eudora's biographer, Suzanne Marrs, points out that "far from embracing the established social order, Chestina Welty herself was a model [to Eudora] for defying convention." Marrs cites the example of Chestina declining to donate to a missionary society because "she did not wish to tell people in other countries what to think." And Chestina joined the Research Club "because she believed in the value of the research projects members actually undertook; the more usual women's luncheon clubs were anathema to her."[24]

Eudora Welty in the garden, undated (c. 1930). © Eudora Welty LLC.

In 1928, the year that her mother claimed her garden prize, Eudora published a poem in the *Wisconsin Literary Magazine* while studying at the University of Wisconsin. When she started her senior year in the fall, Eudora began to write a novella—her first, now lost—that she submitted as her thesis before graduating, in the spring of 1929. That summer, she returned to Jackson, keenly appreciating the place that had, during her college years, clearly defined itself as home. "[E]ven the cut grass in the yards smelled different from Northern grass. (Even by evidence of smell, I knew that really I was a stranger in a way, still, just at first.) And the spring was so much farther advanced. . . . Bloom was everywhere in the streets, wistaria just ending, Confederate jasmine beginning. And down in the gardens! —they were as deep colored as old rugs in the morning and evening shade," she later wrote in her short story "Kin."[25]

In the summer of 1929, Eudora moved home and reconnected with some high-school friends who were planning to attend graduate school at Columbia University in the fall of 1930. She persuaded her parents to allow her to enroll there too, agreeing to her father's condition that she focus on a practical subject—she chose advertising and secretarial studies—so she wouldn't need to rely on an unstable career in the arts.[26]

View into the Weltys' Upper Garden. Photograph by Eudora Welty, 1930s. © Eudora Welty LLC.

Though it was unusual for the parents of young women in Eudora's generation to encourage their daughters to support themselves, the Weltys already had demonstrated their differentness in many other ways. The stock market crash of that fall may have impressed upon her parents that relying on a man, even her father, to provide for her would not be wise.

Eudora wrote for the *Jackson Daily News* through the spring of 1930. In the fall, she headed north, eager to dip into the intellectual and cultural life she craved. Chestina, meanwhile, continued to busy herself in the Garden Lovers group, and in January of 1931, became founding president of the Belhaven Garden Club, one of six chapters of the Jackson Council of Garden Clubs. But later that year she resigned. Christian was diagnosed with leukemia.

Flowers to Go

Everybody for miles around came to the reception. . . . The mayor of Fairchilds and his wife were driven up with the lights on inside their car, and they could be seen lighted up inside reading the Memphis paper (which never quite unrolled when you read it); in the bud vases on the walls beside them were real red roses, vibrating. . . .

—Eudora Welty, *Delta Wedding*

Drivers of early twentieth-century automobiles outfitted their vehicles with special flower vases to freshen the air inside their cars. The vases were six to seven inches tall and tapered to a point at the bottom to fit into brackets mounted on the dashboard. Holding fragrant blooms plucked from the owner's garden, they were especially useful in inclement weather, when sodden mohair or leather upholstery reeked like a wet goat. Made of pressed glass, porcelain, metal, or even wood, the finer vases were sold in jewelry stores and by florists, with more workaday models available from car dealers. As E. B. White fondly recalled in an essay commemorating the Ford Model T, drivers could even purchase "de-luxe flower vases of the cut-glass anti-splash type." The Model T's factory model was called, simply, the auto vase.

Photograph by James R. Haltom

Down with the Fence! Or Not!

As early as 1870, Frank Scott, an ardent champion of the lawn, declared, "It is unchristian to hedge from the sight of others the beauties of nature which has been our good fortune to create or secure; and all the walls, high fences, hedge screens and belts of trees and shrubbery *which are used for that purpose only* . . . show how unchristian and unneighborly we can be."

In the surge of industry after the Civil War, cities overfilled with new immigrants and rural residents seeking work. Behind tenements, backyards still contained cisterns, privies, and the like. Fences maintained privacy and boundaries. But in the 1870s, cities started requiring new houses to be set back a generous distance from the street, and the public front yard came into being, according to landscape historian Christopher Grampp. With the invention of the electric streetcar in the 1880s, suburbia was born. Even then the backyard remained utilitarian, fenced, and private, and the front yard "emerged as a primary target for improvement," Grampp observes in his book *From Yard to Garden: The Domestication of America's Home Grounds* (2008).

By the 1920s, fencing one's front yard was no longer unchristian, but some garden writers thought it un-American: "In democratic America it is not the custom, as it is in some European countries, to have walls about the front of our places," sniffed one writer, in the *Landscape Garden Series* (1921) produced for students of landscape architecture. "We would rather give some consideration to the public and have in the space between the home and the street an area for the view and enjoyment of the passerby."

Garden writers, an opinionated breed, declined to march in step on this issue. One, in the *Garden Guide* (1917), urged homeowners to shun the fad of transparency: "The word 'garden' carries with it the meaning of enclosure. We in America are getting more and more away from having even our own dooryards to ourselves. . . . Marauders have full sweep."

The influential Grace Tabor agreed. "I cannot express too earnestly the belief that nothing worth while will ever be done with suburban or any gardens until we restore the fences and walls so ruthlessly torn down and abandoned around the latter quarter of the last century," she fumed in *Suburban Gardens* (1913). Tabor laid fencelessness at the feet of real-estate developers, who "were responsible for this destruction of boundary markings in the first place," in hopes that "indiscriminating passersby" would spy the attractive grounds and be moved to buy a house.

But Tabor and other dissenters eventually lost the day, steamrolled by the City Beautiful movement, new regulations, and a growing corps of professional landscape architects and planners who, in the words of Grampp, sought to create "an unbroken river of greenery" along suburban streets.

PART II

Summer—1930s

CHAPTER FOUR

"Meeting Death Head On"

[My mother's] gardening was her way of meeting death head on.

—Eudora Welty[1]

In April 1931, Eudora turned twenty-two. Living in New York City with friends from Jackson and taking business courses at Columbia University, she planned to seek work in the city after finishing school. Her optimism about finding employment seems surprising in hindsight, given that New York City was the epicenter of the stock market crash; but at the time, many economists had yet to recognize how severe and lasting the shock waves would be. After all, two recessions had rattled the country since the turn of the century—the brief Panic of 1907–1908 and a longer postwar slump in 1920–1921. Even in early 1931, when the recession showed signs of lingering longer than the one before, few realized that it would plunge America into uncharted financial territory.[2]

The Welty family was on the verge of a more personal crisis. In the spring of 1931, Christian Welty's leukemia worsened, and Eudora came home from New York. In September, in a desperate last attempt to save her husband, Chestina agreed to transfuse her blood into his body—a still experimental procedure. Years earlier, when she had fallen seriously ill, Chestina believed that Christian had saved her life, and now she fervently hoped to save his. While her brothers were at school, Eudora sat

Chestina and Christian Welty, undated (c. 1930). © Eudora Welty LLC; Eudora Welty Collection, MDAH.

Christian Welty, as pictured with his death announcement in the Jackson newspapers. © Lamar Life Insurance Company, courtesy of Eudora Welty LLC.

Publicity shot for Eudora Welty when she worked at WJDX, 1931. Courtesy of MDAH, © Eudora Welty LLC.

with her parents in the hospital as they lay on cots placed side by side. Her father appeared to be unconscious when the doctor ran a tube from her mother's arm to his. But when her blood flowed into him, suddenly "his face turned dusky red all over," and he died. "My mother never recovered emotionally," Eudora recalled. "She saw this as her failure to save his life."[3]

The *Jackson Daily News* reported the death of Lamar Life's president on the front page, describing "C. W. Welty" as a "quiet and unassuming man" who shepherded the company to a new pinnacle of success.[4] Eudora's autobiographical writing reveals an involved, affectionate parent with an aesthetic sensibility—which he engaged chiefly as a photographer, then later as a photography mentor to Eudora when she, too, picked up a camera.

Christian's funeral took place at the Weltys' home on Pinehurst Street[5]; Chestina's friends probably filled the house with flowers from their cutting gardens. Christian Welty had provided for his family after his death, as would have been expected from the president of a life insurance firm. Although Chestina and the children would be able to remain in the house, the nest egg was not large enough to free the family from financial worries with the onset of the Great Depression. The loss of this beloved husband and father also changed the lives of his family in ways that had little to do with money. From then on, Eudora, although traveling often and widely, would live at Pinehurst Street. She and Chestina would be entwined in a close bond that at times chafed both of them, and the garden would become, to some degree, a shared enterprise.[6] Eudora would come to know the garden's poetry and mystery, use its flowers in her fiction, and discover parts of her characters within her gardening self.

In 1931, however, Eudora still had her hopes pinned on a life in New York City. She stayed on in Jackson that winter, finding work at WJDX, the city's first radio station, housed in the Lamar Life building. The station, founded by her father two years earlier, had been part of his plan for the office tower from the beginning. The local newspapers, miffed by the competition, refused to print the program schedule, so the company launched *The Lamar Life Radio News*, published weekly. Editing the *Radio News* became Eudora's first paying job, although it occupied her for only a few hours a day.[7] During this period, she made sporadic forays to New York. "I would save my money and go up there for a couple of weeks, looking for work," she said.[8] But the reality of the economic decline was now inescapable; Eudora could not find a job. She remained at WJDX until 1933, a period in which the news included Al Capone's imprisonment for tax evasion, Amelia Earhart's solo transatlantic flight, the Nazi Party's rise to power in Germany, and the kidnapping and murder of Charles Lindbergh's infant son.

At home, she helped her mother in the garden, watching Chestina expend her grief and guilt in relentless toil. As she observed her mother's labors from a literary remove, Eudora discovered the solace of gardening for herself, and a kind of joy:

After the death of my father, my distraught mother worked all day long most days in her flower garden behind the house. I would be downtown at my part-time job, and my brothers were away at school.

She had always grown flowers, but now she made a garden out of the whole green slant of our back yard, deep borders in the light and dark of their natural surround of old pines and hardwoods. Now, her garden filled all her daylight hours; in becoming her never-ending work, it became her solace. She went to books, of course, and learned her flowers' true names and species, their genealogy and cultivation. "Hemerocallis: beauty for a day," she'd say, cupping one of that day's blooms in her hand. She kept a daily record with all specifics, rather as she had kept the logs and mileage of our old summer trips, and she drew diagrams of her borders, careful to plot their plantings, their seasonal rotations—and I thought of her schoolgirl diagrams of Heaven and Hell for *Paradise Lost*.

In our red clay she discovered what that clay would nourish; and what it would not, she fed the clay to grow and flower the best in spite of itself.

Our garden was a succession of bloom. It was changing and renewing itself every month of the year. It drew me into it, too.

The sight of that garden, and its scent! If work hadn't proved it real, it would have been hallucination; in this sense gardening is akin to writing stories. No experience could have taught me more about grief or flowers, about achieving survival by going, your fingers in the ground, the limit of physical exhaustion.[9]

Like the series of yard boys her mother trained, Eudora recounted that she too "learned by doing, rising at dawn, moving along behind her in the borders." In this same passage she went on to capture the first of many transporting moments she would experience in the garden, which took place while observing a fellow apprentice, "a round-faced youth of about sixteen" known by the initials J. W.

A daylily that has survived from Chestina's original border. Photograph by Susan Haltom.

Facing page:

"The whole green slant of our backyard. . . ." The garden at Eudora Welty House, 2009.

[My mother] sent him partway up the stepladder to trim the big Silver Moon climbing rose, when it was concluding its April bloom. It was a thundery day, and he was shining with sweat as he stood transfixed from moment to moment and briar to briar as she called to him again and again exactly what and what not to do. His black moon face looked out from the Silver Moon blossoms and he said—his was a mourning voice—"I wish there wasn't a rose in the world."[10] As I saw him there without a name to his initials, wishing for a world without its roses, but caught in the thick of them, encircled by wide-open Silver Moons and pricked on every side by their strong thorns, with their fragrance and the gold dust of their pollen sweeping his cheeks, it might have been the first time I knew the compulsion to step back and place myself at a story-teller's remove. It seemed to me an archetypal moment of some kind. When the storm broke, it was like a story falling all over the garden. I turned it into one I called "A Curtain of Green," at a considerable remove from our real lives then. It was the first time I had consciously placed myself at a story-teller's remove, right there on the spot.[11]

In the story, a grief-stricken widow, Mrs. Larkin, "worked without stopping, almost invisibly, submerged all day among the thick, irregular, sloping beds of plants." Although Eudora took pains to couch "A Curtain of Green" as fiction, Marrs observes, "Mrs. Larkin's isolation within her community, her grief, her venturing into the garden, and her discovery of some consolation there draw in oblique ways upon Chestina Welty's experience."[12]

As with the character of Mrs. Larkin, it is not likely that the fictional garden in "A Curtain of Green" literally portrays the Welty garden, although the sloping yard and the thickly planted beds bear a resemblance to the Pinehurst Street yard. The bereft Mrs. Larkin "planted every kind of flower that she could find or order from a catalogue—planted thickly and hastily, without stopping to think, without any regard for the ideas that her neighbors might elect in their club as to what constituted an appropriate vista, or an effect of restfulness, or even harmony of color."[13]

Chestina working in her rose bed, date unknown. © Eudora Welty LLC.

Although Chestina fearlessly spurned social conventions she did not respect, such as discouraging young women from intellectual pursuits, she also had shown herself to be an avid student of landscape design who sought to create such effects in her home garden for her own satisfaction. The details that refer to the neighbors and their club reveal how deep into heedlessness the mourning widow has fallen. Shut out by the garden's "border of hedge, high like a wall," the neighbors exist in a separate world where, since the accident, Mrs. Larkin has not been seen.[14]

But where Chestina was concerned, the high garden wall was not to be a permanent fixture. "She gradually re-entered the world," her daughter observed.[15] Though permanently wounded by her loss, she was able to resume her contact with friends and neighbors, starting with her most valued fellowship—the garden club.

Camellias on the Train

When Eudora was studying at Columbia University, in the dead of winter her mother would ship her boxes of camellias on the express train. "It was wonderful to be up there with the ice and snow, and these lovely tropical flowers would come," Eudora recalled in an interview with a Columbia graduate student, Danny Heitman, in 1994. After settling in Jackson following her father's death in 1931, Eudora took up the custom herself, carefully packing blossoms and shipping them to her friends up North.

"I sewed the stems to the inside edges of the boxes so they wouldn't move about or jostle and hit each other. It was my own invention. . . . I only tried to send four or five blooms in a box on overnight express. I'd wrap the stems in wet cotton. In those days, you could go down to the train station and put things on the express and they'd get to New York the next day." (Prenshaw, *More Conversations with Eudora Welty*, 1996.)

Beauty for a Day

In the early twentieth century, a small number of breeders created the first hybrid daylilies from only a handful of wild Asian species such as *Hemerocallis fulva*, *H. lilioasphodelus*, *H. citrina*, and *H. aurantica*, whose flowers opened and died within the span of a day. Like the species, the early hybrids were often fragrant, but they promised a few more hours of bloom time. Yellow

or orange blossoms grew on scapes, or flowering stems, that rose two to four feet high, depending on the variety.

Some bloomed at night, adding luminous glamour to the garden. Eudora's favorite was the night-flowering 'Calypso'. "Every evening between 8 & 9 you can watch the Calypso day lily opening—it is a night day lily—palest pure yellow, long slender curved petals, the color of the new moon," she wrote to her agent, Diarmuid Russell, in 1942. "To see it actually open, the petals letting go, is wonderful, and its night fragrance comes to you all at once like a breath. What makes it open at night—what does it open to? In the same progression as others close, moment by moment. Tell about night flowers."

Gardeners found daylilies hardy and easy to grow in a wide range of climate zones, making them favorites for summer borders. Because few flowers are better suited to hybridizing—their large flowers clearly display their reproductive parts—many amateurs found it irresistible to try their hand at hybridizing these one-day wonders. Eudora mentioned that her mother had done so, perhaps in their basement. Daylilies also are easy to share by division and to propagate by planting proliferations, plantlets that grow on the scapes.

Daylilies in the Welty garden in the 1930s and '40s included lemon lily (*H. lilioasphodelus*) and other cultivars including:

'Amaryllis' (1932)*	'J. A. Crawford' (1929)
'Apricot' (1892)	'Mandarin' (1924)
'Calypso' (1929)	'Modesty' (1929)
'Cressida' (1929)	'Mrs. W. H. Wyman' (1929)
'Dr. Regel' (1904)	'Ophir' (1924)
'Florham' (1899)	'Sovereign' (1906)
'George Yeld' (1926)	'The Gem' (1929)
'Hyperion' (1925)	'Wau-Bun' (1929)

* Year introduced shown in parentheses

When Susan Haltom started excavating the overgrown garden in 1994, about twenty large clumps of daylilies were all that remained of Chestina's complex border design. Decades after their original planting, they still survive in the restored border.

CHAPTER FIVE

"Medicine to the Soul"

Flowers always make people better, happier, and more helpful; they are sunshine, food, and medicine to the soul.

—Luther Burbank (1849–1926)[1]

Precious indeed is the heritage of the boy or girl who in later life can say, "I remember my mother working in her garden."

—*The Garden Club Manual*, 1931[2]

In 1933, the Belhaven Garden Club reported, "Mrs. Welty offered to take care of all yearbooks and books on flower growing belonging to the club." Chestina had reentered the club activities that had sustained her before her husband's death. She would be elected president in 1936 and again in 1946. Curious, hard-working, experienced, willing to give programs, accepting of leadership positions, Chestina would appear to have been a model garden club member; but she would brook no foolishness. Eudora said that her mother once quit a club because the members began to spend their time "drinking tea and eating strawberry cake."[3]

Meanwhile, enrollment in the Jackson Council of Garden Clubs, which Chestina had cofounded in January 1931, had soared beyond the founders' imaginings. By May of that year, 550 members had joined various garden clubs, which had begun at the neighborhood level. Ten years later the membership had doubled, although the population of Jackson had increased by only 22 percent (to 62,107) during that decade. "Circles literally

Chestina Welty in her garden, undated. © Eudora Welty LLC.

sprang up, women became garden minded and flower conscious and the enthusiasm demonstrated both surprised and delighted the organizers," observed one contributor to the city's garden club history.[4]

In the early 1930s, rural Mississippi had started sinking into the Depression, but Jackson had yet to be hard-hit, buffered by the discovery of natural gas. Even in other parts of the country, garden clubs were popping up in medium-sized cities from Chapel Hill and Charlottesville to Baltimore and Sioux City. "This manifestation of garden interest is nation-wide and is evidenced in every walk of life," wrote Edith Fisher in *The Garden Club Manual*, a guide offering detailed instructions for starting a club. "With this interest in gardening has come the Garden Club movement."[5]

Ladies of the Marigold Garden Circle, a Jackson garden club, united in a demonstration for a cause now lost to history, 1939. From *The Jackson Council of Garden Clubs Scrapbook*, courtesy of MDAH.

By this time, the movement had spread beyond the Garden Club of America and the Women's National Farm and Gardening Association. Representing this grassroots trend, a plethora of neighborhood garden clubs formed in Jackson during the 1930s, adopting names like the Diligent Diggers, the Beauty Lovers Circle, the Flower Lovers, the Friendly Diggers, the Glad Circle, and the Sunnywild Circle. As such local clubs proliferated, some saw advantages in banding together in state federations, which then organized at the national level. The National Council of State Garden Clubs (now the National Garden Clubs), formed in 1929 to coordinate state-federated garden clubs. In 1935, in the thick of the Depression, the organization had enough resources to set up headquarters in New York City's Rockefeller Center. And by 1932, men also were gardening in numbers large enough to found their own organization, the Men's Garden Clubs of America (now the Gardeners of America/Men's Garden Clubs of America), which added about ten clubs a year through the remainder of the Depression.[6]

The clubs were the driving force behind civic beautification, planting

street trees and brightening gas stations with flowers. "We all know that the gasoline station is here to stay but it need not continue to be so ugly as it is at present," observed Fisher. "Trees, shrubs, grass, vines, window boxes and flowers will all help to improve the appearance of stations."[7] The spreading scourge of roadside billboards—another blight associated with automobiles—drew the most concerted activism. In 1938 the Federated Garden Clubs, Federated Women's Clubs, and the Council for Roadside Improvement united to present a "highway safety" bill to the Mississippi legislature. The bill aimed to "get rid of the dangerous, obnoxious, and unattractive signs and billboard that clutter the roads, veritable eyesores to all who behold them."[8]

Most garden club activities, however, focused on proactive measures. In Jackson, even before the founding of the first garden clubs, the former Garden Lovers group "sponsored flower shows at the State Fair; helped stage and judge flower shows; assisted various public projects in landscaping; co-operated . . . in planting 1000 Paul's Scarlet roses along the highway; and with the Chamber of Commerce in planting Crape Myrtles along various streets," Chestina noted with pride. Eudora mentioned that several of her mother's exhibits in the state fair won ribbons for "Best Other Than Named," a category for more creative and risk-taking entries.[9]

Larger trends were propelling this massive planting push. America, wedded to the automobile after a passionate courtship in the early 1920s,

clockwise from top left:

A garden club flower show held in a private home in Jackson, early 1930s. Hand-colored glass slide, courtesy of Eudora Welty LLC.

Rose plantings at Livingston Park, Jackson, early 1930s. Hand-colored glass slide, courtesy of Eudora Welty LLC.

Pink crepe myrtles planted in front of the Welty house, early 1930s. Hand-colored glass slide, courtesy of Eudora Welty LLC.

Spreading the Word:
State Fair Flower Shows

An award-winning design in a flower show at the
Mississippi State Fair, early 1930s. Hand-colored
glass slide, courtesy of Eudora Welty LLC.

Beginning in the 1930s, Jackson garden clubs exhibited flowers at the state fair. In parts of the country without organized horticultural societies, garden clubs often exhibited at state fairs to showcase the latest flowers and trends to the broader public. Such was the case in Jackson, the capital of a predominantly rural state. "It is perfectly natural, if one has grown a beautiful rose or dahlia, a fine egg-plant or a good bunch of grapes, to enjoy showing it in competition with similar products grown by others. . . . The contest has all the joys of pure sport," observed a writer in *The New Garden Encyclopedia* at the time.

"To get Jackson interested in flowers, we had competitions at the state fair," Eudora recalled. "We had ribbons of red, blue, and white. I know this because I did the publicity. Mother complained about the contest—she knew that growing things was not competitive. They were grown for their own sake." In the end, Chestina decided that if people were going to compete, she was honor bound to train as a judge—because, her daughter explained, "she knew the standards she held."

Yardman tending a heav-
ily ornamented outdoor
room, early 1930s. Hand-
colored glass slide, courtesy
of Eudora Welty LLC.

was by the end of that decade rolling out new suburbs almost as fast as vehicles clattered off Detroit's assembly lines. No longer limited by the length or direction of the trolley line, car commuters drove ever-greater distances to bed down for the night in a suburban slice of green. Land was cheaper beyond the bus and trolley routes, which meant homeowners could afford lot sizes up to two thousand square feet larger than the average lot in a streetcar suburb like Belhaven. After the 1929 stock market crash killed the housing boom, federal policies of the mid-1930s encouraged developers to build large-scale subdivisions featuring stand-alone houses. These were set in a fixed relationship to the street, on cookie-cutter lots.[10]

Garden rooms exhibiting different levels of sophistication, Jackson, early 1930s. Hand-colored glass slide formal garden with pool and fountain, courtesy of Eudora Welty LLC. Lightbulb garden, *The Jackson Council of Garden Clubs Scrapbook*, courtesy of MDAH.

With the front yard on display to greater numbers of people, the custom of fence-free front lawns and picturesque foundation plantings evolved into the unofficial law of the land, even in older suburbs.[11] Not just the gazes of strangers, but the noise and fumes of automobiles also made the front yard—and the front porch and front parlor—less hospitable for socializing. And so, by the 1930s, Americans surrendered this space to the public streetscape, shifting social activities and more creative garden design to the backyard. "Large or small, [home] is the one place where we may express our own individuality in terms of beauty. In that expression we create what may be called the 'outdoor living room' or garden, a place where we work and play and learn the moods of Nature," instructed Fisher.[12] Besides, as the Great Depression advanced, many of those fortunate enough to have a backyard could not afford to go anywhere else.

Outdoor rooms required spatial definition and privacy, achieved by hedges and trees, and also by trellises and arbors, which remained popular into the 1930s. Inside the screen of woody plants, gardeners laid out wavy floral borders to enclose their lawns. Other than in rose gardens,

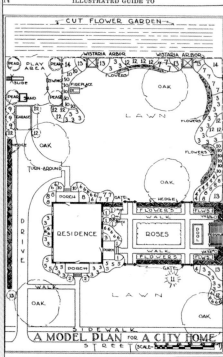

Mrs. W. W. Scott, the wife of Jackson's mayor, in her garden, 1939. From the *Jackson Council of Garden Clubs Scrapbook*, courtesy of MDAH.

Resources from the state extension service helped homeowners in both rural and urban settings plan their landscapes for success. This layout, circulated fourteen years after Chestina Welty's similar design, was a popular template for suburban lots, indicating plant choices and locations. From *An Illustrated Guide to Landscaping Mississippi Homes*, Extension Service Bulletin, December 1939.

which tended to be geometric, the preference for naturalistic form prevailed.[13] These design elements—and a multitude of new nursery offerings—allowed for endless variation. In the hands of a knowledgeable and artistic gardener, the results could be enchanting.

A "PARADE OF BLOOM IN THE BORDER"

After she had laid out the three primary garden rooms, Chestina lavished most of her time on the roses and flower borders, which composed the view from the kitchen, breakfast room, and back bedrooms. In the 1920s and '30s, the gardens behind the house received abundant sunshine, filtered through the airy canopy of tall pines clustered around the house. The sunny exposure—aided by the region's sultry climate, a long growing season, and the Weltys' homemade compost—created favorable growing conditions for a wide variety of plants. With such opportunity came a

The Welty garden, taken from the sleeping porch, probably by Eudora, with 'Silver Moon' rose in foreground, early 1930s. Hand-colored glass slide, courtesy of Eudora Welty LLC.

The restored Upper Garden features several spireas and other shrubs and trees planted by Chestina. Bulbs including leucojum and narcissus 'Avalanche' also survive from Chestina's planting.

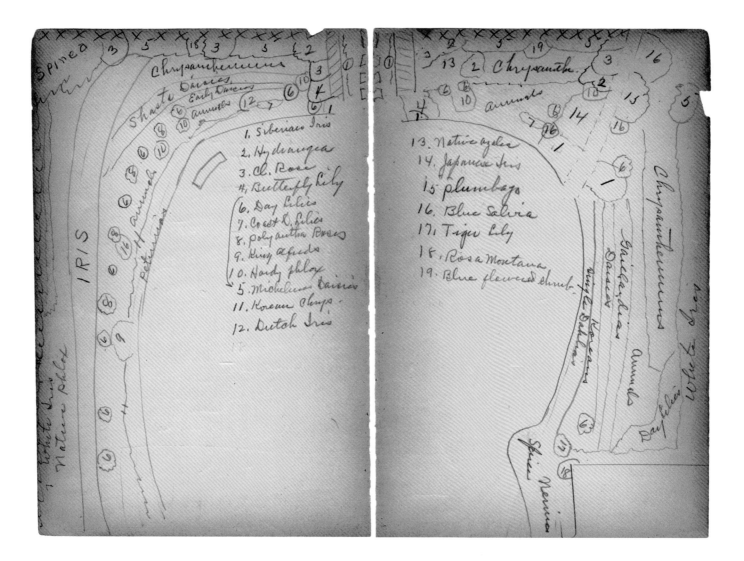

The handwritten garden diagram includes the following legend:

1. Siberian Iris
2. Hydrangea
3. Cl. Rose
4. Butterfly Lily
6. Day Lilies
7. Coast D. Lilies
8. polyantha Roses
9. King Alfreds
10. Hardy phlox
5. Michaelmas Daisies
11. Korean Clumps
12. Dutch Iris

13. Native azalea
14. Japanese Iris
15. plumbago
16. Blue Salvia
17. Tiger Lily
18. Rosa Montana
19. Blue flowered shrub

sense of responsibility. As one southern garden writer noted, "The richness of the vegetation of this territory makes it not only a privilege but a duty to have beautiful gardens all the year. . . ."[14]

The Weltys' side yard showcased a few camellias in the early years, and later, Eudora expanded the collection of her favorite plants in this spot. In the Upper Garden, the border curved from left to right, backed by a fifty-foot-long sweep of tall bearded irises in a rainbow of colors. Behind the border were white, spring-flowering spireas, including early bloom-

Diagrams for the border in the Upper Garden and the cut-flower garden, from Chestina Welty's garden journal, late 1930s. © Eudora Welty LLC.

Original Lady Banks rose (*Rosa banksiae* var. *lutea*) in the restored Welty garden.

The cameo pink 'Dr. Van Fleet' climbing rose, introduced to gardeners in 1910, is a profuse bloomer and the parent of 'New Dawn', the first patented rose (1930). It has been restored to the Welty garden, where it blooms in April, the month of Eudora's birthday. Photograph by Susan Haltom.

Right: The Historic Iris Preservation Society donated these heirloom bearded irises to the Welty garden restoration in 2000. The line of tall bearded irises (*Iris* × *germanica*) was an important part of Chestina's border design, but increased shade and hot, humid summers have made growing conditions unfavorable for irises in the garden today. Photograph by Susan Haltom.

A native 'Florida Flame' azalea (*Rhododendron austrinum*) flourishes at the front corner of the Welty house. Eudora said that she saw some blooming from a train window and sought it out for the house.

Blossoms of an indica azalea (*Rhododendron indicum* 'Gulf Pride') that grows beside the steps leading to the Upper Garden. Photograph by Susan Haltom.

ing *S. thunbergii*, which sprouts tiny white flowers along arching branches (Chestina called it "breath of spring"), and the later blooming bridal wreath (*Spiraea × vanhouttei*) with its confetti-like white petals. The trellis supported climbing roses, including the buttery yellow Lady Banks (*Rosa banksiae* var. *lutea*), the pale pink 'Dr. W. Van Fleet', the creamy white 'Mermaid', and a deep pink climbing 'American Beauty'. In front of the irises, which bloomed at a height of nearly four feet, Chestina planted successive bands of other perennials, mostly spring bloomers, but also summer- and fall-flowering plants.[15]

April is typically the peak month of bloom in Jackson, and Eudora, who was born on April 13, looked forward to its annual reprise. "I never want for anything in winter either, except spring," she once wrote in a letter to her literary agent, Diarmuid Russell. "I think our feelings must keep closer than we imagine to the parabola of the seasons, and that as we have to wait for the spring we feel that much older (really ancient) in its opposite. O Persephone!"[16]

In their spring garden, Eudora and Chestina grew camellias (*Camellia japonica*) in shades of white, pink, and red; white spireas, azaleas in pink, yellow, and lavender; white mock orange (*Philadelphus coronarius*); white

Garden Musings: Chestina's Journal

Chestina Welty's garden journal contains snatches of notes from garden club programs and diagrams and reports on her garden during the late 1930s and early 1940s. The following excerpts also hint at the kind of gardener she was.

I still don't know what to think of the weather nor what to expect. First jonquils nearly gone. Empress beginning. Peonies, phlox – everything is putting on growth. Rose foliage is very luxuriant and Birdie Bly is covered with Black Spot. Use Bordeaux in February? It is still very wet.

February 19th

Still raining! I have worked a little though. Moved the big privet from my garden to form a screen in front of the next door garage. Moved some cape jasmines and orange

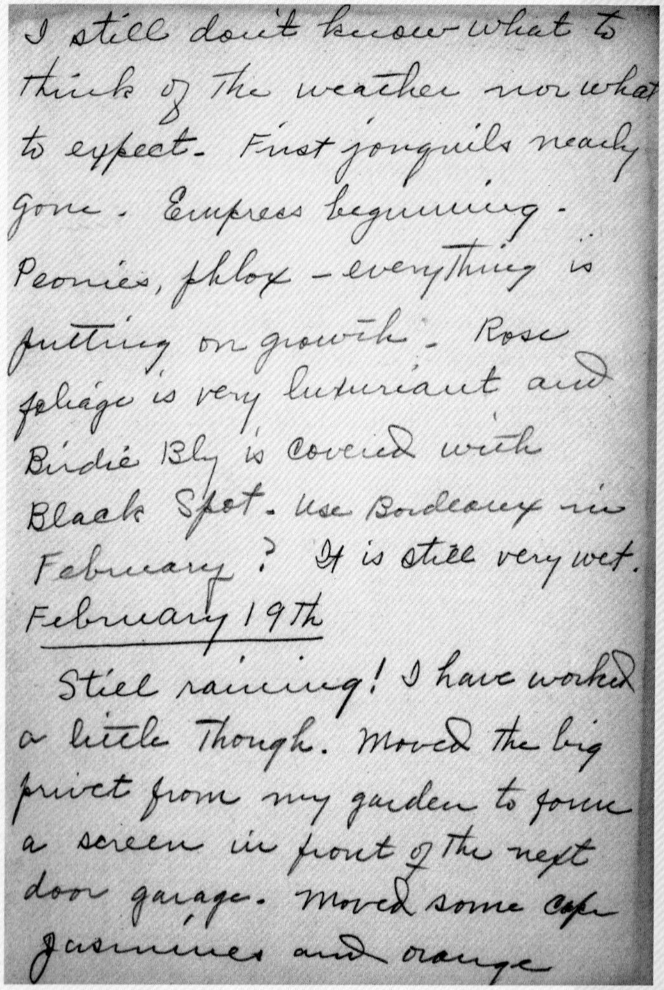

Jan. 10th 1937

Planted Eudora's "Campernelles" yesterday. The little early jonquils are in bud also a few of that double kind. "Butter and Egg" sorts are all up but no sign of bloom. . . .

Jan. 11th 1937

Bought eight Texas Blue-Bonnet plants from a smooth-talking salesman from Texas. Wonder what they would do here? Still raining!

Feb. 19th 1937

Still raining! I have worked a little though. Moved the big privet from my garden to form a screen in front of the next door garage. Moved some cape jasmines and orange Day Lilies, extended the west border down beyond the lattice to form a small border for Eudora to plant. Made a plan for this west border which I have begun with the Day Lilies and daisies. Bought and planted two beautiful camellias—Gloire de Nantes and Chandlerii Elegans. I am very proud of them and hope they will do well for me.

May 9th 1937

Have been too busy to keep records. . . .

October 14th 1937

My garden diary always plays out about the first week in May, but I'll begin in the fall this time. My borders looked fairly nice all summer and I had something to cut for the house all the time tho' I never had a wealth of flowers at any time—never things to give away as I would like to have. But have resolved to stop trying to grow annuals. I am going to have perennials in my borders to keep blooms of some sort all the time and try to plan a good succession of blooms. To this end I have made planting plans for all except the North border—which has looked fairly well all summer. I have bought a dozen new Iris and ordered a collection of Day Lilies and one of Japanese Iris. Then I plan to buy a dozen new roses. I have had better roses this year than I've had in a long time. . . .

February 3rd 1938

The lowest temperatures of the winter this week—around 20. My single camellia was in full bloom so all were lost. The other camellias were hurt but still have some buds that I think will bloom. . . .

I resolved not to grow any more annuals—but today I ordered $1.35 worth of seeds. Found a lot

of small Texas Blue-Bonnets and have transplanted them to North border. I liked them very much last year and am proud that I saved some of them. . . .

March 13th 1938

Beginning to feel safe about a freeze. Surely we will not have one now! Everything looks lovely. Wisteria and azaleas better than they have ever been. . . .

dogwood (*Cornus florida*), banana shrub (*Michelia figo*) with a cream-colored flower that exudes a banana scent; roses in all colors; and Carolina jessamine (*Gelsemium sempervirens*, also known as yellow jasmine). Perennials and annuals flowered in a riotous groundswell: pale blue Spanish bluebell (*Hyacinthoides hispanica*); irises in several varieties and colors; bright blue cornflower; annual phlox in bright red, pink, and white; white sweet alyssum; a mix of pink, purple, blue, and white larkspur; and pink Shirley poppies, among other flowers.[17]

"My mother always wanted a parade of bloom in the border," Eudora said.[18] To fill the gaps between perennials in the long growing season, Chestina used annuals—multicolored zinnias and bright yellow marigolds—along with tropical pink cannas and other herbaceous plants to carry the bloom through fall. Although gardeners all over the country used many of these same plants, the timing and successive combinations of bloom stamped each region with its own sense of place.

Chestina's daylilies, even when not in bloom, dominated her border: "I have more than thirty varieties of this plant and from early May until the end of June you might look at my border and exclaim 'It is a garden of day-lilies.' But you would be mistaken," she wrote.[19] In fact, her orange and yellow daylilies alternated with polyantha roses, whose clustered pink blooms reappeared every six weeks. Near the front of the border, an early, low-growing variety of daylily ran the entire length, interspersed with clumps of blue stokesia. White perennial phlox extended the period of bloom. In October, chrysanthemums and asters took their turn. Chestina conducted her perennial border like a symphony, with each movement calling on a different instrument section in succession.

Besides orchestrating the timing of all these flowers, the designer of a successful perennial border must choose for height, color, and texture, striving for contrast, harmony, and unity. Finer-leafed plants in the front of the border contrasted with the sword-like iris foliage. Chestina chose her pink cannas for their five-foot height and their big, glossy leaves. "I have tried to show that while there are at least four periods of profusion of bloom in my little garden these periods overlap sufficiently so that the

Clockwise from top left:

———————

Carolina jessamine and spireas bloom near the cold frame in the early spring. Photograph by Susan Haltom.

———————

Phlox drummondii, a Texas native, blooms in the curving border of the Upper Garden in spring. It was a popular garden plant of the 1920s and '30s. Photograph by Susan Haltom.

———————

Cornflower 'Jubilee Gem' grows in the restored cut-flower garden. It was an All America Selection in 1937. Photograph by Susan Haltom.

Chestina in the garden, undated. © Eudora Welty LLC.

Above: Original daylilies bloom in the Upper Garden.

Right: Blue stokesia, shown in the 1944 Wayside Gardens catalog, has been restored to the Welty garden. Collection of Susan Haltom.

Above: Pale pink, single, daisy-flowered chrysanthemums bloom in October in the restored Welty garden. Photograph by Susan Haltom.

border is never bare of bloom," Chestina concluded in her notes for a
garden-club talk, "and from early February until after Thanksgiving there
are always spots of color and something of interest to be found."[20]

Her selections—from native species such as Indian pink (*Spigelia
marilandica*) through old-fashioned bulbs (*Jonquilla simplex*) and modern hybrids like the daylilies—reveal that Chestina was open to all sorts
of plants, not only the newest hybrids or the most traditional varieties.

Pink canna appeared on Chestina Welty's garden diagram. This variety, 'Mrs. Pierre S. du Pont', was pictured in *Garden Bulbs in Color*, J. Horace McFarland, L. H. D.; R. Marion Hatton; and Daniel J. Foley, 1938.

Above: Spigelia, or Indian pink, grows wild in the Mississippi woodlands. Eudora and Chestina discovered this specimen growing along a dirt road and planted it by the driveway, where it continues to pop up every year. Photograph by Susan Haltom.

Left: Native pink azalea has been restored and grows near the trellis in the Welty garden. Photograph by Susan Haltom.

But she refused to coax plants to grow in unsuitable places, or to force them to bloom out of season. Where the garden was concerned, "fashion meant zero to her," her daughter said. Some of her plants, like the pink native azalea (*Rhododendron canescens*) near the arbor seat, she dug up in the woods. When the two women realized how this practice was depleting Mississippi's native plants, particularly the signature woodland dogwoods, they put a bumper sticker on their car that read "Leave the dogwoods for others to enjoy."[21]

As Chestina poetically put it, beyond the border, "a small rose garden runs away down the hill to meet the trees."[22] Here she raised her choice roses and checked them continually, pruning them in February, spraying and clipping, in order to have flowers to arrange and share. Chestina was busy with her roses nearly year-round, since in Mississippi they often bloom until Christmas and start again in April.

Suzanne Marrs suggests that Chestina relished working in the garden precisely because it was "always a work in progress," never perfected. Eudora said her mother believed that "a gardener needs patience above all," and she rarely showed frustration when a gap appeared between her vision for the garden and its reality. "In the garden she was pretty hard to lick," Eudora recalled.[23]

As Chestina herself explained:

> Curiously enough, the vision of the gardener seems to grow faster than the garden. He who finds profusion of bloom with no attempt at garden design satisfying this spring will likely be planning to bring about a more ordered arrangement next year, and the gardener who thinks of his garden as a beautiful picture or a carefully planned retreat may soon be digging and fertilizing in an effort to secure more and finer blooms in his well-designed plot. Thus does the gardener grow up to his garden, and thus does the garden continue to be satisfying though never perfect.[24]

The hybrid tea rose 'Etoile de Hollande', introduced in 1919, was the standard of excellence among red roses. It inspired the character's name Etoyle in Welty's story "Moon Lake," and was used again in her novel *Losing Battles*. Photograph by Susan Haltom.

Above: 'Radiance' and 'Red Radiance', two of the most popular roses of the 1930s. From *How to Grow Roses*, Robert Pyle, J. Horace McFarland, and G. A. Stevens, 1930.

The hybrid tea rose 'Dainty Bess', introduced in 1925, has a single (five-petaled) blossom and prominent, cinnamon-colored stamens. Welty referred to this rose in *Delta Wedding*. Photograph by Susan Haltom.

Chestina's Roses

Chestina Welty loved many flowers, but "she loved roses better than anything," according to Eudora. Throughout her life she often posed for photographs among the roses: as a young woman in West Virginia, as a young mother with a climbing rose adorning one of the columns at her first home, as a gardener working among the hybrid teas in her Pinehurst garden, and as a flower arranger in her home. Two of her brothers in West Virginia also grew roses, and the three of them swapped rose culture information and cuttings.

Climbing roses draped Chestina's garden trellises and provided a lush and beautiful background for springtime borders, but her utilitarian rose bed was screened from view. Here she grew a combination of old garden roses (including 'Maman Cochet', introduced in 1893; 'Duchesse de Brabant', 1857; 'Lady Hillingdon', 1910; and 'Louis Philippe', 1834) and the newest hybrid teas, which were bred for longer stems and blossoms that held their heads upright, so they looked good in a vase. These hybrids, however, require coddling and spraying, so years later the two women reinstated more of the older, hardier varieties.

On at least one occasion, Chestina presented a program on rose growing to her garden club, offering her own best advice. She knew that for roses to thrive they must be watered deeply, and Eudora said her mother "remembered the classic advice given to

Chestina in her rose garden, undated. © Eudora Welty LLC.

rose growers on how to water their bushes long enough: 'Take a chair and *St. Elmo*'"—a long, popular Victorian novel set in the South.

Although Chestina preferred organic fertilizers (manure, liquid manure, and cottonseed meal) on her roses, she did use Bordeaux mixture for fungal diseases (it could be made at home with blue vitriol or copper sulfate, lime, and water), and arsenate of lead and tobacco dust (boiled or ground tobacco stems mixed with water) for insect pests.

Near the end of Chestina's life, when she was bedridden, her beloved roses died virtually overnight. Eudora did not have the heart to tell her.

Annuals: No Two the Same Kind

"... I happen to know where I can send in a box top and get a packet of one thousand mixed seeds, no two the same kind, free."

"Oh, where?" Mama wants to know.

But I says, "Too late. You tend to your house, and I'll tend to mine. . . ."

—Eudora Welty, "Why I Live at the P.O."

The testy mother and daughter in Eudora's story were talking about annuals, or flowers that complete their life cycles in one season. Typically grown from seed, they are the multitaskers of the flower garden. They rise to all heights, exhibit varying leaf textures, and bloom for weeks longer than the perennials that pop up year after year on their own. The thought of a packet of a thousand different mixed seeds planted in a single garden would make the design-conscious gardener shudder.

Chestina used annuals such as Drummond phlox (*Phlox drummondii*) and Shirley poppies (*Papaver rhoeas*) in her border, to fill in between perennials. In her cut-flower bed, she grew zinnias (*Zinnia elegans*) and marigolds (*Tagetes patula* and *T. erecta*) for their bright accents in bouquets. And she may also have planted nasturtiums (*Tropaeolum majus*) in flowerpots for moveable feasts of color. Eudora wrote in a letter to her agent that she had started cosmos seeds in the cold frame in April.

Americans imported flower seeds from Europe until World War I, when supplies were cut off, prompting the emergence of large American seed companies. Commercial houses with nationwide distribution, such as W. Atlee Burpee (whom the Weltys patronized), Ball, Ferry-Morse, Harris, Michell, and Park, sought to select or hybridize the longest-blooming, easiest-to-grow annuals with the purest colors. Clever seedsmen offered discounts to garden clubs, trumpeting their latest varieties as new and fashionable.

In 1932, the Southern Seedsmen's Association founded the All-America Selections program to develop superior seeds in test gardens, using impartial judges. The idea was to offer this information to gardeners as a credible alternative to the claims made by advertisers. The All-America Selections list contains superior plants grown from seed, and the program continues today. Some varieties from the 1930s are still available in the nursery trade.

Because of the importance of color nuances in early twentieth-century garden design, seedsmen took care to separate certain flower seeds by color. Gardeners who perused the winter catalogues could find Drummond's phlox, China asters, zinnias, portulacas, pansies, sweet peas, and others available in single-color packets. In 1935, Burpee's seed catalogue listed nearly three hundred kinds of sweet peas—an astonishing number, given that more recent catalogues have offered fewer than ten. Also in 1935 the company offered a nasturtium named 'Bur-

pee's Dwarf Giants', a name that surely would have amused Welty. Her fancy certainly took flight when she wrote to Russell about a news item in September 1945: ". . . I read in the Jackson paper that the WCTU [Women's Christian Temperance Union] had a called meeting . . . under their president whose name is Miss Vashti Ishee. I thought you, like me, would want her to marry Atlee Burpee the seed man and have two children, Vashti Burpee and Ishee Burpee (the boy)."

Common names of annuals (and all garden plants) vary according to local custom. While Eudora and Chestina planted ragged robins (*Centaurea cyanus*), to others these royal-blue flowers might have been known as bachelor buttons or cornflowers. Latin botanical names, listed in parentheses after the common name, minimize confusion. Unfortunately, Chestina, never imagining her journals would be read by anyone else, jotted down only common names. Although it isn't certain which annuals the Weltys actually planted, the ones mentioned in Chessie's journals and Eudora's letters include larkspur; marigolds, one of the most popular garden flowers of the 1930s; nasturtiums, design icons of the Arts and Crafts movement; petunias, in pinks, purples, and whites; and zinnias of all colors. More of the Weltys' annuals are listed in Appendix III.

CHAPTER SIX

"You and Me, Here"

If the children are at home, the front yard, creeping unsodded from beneath the porch, is naked and clean. If the children are grown . . . , verbena, old maids [zinnias], phlox, and four-o'clocks, crowd each together for space. . . . Our housewives haven't the time to be always sweeping the yard, so they just plant flowers and "let 'em have it." If the house is in the Delta, and is not the house of a planter, it will not have a yard at all; cotton will grow to within a few feet of porch and eaves.

—*Mississippi: The WPA Guide to the Magnolia State*, 1938[1]

When other parts of America dropped into the Great Depression, Mississippi had so little industry, and its sharecropping tenant farmers had been mired in poverty for so long, that most of the rural population didn't have far to fall. As a result, it took longer for the Depression to take hold in a noticeable way. As Eudora observed, "[P]overty in Mississippi—white and black—really didn't have too much to do with the Depression. It was ongoing. Mississippi was long since poor, long devastated."[2]

Four years later, however, the state's scant fifty-two thousand industrial jobs had dropped to twenty-eight thousand. With textile mills in other parts of the country also shuttering, cotton prices plummeted. The average annual income for Mississippi farmers—already the lowest in the nation, at $287—plunged by 64 percent, to $117. "On a single day in 1932, one-fourth of the state's farm land was sold for taxes," notes one Mississippi historian. By the time President Franklin D. Roosevelt was inaugurated in

Cotton grows right to the doorstep of this sharecropper's cabin in the Mississippi Delta, 1930s. An ornamental garden would have been an unthinkable luxury here. Works Progress Administration photograph, courtesy of MDAH.

A work crew in a Jackson park under the city's Depression-era relief program suggests how many men were unemployed. Courtesy of Steve Colston Photography.

Children at a day nursery in rural Mississippi during the Great Depression. Works Progress Administration photograph, courtesy of MDAH.

January 1933, 40 percent of Mississippi's farms were on the auction block.[3]

In a state where no government safety net existed, Jackson devised its own relief program. For several months in 1931 and 1932, the "One Cent Plan" called on citizens to donate a penny from every dollar they earned to a general fund that allowed the city "to hire unemployed men and women to build roads, cut stove wood, plant gardens, and make general repairs throughout the city." Jackson created sixteen community vegetable gardens for needy residents during the Depression.[4]

Whether or not the Weltys saved money by growing their own vegetables remains unknown. Although comparatively well off, they took steps to augment their household funds. Edward, an architect, built a duplex house on the lot next door to provide rental income, and Chestina took in a boarder at home. A naturalist and pioneering conservationist named Frances (Fannye) Cook shared the Welty household for many years. As an educated and independent woman, Cook found good company in

Chestina and Eudora, who shared her interests in plants and wildlife. Eudora, as usual, found humor in the odd situations that sometimes arose in Cook's vocation. "We would take messages for her and the message would be something like 'Mr. Tackett is out of the swamp,'" Eudora recounted. Once a man came to the house and asked Eudora to stow a dead owl in the refrigerator until "Miss Cook" could dissect it.[5]

Eudora's part-time radio job allowed her to take on more work, and, as she began to concentrate more on her fiction writing, she cast about for other ways to apply her writing skills. For a time, she worked for a local paper and penned a society column for the Memphis *Commercial Appeal*, which provided an irresistible venue for her wit. Her friend Patti Carr Black, a writer and scholar, describes one satirical piece, "Language of Flowers," that made it into print:

> By using historical and straightforward information from an etiquette book concerned with the [Victorian-era] language of flowers, [Eudora] draws the unsuspecting reader slowly into the piece. Suddenly the reader is jolted by the advice that "with London Pride, a Lobelia, and some Laburnum," one can say, "your frivolity and malevolence will cause you to be forsaken by all." Later in the romp, she writes, "The expression of flowers is varied by changing their position. Place a marigold on the head, says the etiquette book, and it signifies mental anguish; on the bosom indifference."[6]

Between 1933 and 1935, she made several trips to New York City, applying for clerical jobs as well as positions at *The New Yorker* and *National Geographic* magazines. Although she had studied advertising at Columbia and written ad copy to earn extra money while in school, that business would have been her last choice. Advertising, she decided, "was too much like sticking pins into people to make them buy things that they didn't need or really much want." Again employment eluded her, but she managed to absorb as much theatre, dance, and jazz as possible with transplanted Jackson friends.[7]

These New York trips proved memorable because she took her camera along. Her father had regularly taken family snapshots, and at some point Eudora bought herself an inexpensive model.[8] As with her writing, to which she devoted increasing amounts of time and energy during the early 1930s, she pursued photography both as an artistic medium and

The unemployed and the apple seller, 1935–1936. Photograph by Eudora Welty, © Eudora Welty LLC; Eudora Welty Collection, MDAH.

a possible vocation. While walking around the city she snapped street scenes, including the unemployment lines and distressed faces of Depression-stricken New Yorkers. Roosevelt's emergency "bank holiday," a forced closure to stop panicked withdrawals, took place while she was there in March 1933. Her memory of people fighting to retain hope and dignity under the stress of prolonged unemployment would echo in the short story "Flowers for Marjorie."

Back in Jackson, she was restless, but not despondent. In the 1930s, and even decades later—after "influxes [of] the Dutch and the Texans, all sorts of people," as she once quipped to a friend—her hometown was far from cosmopolitan. But the high-spirited Eudora didn't lack for witty companions, who were either living in Jackson or returning for regular visits. Budding writers Frank Lyell, Hubert Creekmore, and Nash Burger, and the conductor and composer Lehman Engel—all of whom would go on to lead distinguished careers—were among the worldly, artistic friends who gathered on the Weltys' porch for barbecue dinners and theatrical antics. "We made our own entertainments, and one of our entertainments was to take funny pictures," Eudora recalled, describing how she and her friends photographed themselves dressed up in imitation of the society features in *Vanity Fair*.[9]

In 1934, the friends began calling themselves the Night-Blooming Cereus Club, after the custom of visiting people who announced in the newspaper that their night-blooming cereus was expected to bloom that evening. The opening of this eerie, fragrant flower, a member of the cactus family, is indeed a spectacle akin to performance, as transfixing and exotic as any dance by Martha Graham. As Creekmore described it, "We'd sit,

Night-blooming cereus in a private home, early 1930s. Hand-colored glass slide, courtesy of Eudora Welty LLC.

A close-up of the night-blooming cereus flower. Photograph by Mary Alice White.

mesmerized, as the bud trembled and shuddered while it unwound its long slender white petals and spread them before our incredulous eyes as a delicately incised saucer full of froth." The group's take on this and other improvised entertainments was firmly tongue-in-cheek, as their club motto attested: "Don't take it too cereus. Life's too mysterious."[10]

"A FULLER AWARENESS"

For Eudora, photography, flowers, and fiction converged in the idea of place. At home in Jackson during the 1930s, she documented her mother's garden in a series of photographs that provided a valuable record of the garden. In 1936, while Chestina was sketching new outlines for her borders, Eudora landed her first full-time job, as a "junior publicity agent" with the new Works Progress Administration (WPA), the work relief program established by Franklin Roosevelt. "Traveling over the whole of

"Eudora Welty, WPA Junior Publicity Agent, while traveling through rural Mississippi, meets a Rankin County family." © WPA, courtesy of Eudora Welty LLC; Eudora Welty Collection, MDAH.

Mississippi, writing news stories for county papers, taking pictures, I saw my home state at close hand, really for the first time," she recounted in *One Writer's Beginnings*. "Making pictures of people in all sorts of situations, I learned that every feeling waits upon its gesture; and I had to be prepared to recognize this moment when I saw it. These were things a story writer needed to know."[11]

Although Eudora acknowledged that photography honed "the practice of perception," she did not regard it as a path to writing, but as a parallel pursuit—each art originating in direct experience.[12] Thirty-five years later, in the introduction to *One Time, One Place*, a book of her Depression-era photographs, she described how her brief WPA stint (the position folded in less than a year) had revealed to her the focus and the medium of her art:

In my own case, a fuller awareness of what I needed to find out about people and their lives had to be sought for through another way [than photography], through writing stories. But away off one day up in Tishomingo County, I knew this, anyway: that my wish, indeed my continuing passion, would be not to point the finger in judgment but to part a curtain, that invisible shadow that falls between people, the veil of indifference to each other's presence, each other's wonder, each other's human plight.[13]

In these years, 1935–1936, Eudora set her compass not on home, but on relationships among people living in vividly painted, deeply familiar places; that most of them happened to be in Mississippi is simply because that is where she found herself. As she once asked rhetorically, "How can you go out on a limb if you do not know your own tree?" People were her subject, place their ground. As she later observed, place in fiction, "by confining character, . . . defines it." It was no accident that it was during the months of driving back roads through the varied landscape of her native state that she found "the blessing of the inexhaustible subject: . . . You and me, here."[14]

All the while, Eudora was trailing her mother in the garden, learning. She experienced the "archetypal moment . . . of a story falling all over the garden," as she witnessed the yard boy J. W. battling the thorny tangle of Silver Moon roses. These—along with the pansies and phlox, the trellis and arbors, the camellias, and the overarching pines—made up the landscape of home. "Location is the ground conductor of all the currents of emotion and belief and moral conviction that charge out from the story in its course," she wrote. In this time, this place, her imagination tapped into those powerful currents, for "the stories came, and in torrents, soon."[15]

In 1936 Eudora published her first two short stories, "Death of a Traveling Salesman" and "Magic," in *Manuscript*, a nonpaying literary magazine, and she also exhibited her photographs at a camera shop in New York City. The next year she sold five more stories to magazines.[16] *Life*

Yard man / Clinton. This image resembles Welty's description of the character Plez, in her story "Shower of Gold": "Some of Miss Lizzie's fall roses, big as a man's fist and red as blood—they were nodding side-to-side out of the band of his old black hat. . . ." Photograph by Eudora Welty. © Eudora Welty LLC; Eudora Welty Collection, MDAH.

Washwoman / Jackson / 1930s. Photograph by Eudora Welty.
© Eudora Welty LLC; Eudora Welty Collection, MDAH.

published six of her pictures to accompany a news feature, and the editors of *Mississippi: A Guide to the Magnolia State* (produced by the Federal Writers' Project) chose three of her photos.[17]

By 1937 she had kindled a relationship with John Robinson, a friend from high school. Tall and good-looking, John came from a family of cotton planters in the Mississippi Delta. He was then working in New Orleans as an insurance adjuster, and he started seeing Eudora while he was in Jackson, where his parents had a home.[18] John's company did not seem to interfere with her work, which continued to draw critical accolades. In 1938 one of her stories ("Lily Daw and the Three Ladies") was selected for that year's volume of *The Best American Short Stories*, and she published "Old Mr. Marblehall," "The Whistle," and "A Curtain of Green," which would appear again in *The Best American Short Stories 1939*.[19]

"The Whistle" bears out Eudora's intention "not to point the finger in judgment but to part . . . the veil of indifference," Marrs comments. Welty wrote this story after staying with a well-to-do friend in Utica, Mississippi, whose family owned land worked by tenant farmers. In the night, a loud whistle signaled a freeze, and the next day she was astonished to see blankets, quilts, and clothing strewn over the tender crops to shield them from the cold. The contrast between her comfortable accommodations and this desperate scene moved her deeply.[20]

In this story Welty uses the landscape, among other images, to depict the deprivation of tenant farmers Jason and Sara Morton: "A farm lay quite visible [in the moonlight], like a white stone in water, among the stretches of deep woods in their colorless dead leaf." The Mortons are already battered by the cold when the freeze whistle awakens Sara, who lies in bed with a momentary fantasy "of colors of green and red, the smell of the sun on the ground, the touch of leaves and of warm ripening tomatoes." Then she and Jason trudge out into the frosty fields, Sara carrying their bedclothes. "Stooping over the little plants, Jason and Sara touched them and touched the earth. For their own knowledge, by their hands, they found everything to be true—the cold, the rightness of the warning, the need to act."[21] The story exposes their poverty and misery, but also reveals the dignity born of their fierce defiance of the cold, and of their deep connection to the land.

Of the other stories that poured out of Welty during the Depression years, several in addition to "A Curtain of Green" are filled with images of landscape, gardens, and flowers. In "Old Mr. Marblehall," for instance, the title character is leading a double life. In the same city he keeps two families, one in a grand house in the wealthy part of town, the other in a row of "little galleried houses" on its outskirts. So secure is he in the class divide separating the two families that he makes no attempt to conceal himself. He "can easily be seen standing beside a row of zinnias growing down the walk in front of that little house. . . . Of course he planted them!" He has sowed the inexpensive flowers—annuals, dispensed from a seed packet—as brazenly as he has this second, lesser family, with its braying wife and cunning son.[22]

And though she wrote the novel *Losing Battles* over a period of fifteen years and did not publish it until 1970, Eudora chose to set it during the Depression, in the hardscrabble hill country of Tishomingo County, that touchstone of her WPA days. "I wanted the characters to be down to bedrock—no money, no education, no nothing, except themselves—the rest being all cleared away to begin with. . . ."[23]

Eudora used her knowledge of people, place, and gardening to establish most of that in a single paragraph:

From the waterless earth some flowers bloomed in despite of it. Cannas came around the house on either side in a double row, like the Walls of Jericho, with their blooms unfurled—Miss Beulah's favorite colors, the kind that would brook no shadow. Rockets of morning-glory vines had been trained across the upper corners of the porch, and along the front, hanging in baskets from wires overhead, were the green stars of ferns. The sections of concrete pipe at the foot of the steps were overflowing with lacy-leaf verbena. Down the pasture-side of the yard ran a long row of montbretias blazing orange, with hummingbirds sipping without seeming to touch a flower. Red salvia, lemon lilies, and prince's-feathers were crammed together in a tub-sized bed, and an althea bush had opened its flowers from top to bottom, pink as children's faces. The big china trees at the gateposts looked bigger still for the silver antlers of last year's dead branches that radiated outside the green. The farm track entered between them, where spreading and coming to an end it became the front yard.[24]

clockwise from left:

Milk and wine lily (*Crinum* sp.), golden glow (*Rudbeckia laciniata*), and morning glory 'Heavenly Blue', were among the popular southern pass-along plants of the 1930s. Photographs by Susan Haltom.

To a sophisticated southern gardener like Welty, the gaudy mix of hot colors—yellow, orange, magenta, and red—signals an uneducated eye. The gardener has lined up her cannas and montbretia in single and double rows, like a crop farmer. The plants are a combination of inexpensive annuals and pass-along perennials, hardy and low-maintenance. Farm women of the South knew where they would spread to best effect and how to contain them. To that end, this gardener has used cheap but lovely morning glory vines to make a cool bower of the porch and reused sections of humble concrete pipe as planters. Raised off the ground even a little, these allow the verbena to trail over the sides, creating a feeling of abundance. Abundance does, in fact, spill out from within, and as the "children's faces" of the althea suggest, it is an abundance of family. Altogether, the plants of this garden—lined up, paired, and potted—form a veritable fortress of female guardianship.

Welty painted this scene knowingly and deliberately, recognizing that this garden speaks of the desire to make the home place beautiful, an act all the more valuable in downtrodden times. These details lay dormant in Welty's imagination, stored in her memory until they streamed out more than a decade later.

As the 1930s drew to a close, Welty's career was launched, but rejections still showed up in the mailbox. Even as publishers started to recognize her talent, they wanted novels, not the short stories she felt compelled to write. The garden, her friends, and the attentions of John Robinson offered comfort and consolation, but she still felt hampered by this barrier she could not seem to hurdle.

Welty's Garden Photography

How exciting it must have been for an amateur photographer of the early twentieth century to capture her own garden in print. As Welty once wrote to Diarmuid Russell during a winter cold snap, "I got out some old pictures of the garden in spring to restore my faith. I will send you one—iris and hemerocallis, with some roses—April." A visual record cheered her during the winter and also pointed out design flaws to be remedied, come spring.

Welty photographed the garden to document it, climbing out onto the roof to better capture its spatial relationships. All of her images proved invaluable when the garden was restored. Welty, who photographed people in their home settings, also captured her mother working in the garden—spreading grass seed, spraying the roses, admiring a blossom.

Langdon Clay, who photographed the restored Welty garden for this book, says that capturing the right light is the most important thing. He also strives to show the garden structure as a compositional element; vary framing, distances, and angles; and shift focus, scale, and distance to create drama and tension where it does not naturally exist.

PART THREE

Fall—1940s

CHAPTER SEVEN

"The Subject Was Flowers"

... hundreds of artists, and indeed people who are not artists at all, will tell you how clearly they see in their dreams.

—Æ Russell, *The Candle of Vision*[1]

Portrait of George (Æ) Russell by Mary Duncan. The Irish mystic, artist, and writer was Diarmuid Russell's father. Courtesy National Library of Ireland.

facing page:

Diarmuid Russell, Katonah, New York, 1940s. Photograph by Eudora Welty. © Eudora Welty LLC; Eudora Welty Collection, MDAH.

In 1929, when Welty was preparing to graduate from the University of Wisconsin and her mother was busy with the new Garden Lovers group in Jackson, a twenty-seven-year-old engineer named Diarmuid Russell emigrated from Ireland to America. He found a job in his field in Schenectady, New York, but neither the place nor the work suited him. He left his job in the depths of the Depression and wandered to Chicago, where he worked in a bookstore, fell in love, and married. He and his wife, Rose, moved to New York, and in 1935, he landed a job with a publishing company, G. P. Putnam, in Manhattan. That year in Mississippi, Welty roamed her home state for the WPA, started to write in earnest, and still harbored the dream of moving to New York City. The meandering paths of these restless spirits would soon cross.

Diarmuid (pronounced DER-mid, Gaelic for "without enemies") seemed preordained for a literary occupation, whether he intended it or not. His father, George William Russell (1867–1935), was an Irish nationalist, poet, artist, editor, and religious mystic. He adopted the name Æ, short for Æon—sometimes written AE or A. E.—after it came to

Eudora Welty, 1940s.
© Eudora Welty LLC.

him in a vision. An art-school friend of William Butler Yeats, to whom he later introduced the young James Joyce, Æ personified the term "literary lion." Tall, big-shouldered, and with a beard to rival Rasputin's, he stood at the center of the Irish Literary Revival of the early twentieth century. His collection of autobiographical essays, *The Candle of Vision*, described, among other things, his mystical experiences, his rejection of urban life, and his spiritual bond with the natural world.[2] Nonetheless, the Russells lived in Dublin, where the city's intellectual firebrands habitually stopped by their house to argue politics, religion, poetry, and art. Michael Kreyling, in his book *Author and Agent*, which chronicles the partnership of Welty and Russell, observes that Diarmuid had, "by virtue of his birth and rearing, one of the finest literary educations available at the time." After working for three years as "sub-editor" under his father's demanding tutelage, however, the younger Russell opted to pursue a career in science.[3] Fortunately, the rebellion did not hold.

In 1940 Welty, living hundreds of miles from the center of the American publishing world, found herself at a frustrating impasse. Her creative outpouring continued, and it continued to take the form of short stories. At thirty-one, she had succeeded in publishing her stories in low-paying, if prestigious, literary magazines; some did not pay at all. To pursue writing as a full-time career would require breaking into higher-paying publications, such as the esteemed *Atlantic Monthly* and *Harper's Magazine*, which also preferred to publish work by novelists, and sometimes printed novels in serial form. Welty pitched book publishers the idea of combining her stories and photographs as a book, but this too met with multiple rejections. With or without the pictures, a volume of stories held no appeal for publishing houses, where editors viewed stories as "snack food, not the entrée"—even though readers showed a healthy appetite for the snacks. Until she proved her mettle as a novelist, she would remain an outsider. John Woodburn, a literary scout for the New York publisher Doubleday, Doran, had taken up her cause with his editors as well, as yet to no avail.[4]

Meanwhile, Diarmuid Russell, back in New York, was relieved from his job at G. P. Putnam, after upbraiding his boss for writing a publishing contract that placed the publisher's interest over the writer's. Although he was then thirty-eight and working in the capitalist center of North America, if not the world, Russell, true to his upbringing, was genuinely outraged by the idea of making money at the expense of an artist. Spurred on by the likes of Maxwell Perkins, the legendary editor at Scribner's, Russell started a literary agency with a partner, Henry Volkening, in spring 1940. John Woodburn passed along the name of Eudora Welty as a prospective client. Russell wrote to her in late May, offering to represent her and describing himself as a "benevolent para-site." Welty wrote back within days: "Yes—be my agent."[5]

Thus began a thirty-three-year relationship that merged business with friendship until Di-armuid Russell's death, in 1973. His introductory letter mentioned that his father was Æ Russell. Eudora responded that *The Candle of Vision* had thawed her heart during a "shivery winter" in Wisconsin.[6] They soon discovered that they had even more in common. Welty and Russell sealed their literary partnership in their mutual passion for gardening. In August 1940, only months after signing on with Russell & Volkening, Welty met with Russell in New York City and visited the Russells' home in Kato-nah, north of the city. Not only was her agent a gardener, but an amateur horticulturist with a keen interest in wildflowers.[7] Russell's garden was his respite from the city and his reward for tolerating it during the work week.

Diarmuid and Rose Russell in their garden in Katonah, New York, 1940s. Photo-graph by Eudora Welty. © Eudora Welty LLC.

From then on, the two swapped plants and news of what was blooming in their very different climates. At a time when long-distance telephone calls were costly, they sometimes wrote several times a week. After Rus-sell sold two of her stories ("Powerhouse" and "A Worn Path") to *The*

Atlantic in December 1940,[8] Welty confessed that she had "spent a great sum of my new gains on flower seeds from Burpees." And the following month, when Russell struck a deal with Doubleday to publish her first collection of short stories, she wrote back to say that when she received his letter, she had been "digging in the woods—whenever I get good news from you I seem to have to sit down covered with dirt and leaves to tell you, but I feel like chiffon and jewels." Another time, when frost was still a danger, she reported, "My mother and I are in two different schools about covering up plants—she thinks they should learn to be Spartans, and I hold that nothing should be Spartans, and that one should not impose one's will over any thing, especially a helpless bush."[9]

In February, Welty boasted that seeds were sprouting in baked dirt (to sterilize it) on her back steps:

> A girl in her garden no sloven
> Once baked all her dirt in the oven—
> But they said what you bake
> Is not tart and not cake,
> Macaroon, macaroni, or muvven—[10]

Diarmuid Russell and Henry Volkening, Welty's literary agents. Photograph by Eudora Welty. © Eudora Welty LLC.

When spring finally showed itself in the North, Russell felt the stirrings. "Flowers are getting more and more in my thoughts these days. I can't speak about them in the office because the others don't know much about them," he wrote. "Henry [Volkening], who is a remarkably fine and intelligent person, didn't know what a pink was when I mentioned the name to him today and it filled me with horror that a human being and a good human being should not know this."[11]

Soon after that Welty mailed him a camellia cutting (*Camellia japonica* 'Herme') and a note to tell him it was on the way. "There is danger that I will pour all my riches into camellias," she said, "I have just been waiting for the chance. . . ." And in April: "My mother speaks out now and then from her meditations on the garden to state that this is going to be a good iris year. Do you agree?" The report continued:

Chestina Welty, 1940s. Photograph by Eudora Welty. © Eudora Welty LLC; Eudora Welty Collection, MDAH.

> I've been working in the backyard so long and hard that when I finally shut my eyes at night I see certain kinds of leaves in my head—I see leaves the way Lady Macbeth saw spots. . . . I am trying to grow delphiniums, which are not for us, and they have already sent up flower spikes, being all hopped up on vitamins so they don't know what they're doing. I saw some grand manure the other day and thought of you. . . . It was well rotted manure—practically antique. But I had no way to make off with it. I carry scissors, diggers, and hatchets, but no manure compartment in my car.[12]

Sweetpeas in the restored garden. Photograph by Susan Haltom.

Clearly, by now Chestina's "yard boy" had graduated to full gardener status. This letter also aired some playful thoughts about her upcoming summer writing retreat at Yaddo, an artists' community in Saratoga Springs, New York: "Maybe they have it fixed up to force writers, with warm moist rooms and a sprinkling of vitamins on the soup, and we will all write exotic large-scale things that you will have to sell to strange little men in back rooms. Maybe I will send you . . . giant, double-size, everblooming stories with which you cannot fail."[13]

A few weeks later a searing early heat settled over central Mississippi. The sun was "smiting everything," and Welty was putting "little paper hats over my new plants at break of day, to shade their brows." At the end of April, the garden sent up great wafts of "ambrosial" fragrance to her bedroom: "Under my window is a Magnolia fuscata tree [commonly known as banana shrub] and I can smell it anytime by just drawing my breath. . . . Everything that smells good is in bloom now, irises, roses, honeysuckle, lilies, pinks, sweetpeas. . . ."[14]

From the New York writing retreat that June, Welty relayed garden gossip sent by her mother: "The delphiniums I planted in my ignorance have all bloomed like everything and are getting ready to bloom for the second time and Mother says the ladies of the garden club come over each day to worship and grit their teeth."[15]

Much discussion passed between them on gardening topics, some of it witty, some poignant. But for both author and agent, gardening was more than a rewarding pastime; it was a form of communion with nature that uplifted them and inspired creativity. Their letters reveal that for both,

Delphiniums tower over Chestina Welty in the cut-flower garden. © Eudora Welty LLC; Eudora Welty Collection, MDAH.

Eudora Welty at Yaddo, 1940. © Eudora Welty LLC.

"the garden and writing were linked at some profound level," as Marrs observes. From Russell's perspective, says Kreyling, a writer was "a sort of seer or philosopher with a vision that prompted the words.... A story or novel or poem was the visible product of a seamless vision, moment, or mood."[16] Such moments often arose for Welty when she was outdoors, and often in the garden. She had long been solitary in the act of writing, and the fellowship with a kindred spirit released a stream of reveries, musings, and occasional flights of mystical communion:

> Every evening when the sun is going down and it is cool enough to
> water the garden, and it is all quiet except for the locusts in great waves
> of sound, and I stand still in one place for a long time putting water on
> the plants, I feel something new—that is all I can say—as if my will went

out of me, as if I had a stubbornness and it was melting. . . . when I feel without ceasing every change in the garden itself, the changes of light as the atmosphere grows darker, and the springing up of a wind, and the rhythm of the locusts, and the colors of certain flowers that become very moving—they all seem to be a part of some happiness or unhappiness, an unhappiness that something is lost or left unknown or undone perhaps—and no longer simple in their beautiful but outward way.[17]

"I think I understand the feeling you speak about," Russell replied. "I have had it myself on several occasions but [it] comes and goes so quickly that no memory can ever recapture it. . . ." Of course, the son of Æ Russell would identify with these perceptions, which echoed not just his own experiences, but also his father's ecstatic relationship with nature: "As I walked in the evening down the lanes scented by the honeysuckle my senses were expectant of some unveiling about to take place. . . . Every flower was a word, a thought. The grass was speech; the trees were speech; the waters were speech; the winds were speech."[18]

In the way each of them worked, too, Welty and Russell relied more on intuition and imagination than on analytical thought—although Russell did encourage his client to embed a clearer sense of "logic" in some of her early stories. "Story writing and critical analysis are indeed separate gifts, like spelling and playing the flute . . . ," Welty declared in an essay. Like her mother, she was the kind of reader who sank into novels with a "sweet devouring," and the kind of writer who let her imagination carry her away— the opposite of one who composed with the orderly mechanics she called "craft": "I would just as soon write out of a dream, out of music, out of love, out of a beautiful day, out of anything except out of craft—because I think [stories] . . . seem more like a little road, leading from one thing bigger than the writer into some other thing which should be also bigger than the writer. Perhaps it is all because I love magic things instead of clever things. . . ."[19]

She did spin elegant magic out of her imagination, but even the wildest flights touched ground. In August 1941, after spending two months in

Saratoga Springs, she returned home to parboiling heat; her delight in being there reached out from the garden to embrace the larger sense of her home place: "The heat is on here and I go out at 6 to water the garden a few hours so it will live through the day, then I myself fall under the butterfly-lilies and go into a trance. . . . A little parade of country people goes by the house yelling 'Blackeyed peas and okra!' . . . Blackeyed peas should be grown everywhere, it is the dish you're supposed to eat on New Years Day and you will never go hungry—We always take out this insurance. . . ."[20]

As Michael Kreyling observes, "In deep and mysterious ways Mississippi was home, and the garden an intensification of home."[21] A week later, the garden rapture crept into her sleep. A letter that began with descriptions of plants blooming in her garden ended with an account of an astonishing dream:

> . . . it is a kind I have now & then, of listening while someone reads me some long wonderful thing, really chants it—the dream is all words and seems to last all night long. Sometimes the one giving it has it written down & sometimes it is a chant, but always it is something before which I simply recline and marvel. (A grand kind of dream, nobody has to move.) Anyway this one was yours, it was read off from notes & augmented by something like oratory, it was very important & nothing was left out—the subject was flowers, and I think you should go on and write it. It took up all kinds, one by one, but there was more to it than just descriptions & cultivation—the structure & anatomy, very particular, and since I am unfamiliar with that it impressed me greatly, and the history going back to the beginning, like with the fleur-de-lis, and the symbolic flowers, like the blue water-lily of the Nile and Solomon's Seal, and the lotus, and the category of flowers people have been changed into or out of—all including the cultivation & care, & the use of Vitamin B-1—in other words, complete. I can't tell you how far-reaching it was. All the real, legendary, decorative (like in illumina-

tions), primal, symbolic, and imaginary flowers were there—a lot I had never heard of—I didn't know Solomon's Seal was a plant but I looked it up in the dictionary this morning.[22]

Russell wrote right back: "Solomon's Seal was one of the earliest plants I knew. . . . The name comes from the markings on the roots which are supposed to represent the seal of Solomon. . . ."[23] Russell had recently explored the relationship of dreams and creativity in an attempt to write a story. He related his experiences in an article for *Harper's Magazine*, concluding that an "interior intelligence" inspired creativity and imagination through sleeping dreams and "daylight vision[s]." His repeated conscious attempts to tap this mysterious intelligence helped to spark his imagination.[24]

Regardless of how Welty and Russell interpreted the meaning of their dreams, for Welty, the simple fact of having a close friend who understood how the garden might serve as a creative inspiration, and who respected the dream as a creative medium, may have been comforting as she felt increasing anxiety about the escalating hostilities in Europe. In one letter she complained that she felt as if her bones were "being ground to pieces" by the drone of military airplanes flying over the house; but the injury may have been more to her nerves—the increasing air traffic signaled a build-up in military preparedness, filling her with foreboding.[25]

On December 7, 1941, the Japanese bombed Pearl Harbor, and the United States and England entered the war. With her brothers, her sweetheart, John Robinson, and several close male friends eligible for military draft, Welty wrote, "I cannot wish for destruction of anyone but O Lord how I want to protect the rest. To keep a few separate and apart. . . ." Then she added a sentence that expressed one of her life's guiding principles: "People must be taken one by one in the world, that is the way they are loved, believed, or understood, and when we are told to think in masses, we are lost for the one thing that is the essence and holy is gone. . . ."[26]

Later in this long letter, she recounted another "wonderful dream." This one swirled around her favorite flower, the camellia:

"First there were all the billions of camellias in the world. . . ."

First there were all the billions of camellias in the world, that was how it started. Then these just narrowed themselves down to millions, each showing how it was a variation of what, then these narrowed themselves down, and so on, back and back, further and further, and all the time I had to hold on fast (it was like being in a strong wind) or I could never keep it straight or learn it exactly. It was like a wonderful problem in deduction but it had all kinds of importance attached, I forget what. So the plants narrowed down, and narrowed down, all night, and finally there were only three left and still I held on, and then all of a sudden there was only one, the original bush, and I looked and the leaves stirred and I got to see it. But immediately there was a little sound like the closing of a jewel box, fast and final, and that was the end.[27]

It is tempting to imagine that the masses of flowers "narrowed down and narrowed down" to the sense of a jewel box holding "one thing that is the essence and holy." This glimpse of something rare and essential did, in fact, snap shut, at least for a time, as Welty's anxiety crowded out her creativity. If her fears ran high during the build-up to war, they threatened to consume her now that America had joined it.

Camellias: "Such Grandeur"

Of all the plants she cherished, the camellia was probably Eudora's favorite. She purchased them from private growers out in the countryside as well as from well-known nurseries elsewhere, such as Overlook Nurseries in Mobile and Fruitlands Nursery in Augusta, Georgia. The nurseryman G. G. Gerbing's book *Camellias* (1943), with its color plates throughout, was in her bookshelf, and she may have used it as a guide to her selections for the garden. She wrote about these flowering shrubs often to Diarmuid Russell and John Robinson, and she collected and took cuttings, planted seeds, and even learned to graft in order to increase her collection.

In 1945 she told Diarmuid that she was creating a camellia garden of her own: "My plants look all right, though they have been frozen, sleeted on, snowed on, and came through a terrible drouth just before. The outdoor plants look more pleasing and symmetrical than those grown in pots, because just as you say all the plant goes to the flower, indoors. When they get to be trees they are something like the holly tree in form. In about ten years or so there will be a tall hedge of camellias all the way around the yard on one side, if they keep thriving, and I will put a bench out then, and you must expect to sit on it and enjoy such grandeur. There are fall and spring flowering, early and late, single and double, red, white, pink, solid, striped, and variegated, though of course just a small representation of the family. Most of them stand for some story sold, though some are raised tenderly from stolen cuttings."

Although there are many species of camellia, including the popular fall-blooming *Camellia sasanqua* and the tea plant, *Camellia sinensis*, the most popular camellia in the South is *C. japonica,* and these compose the bulk of Eudora's collection. They are native to regions of Japan and China, where they were revered for hundreds of years before being exported to the West.

The first recorded specimens of *C. japonica* to arrive in England were the white 'Alba Plena' and an unnamed variegated type, transported in 1792 by East India merchantmen. Interest in this beautiful plant ignited, and by 1800 camellias had made their way to the eastern United States. By the late 1830s a grower in the Boston area listed 150 varieties. A decade later, Philadelphia was the leading camellia center in the country.

Originally thought to be tender, camellia plants were coddled by growers in the northern United States, but once glass became easier to obtain, the shrubs luxuriated in greenhouses. When nurserymen found that camellias thrived outdoors, the plants quickly became ubiquitous in southern gardens, where they thrived in the filtered shade and acid soil under loblolly pines, sometimes growing more than ten feet tall.

An assortment of camellias
from the Welty garden. Photograph by Susan Haltom.

The last half of the nineteenth century saw a decline in camellia cultivation. The Civil War interrupted their importation through southern ports including New Orleans, Mobile, and Charleston, South Carolina, and after the war they fell out of favor as exotic Victorian bedding schemes came into fashion. Hundreds of older camellias across the South survived this period of neglect to attain huge size, but in many cases, the names of cultivars were lost or confused. Over time, local nurseries simply made up new names for the old stock they continued to propagate, which accounts for the thousands of camellia names in existence today. The International Camellia Society completed a forty-year project of camellia nomenclature in 1993 with the publication of the two-volume *International Camellia Register*. This invaluable resource includes both Asian names and Western synonyms, along with plant descriptions and dates of introduction. Since then, researchers have cracked the DNA code for the genus *Camellia*, so in the future one might be able to send a leaf to a laboratory for precise identification.

Eudora noticed the spread of camellias through her home state, with certain towns known for their particular flower. In 1942 she wrote to Diarmuid, "When you go around the countryside you see that each community of any age has its own variety, grown from seed by some lady once and cuttings given away, and there you will see a great parent bush in some yard and little and middle-sized ones scattered in the yards around it, all a camellia known only to the one place. I am trying to collect cuttings of the ones that are the nicest and after years go by I'll have them all in one place—whatever kind of instinct that may be."

Camellias regained their star status in the 1920s and 1930s, appearing with azaleas in large display gardens throughout the South, including Avery Gardens in Louisiana, Bellingrath Gardens in Alabama, and the historic Magnolia Gardens in South Carolina. The founding in 1945 of the American Camellia Society (ACS) established a national venue for growing and showing. The ACS has created a Camellia Trail, linking noteworthy collections accessible to the public, primarily along the nation's coastlines (www .camellias-acs.com).

In temperate zones *Camellia japonica* blooms outside throughout winter, with early flowering varieties beginning in October and the latest bloomers in April. February through March is peak bloom time in Mississippi. More than forty camellias growing in the Welty garden today were planted by Eudora and Chestina, and many of these plants have reached a commanding stature. Varieties include 'Lady Clare' (which Eudora used as a character's name in her novel *Delta Wedding*), 'Berenice Boddy', 'Magnoliaeflora', 'Imura', 'Tricolor', 'White Empress', 'Elegans' (planted in the cemetery in *The Optimist's Daughter*), 'Dr. Tinsley', 'Herme' (sent to Diarmuid Russell), and 'Mathotiana'. Because they date to the early part of the twentieth century, this constitutes a historically significant collection.

CHAPTER EIGHT

"In the Fall I Will Miss You Then"

The loved garden is always satisfyingly responsive to moods. It flaunts its colors joyously when we are glad, its peace and [f]ragrance are soothing to frayed nerves when we are weary from contact or perhaps conflict with the everyday world, and its recurrent beauty whispers a message of comfort and hope when our hearts are lonely or sorrowful that "steals away our sadness ere we are aware."

—Chestina Welty, "The Perfect Garden"[1]

The day after the bombing of Pearl Harbor, Welty wrote to Russell, "now the teeth-grit of war is to begin."[2] Like other Americans, she felt deep anxiety about the safety and well-being of her loved ones. In January 1942, her gloom about the war interrupted even her cherished winter ritual of perusing seed catalogues. "[T]hings seem so grave and desperate sometimes that you find yourself deliberating over what plants you can have or can't as if the weight of the world were in that too—this isn't right, we should have them all, some things are better than any weight," she wrote to Russell.[3]

The weight of the world was hard to ignore. "I'm afraid my brother [Edward] will have to leave this month for the army, and three more of my friends," she told Russell the following month. "There's not much to be found out about it—all I know is that it will be soon and far from here and that all their hearts are gentle." She added that she had been

A Mississippi Marine Corps battalion departing for service. Courtesy of MDAH.

Above: Military parade,
Jackson, World War II.
Courtesy of MDAH.

Top and bottom left: Walter
Welty entered the navy and
Edward Welty served in the
army during World War II.
Photograph of Edward Welty
courtesy of Eudora Welty
LLC. Photograph of Walter
Welty © Eudora Welty LLC.

approached to "'popularize' and 'sell' all local war doings in the paper and radio." Feeling firmly antiwar at this time, Welty declined.[4]

It was a difficult time to take such a stance. After Pearl Harbor, the army air force built airfields throughout the gulf states in anticipation of enemy submarines prowling the Gulf of Mexico. Thousands of servicemen poured into Mississippi for flight training at Jackson Army Air Base (today Hawkins Field) and reported to nearby Camp Livingston for training. Similar military activity around the country produced the most noticeable effect of the war's early years—the end of the Great Depression. In the six years between 1939 and 1945, national unemployment dropped from 17 percent to less than 2 percent.[5]

Welty was among those whose financial fortunes rose in the 1940s. After a slow start, Russell regularly sold her stories to high-quality magazines, sometimes as fast as she could write them, and he negotiated with publishers to bring out three books of short stories—*A Curtain of Green* (1941), *The Wide Net* (1943), and *The Golden Apples* (1949)—a novella, *The Robber Bridegroom* (1942), and her first novel, *Delta Wedding* (1946).[6]

Taken as a whole, Welty's prolific output does not reflect her emotional turmoil, which taxed her ability to write for months at a time. During this period, Welty's immersion in the garden was intense, similar to her mother's after being widowed. She also tried to stem her anxiety in other creative ways—listening to music, painting, making rugs, and knitting. But it was gardening that "allowed her to create order and beauty rather than dwelling on war." Welty was frank with her agent about this shift in focus. In early 1942, she confessed to him, "I have lots of energy and full days working, but on flowers, not stories—there is so much to do outside that I may never get through and never get to stories. I only think about the kind of day and the feel of the earth that day, and the planting and transplanting and spading and digging and weeding and watering, and then I am asleep and doing the same thing in my sleep."[7]

Not long afterward, Welty seized a moment of inspiration and wrote her short story "Livvie," about a young black woman married to an older man. Two very different gardens are featured in this story: the husband's bare and leafless grove of bottle trees, designed to catch harmful spirits, and Livvie's swept yard, with its "blood-red roses blooming every month." Russell immediately sold the story to *The Atlantic*.[8]

Between the writing and the selling of "Livvie," Welty had another of her spellbinding dreams, which seemed to bear out her sense of gardening in her sleep; it was not digging and planting that dominated the dream, however, but a magical iris, one of Russell's favorite flowers:

> The flower floated for the whole dream in front of me, in slight motion and a little larger than life so that all the pattern of it was shown closely —then going off from it stamped or printed in the air were fainter images of the iris and it showed how by giving off its form or its qualities of color or fragrance, all these being distinct images each one, it set people to paint or to dance or to plan structures and systems or to follow after some romantic thing, all depending on the image thrown off by the iris, and then it suddenly appeared in cross section and was identical with the floor plan of a great church. . . . I had the feeling that it could go on giving off images like a fountain, for as long as I could dream it.[9]

In an answering letter, Russell suggested that the iris form was similar to the fleur-de-lys (lily flower) of medieval French heraldry. Welty replied:

> I suppose the subconscious mind as well as the conscious can take a great liking to some time and place in history and see it in everything— but why? Isn't it mysterious? I have never known much about the thirteenth century in France, though I like it very well. . . . There may be somebody in the world now thinking so hard on the 13th century that in my openness of dream and vacancy of mind I caught it. I guess it will pass—although now I am determined to read and ponder all I am able on the time and force the connection through and see what is so marvelous to me. . . .[10]

"The flower floated for the whole dream in front of me. . . ." Photograph by Susan Haltom.

Welty's garden, and her relationship to flowers, now filled several roles in her imagination. At various times it took on almost mystical powers—a place where her hopes could be made real, and an oracle of sorts. When she was worried about loved ones entering the service, she told Russell, "Six yellow rain lilies opened this morning—they never did bloom in their lives before and while I was weeding they opened right under my eyes—

lovely, clear, and fragrant with a cool fragrance—I took them as a sign. I feel as if I could just turn into something that would keep people safe, if I knew how. . . ."[11] This is not to suggest that Welty consciously practiced religious rituals in the garden; it seems clear, though, that she related to the garden as a creative touchstone where her imagination, dreams, and memories mingled and flowed.

Eudora Welty, 1940s. © Eudora Welty LLC.

Knowing how hard his client was laboring under the weight of her anxiety about the war, Russell expressed concern, but he had too much respect for the creative process to prod her. During spring and summer of 1942, she managed to write two stories in addition to "Livvie"—"A Still Moment" and "At the Landing." Spring, her favorite season, briefly buoyed her spirits. "O God, what a day, too grand, I had a digger poised but will lay it down and work on [the short story] the Winds," she wrote, adding, "The brain has not been working lately and all I can do is make rugs, but I have made two—that's enough—it must be my brain hibernates in winter. In bloom—crocuses. Hyacinths on the verge."[12]

In the days when "endangered species" had yet to enter the gardener's vocabulary, spring's arrival also meant foraging for wild flora. "Now is the time when all the swamps will be filled with strange rare things," she told Russell in March. "Do you think I could buy a ticket on the bus and get on carrying a bucket and spade and wearing hip boots and patting a snake-bite remedy in my pocket, and get off in the middle of the swamps; and get back on the night bus hung with lilies and irises and orchids and snakes and with water hyacinths in my hair, and not attract unfavorable attention?" A passing comment suggested how Chestina Welty handled her daughter's whimsy: "My mother will not even answer this question, much less say 'Use the tires and go, rather than that.'"[13]

Welty's letters to Russell convey the robust sense of humor that buoyed her spirits during these stressful times, and, like their references to flow-

"Bulbifying" montbretia corms. Photographs by Susan Haltom.

ers and gardening, it was a consistent thread in their correspondence. The topic of bulbs, in particular, caught Welty's fancy: "Today I have something beautiful in flower . . . It is Eustylis Purpurea . . . the tiniest bulb I have ever seen—no bigger than this * . Maybe a little bigger, but for some reason there is not a thing on this typewriter the size of a eustylis bulb—they ought to have a bulb keyboard, with bulb drawings on the top row and italics below. I can no longer write to you on this typewriter."[14]

In the same letter she boasted, "Something I did turned out to be smart. I wrote to Oakhurst Gardens in California, one of the strange bulb clip joints, and offered to exchange with them—I would send them spider lilies [prolific to the point of nuisance] and they could send me something wonderful out of their catalogue. I made it casual and unsuspicious." The company made her a deal.[15]

Another missive described digging 986 montbretia bulbs out of a four-foot-long bed. "If things can be said to petrify, what this dirt did was to

W elty's crowning witticism on bulbs unfolded in the form of a poetic homage to William Blake, posted on a stick in the garden:

Squirrel squirrel burning bright,

Do not eat my bulbs tonight!

I think it bad and quite insidious

That you should eat my blue tigridias.

Squirrel, Sciurus Vulgaris,

Leave to me my small muscaris.

Must you make your midnight snack, mouse,

Of Narcissus Mrs. Backhouse?

When you bite the pure leucojum,

Do you feel no taint of odium?

Must you chew till Kingdom Come

Hippeastrum Advenum?

If in your tummy bloomed a lily,

Wouldn't you feel sort of silly?

Do you wish to tease & joke us

When you carry off a crocus?

Must you hang up in your pantries

All my Pink Queen zephyranthes?

Tell me, has it ever been thus,

Squirrels must eat the hyacinthus?

O little rodent,

I wish you wo'dn't![17]

Camellia 'Catherine Cathcart'
(a.k.a. 'Leila'). From *Camellias*, G. G. Gerbing, 1943.

John Robinson, early 1940s.
© Eudora Welty LLC.

bulbify," she quipped. "Each one sends out long rays of root like a star, and each star end becomes a bulb, and then sends out its own rays, a whole universe down there."[16]

Welty's struggle to write intensified in the summer of 1942, when John Robinson, with whom she was in a serious relationship, enlisted in the army air corps.[18] Robinson not only shared Welty's interests in literature, art, and music; he also was a talented writer and a sophisticated gardener. The plants he gave her were her joys in the garden, especially a pink-blooming camellia cultivar called 'Leila' (a. k. a. 'Catherine Cathcart'). As Robinson prepared to leave for his training and, eventually, his duty overseas in military intelligence, Welty wrote to him in a voice already tinged with sadness:

A Welty camellia staked and ready for slipcovers against freezing. Photograph by Eudora Welty. © Eudora Welty LLC.

It is a still morning, rains every day, I think with pleasure and comfort of my little plants and the roses are growing and blooming. When it is just a little cooler and they all come out the way they do in the fall I will miss you then. Leila had a number of real buds, I will not count for it's bad luck, but around a dozen and more coming every day. . . . I go over bulb catalogs every night and order and some have come. There is a chance you might see the flowers come up in spring—there is the feel of dirt for you, and what it does, it makes your hopes seem matters of truest fact. Well, flowers are older than war.[19]

In November, she told him that she had been watering the camellias and "making stakes to put their covers on over," referring to the sacks she sewed, each with a generous hem, to shield them from frost. As the shrubs grew taller, she would let down the hems for more coverage. She added a wry note about her mother blaming her for "a bad chrysanthemum plague" afflicting the garden after Welty had returned from visiting Robinson at his base in Florida. "Six different bugs by count (mother's) are on our flowers—though I think some of them are after the other bugs by this time and have lost sight of the chrysanthemums. . . . Mother said one day that she just thought I had brought those bugs back from Florida—all 6, one of each on my hat no doubt. . . ."[20]

Chestina Welty, a hardened battler of plagues and pests, marshalled an arsenal of chemicals that she mixed in the basement according to recipes clipped from magazines and passed along by other gardeners. "[I] spent all day yesterday spraying bad concoctions mixed by my mother," Welty once remarked to Russell. On another occasion she told him she and her mother were applying cottonseed meal, "a very fumey dust," to fertilize their camellias: "I scarce like to enclose it—it turns you chartreuse yellow—if your secretary . . . chanced to slit the mail open she would be whiffed out flat—of course you probably expect things like that & look out for them."[21]

EUDORA WELTY
1119 PINEHURST ST
CITY

The MISSISSIPPI MARKET BULLETIN

PUBLISHED BY THE MISSISSIPPI   DEPARTMENT OF AGRICULTURE

SI CORLEY   COMMISSIONER

VOLUMES 37 (N. S. Volume 87)	JACKSON, MISSISSIPPI, MARCH 1, 1944	NUMBER 1

POULTRY	FOR FARM WOMEN	NEW EDITOR	Machinery Equipment	FARM CROPS
LEGHORNS	**FLOWERING PLANTS**	This being the last issue of the Market Bulletin under the direction of Jim Buck Ross for the duration of the war, we desire to express our sincere appreciation to the 54,000 readers of the Bulletin for the splendid cooperation given us during his tenure as editor.	**FIELD EQUIPMENT**	**BEANS AND PEAS**

FOR SALE—24 white leghorn hens, March hatched, one year old. AAA grade, breeding certificate, from Miss. Hatcheries. Price $1.50 at farm, Mrs. J. I. Hatton, Bassfield.

FOR SALE—7 AAAA white leghorn roosters, one 1 1-2 years old and one year old. $1.50 each at farm or $1.75 delivered, to Newton Express office. Money order please, Mrs. F. H. Bostick, Newton.

FOR SALE — 35 White Leghorn hens and 2 cockerels. All for $31.45 crated and shipped from Noxapater. At yard $27.00. Write before you come and I will have them penned. Reason for selling ill health. Will S. Stokes, Rt. 1. Box 50 Noxapater.

FOR SALE — Hardy Snapdragons, can stand the coldest of winters and are ready to start blooming in early spring. Write for prices. All colors and many variegated ones. Mrs. James Hunt. Ackerman.

CHRYSANTHEMUMS all colors and hardy 25 for 50c or 75 for $1.00. Mrs. James Hunt. Cakerman.

NOTICE — I do not have any more named Iris bulbs for sale. Now only have the purple and white ones. Mrs. James Hunt. Ackerman.

FOR SALE — White swamp violets for 50c per 100. Postage prepaid. No stamps or checks. I have Mimosa trees for 24c plus 6c for postage. Mrs. C. L. Cain. Rt. 2. Brookhaven.

When war was declared, Mr. Ross, who was a Reserve Officer, immediately reported for duty, but failed to pass the physical examination. The physical disability having been corrected, he then volunteered and has been accepted as a private.

We are happy to announce that we have secured the services of Mr. Ross' wife as editor of the Market Bulletin for the duration of the war. Mrs. Ross, the daughter of a farmer, is a graduate of MSCW...

FOR SALE — One garden planter, that will plant all garden seed, from mustard to bean's and peas. This seeder is same as new, has only been used about 2 days. Sears Roebuck Seeder, has fertilizer distributor. $11.50, crated to ship. A. P. Anderson. Rt. 2. Box 65. State Line.

FOR SALE — Farm trailer, 3-4 ton heavy duty with solid rubber tires, ball hitch, first $45.00, takes it. C. E. Bogren. Ovett.

FOR SALE — One old style Fordson tractor, in first class shape and also one pulley for it and 1 tractor disc needs some repair. Will sell all together for $300.00. Prentis Cleveland. Golden. Rt. 1.

FOR SALE — Deep well pump for sale. Complete—stand, brass cylinder, 45 feet pump rod, new

FOR SALE — Bunch Butterbeans. White and speckled. 1-2 pound 20c, pound 35c postpaid in 1st and 2nd zone. Grown last year. sound and well matured. Mrs. D. M. Gean. Rt. 4. Box 43. Oxford.

FOR SALE — About 65 bushels of Arksoy beans. $2.75 per bushel. Rt. 1. Marietta. Curtis Barron.

FOR SALE — 200 pounds creole English pea seed. $20.00 per hundred or 25c per pound F.O.B. Jackson. J. W. Storment. Rt. 1. Box 205. Jackson.

FOR SALE — Sound garden seed. White and colored pole butterbeans, colored bunch butterpeas, Golden Bantam Sweet corn. 25c per package of each kind sufficient for planting several average rows. 5c liberal package white

---

ELIZABETH LAWRENCE AND THE MARKET BULLETINS

The Mississippi Market Bulletin. Courtesy of Mississippi Department of Agriculture and Commerce and MDAH.

Another Welty correspondent who shared her humor and passion for gardening was Elizabeth Lawrence, a gardener, garden designer, and writer—most famously, of the first major garden handbook for the South, *A Southern Garden* (1942). Lawrence was trained as a landscape architect, but she once declared, "I design gardens but cannot bear to be called a Landscape Architect." The women probably met through their mutual friend Frank Lyell, who taught at North Carolina State College in Raleigh, where Lawrence was living in the late 1930s. In addition to their shared connection of gardening, both women were single, educated, and well-traveled. Both also lived at home, caring for their aging mothers, and were about the same age (Lawrence was five years older).[22]

Welty put Lawrence and Russell on the mailing list for the *Mississippi Market Bulletin*. Published by the state's Department of Agriculture, the publication advertised everything and anything farmers wanted to buy, sell, or swap—from hay and hogs to jams and buttons. With the bulletin reaching more than fifty-four thousand readers by 1944,[23] farm women conducted a brisk trade in seeds, bulbs, and cuttings:

Elizabeth Lawrence, undated. Courtesy of Emily Wilson by permission of Warren W. Way III and Elizabeth Way Rogers.

"All colors of mums (with nice roots), six false dragons, two St. Joseph's lilies, and one small grandad greybeard, for two 100-pound feed sacks (print or white) free of snags and mildew."

"[Will swap] anything I have, for three wandering Jews."

"Will give a large pink oleander to anyone who will haul it away and provide several buckets of good dirt to fill the hole."[24]

Welty and Lawrence, a born botanical detective, loved tracking down the true identity of plants offered for sale under what Lawrence called their "sweet country names": Eli Agnes (Eleagnus), Festive Maxine peony (*Paeonia lactiflora* 'Festiva Maxima'), Virginia's Philadelphia (*Philadelphus* × *virginalis*, sometimes called mock orange), and wiggly rose (*Weigela florida*). Welty once sent away for a "Blue Wonder Lily" and probed the seller for more information. She reported to Robinson, "[T]he lady replied to my question that it has never bloomed and that was why she wondered—will let you know."[25]

To Welty's keen ear, the rhythms of speech, the flower names and the names of the advertisers—Rhunella Johnson, Viva Mae Pipkins, Zettie May Sanders, Lula Gammill—all sang of rural Mississippi. Some of her characters' names—Maideen Sumrall, Billy Texas Spights, Eva Sistrunk—seem clipped from the publication's pages. In her story "The Wanderers," Virgie Rainey aimed to get married on her "bulb money," and during her mother's last moments, Virgie fanned her with the *Market Bulletin*:

> Dying, Miss Katie went rapidly over the list in it, her list. . . . Purple althea cuttings, true box, four colors of cannas for 15¢, moonvine seed by teaspoonful, green and purple jew. Roses: big white rose, little thorn rose, beauty-red sister rose, pink monthly, old-fashioned red summer rose, very fragrant, baby rose. . . .
> Faster and faster, Mrs. Rainey thought: Red salvia, four-o'clock,

pink Jacob's ladder, sweet geranium cuttings, sword fern and fortune grass, century plants, vase palm, watermelon pink and white crape myrtle, Christmas cactus, golden bell. White Star Jessamine. Snowball. Hyacinthus. Pink fairy lilies. White. The fairy white.[26]

Welty did not read the bulletins merely as homespun literature; she was a frequent and eager customer. "I hear the ladies in the market bulletin are beginning to spade up looking for their bulbs—hope they save me some hyacinthus," she wrote to Robinson.[27]

Lawrence struck up long-running correspondences with several advertisers, joining a rural network of seed swapping and letter writing that connected women like Mrs. U. B. Evans, who gardened in isolation "about twenty miles from Natchez, and nine miles from the highway and the nearest telephone." In "Livvie," the young bride's husband carries her "twenty-one miles away from home . . . away up on the Natchez Trace into the deep country."[28]

Another of Lawrence's regular correspondents, Lucy Stamps, of Bogue Chitto, Mississippi, told her: "I love to work with flowers, advertise, and get letters from people. Some people write letters when ordering, some send free seed along. I give good measure and free seed, too. I turn my flower money back into more flowers. I have a friend in Texas that swaps plants with me, and a pen pal in Indiana that sends me peonies and lilies. As long as I can, I'll work with my flowers. . . ." Lawrence recognized the richness of these connections. "Like Eudora's novels, the market bulletins are a social history of the Deep South," she observed in her book *Gardening for Love: The Market Bulletins.* "[M]y own life would have been a bit poorer without these things, for which I will always thank Eudora Welty."[29]

Blue French Roman hyacinth blooming in early February in the restored Welty garden. Photograph by Susan Haltom.

Precautions Against Spirits

. . . coming around up the path from the deep cut of the Natchez Trace below was a line of bare crape-myrtle trees with every branch of them ending in a colored bottle, green or blue. There was no word that fell from Solomon's lips to say what they were for, but Livvie knew that there could be a spell put in trees, and she was familiar from the time she was born with the way bottle trees kept evil spirits from coming into the house—by luring them inside the colored bottles, where they cannot get out again. Solomon had made the bottle trees with his own hands over the nine years, in labor amounting to about a tree a year, and without a sign that he had any uneasiness in his heart, for he took as much pride in his precautions against spirits coming in the house as he took in the house, and sometimes in the sun the bottle trees looked prettier than the house did.

—Eudora Welty, "Livvie"

House with bottle-trees / Simpson County / 1941. Photograph by Eudora Welty. © Eudora Welty LLC; Eudora Welty Collection, MDAH.

Before she wrote this story about youth and old age, Welty photographed the bottle tree during her travels for the WPA: "a bare crape myrtle tree with every branch of it ending in the mouth of a colored glass bottle—a blue Milk of Magnesia or an orange or green pop bottle; reflecting the light, flashing its colors in the sun, it stood as the centerpiece in a little thicket of peach trees in bloom," she wrote, in *One Writer's Beginnings*, as she discussed how photography helped her "to capture transience" and "to hold transient life *in words*."

She continued, "I know that the actual bottle tree, from the time of my actual sight of it, was the origin of my story. . . . In 'Livvie,' old Solomon's bottle tree stands bright with dramatic significance, it stands vulnerable, ready for invading youth to sail a stone into the bottles and shatter them, as Livvie is claimed by love in the bursting light of spring. This I saw could be brought into being in the form of a story."

Elizabeth Lawrence at work in her iris bed. Courtesy of *The* (Raleigh, N.C.) *News & Observer*. Welty may have been thinking of her friend when she described a character in her unfinished story "Nicotiana" or "The Last of the Figs": "She was of that cleanness only achieved by people who have gardened all day and rub off the dirt by excessive scrubbing."

Welty repaid the compliment by making *A Southern Garden* a well-thumbed, scribbled-in staple of her garden library. Later in life, when Welty was asked what gardening magazines and books she and her mother consulted, she replied that they relied most on Lawrence, Vita Sackville-West, and Rodale (the Pennsylvania-based publisher). "Elizabeth Lawrence was a record keeper, not a hit or miss gardener," Welty observed. Like Lawrence, Chestina Welty was a scientific gardener, comparing garden notes from year to year. Chestina pounced on Eudora's copy of *A Southern Garden* before Eudora had had a chance to read it, confessing this and declaring her admiration for the book in a fan letter to Lawrence. "She and Elizabeth approached the garden in the same way: as teachers in a classroom, passionate and opinionated about their subject," observes Lawrence's biographer, Emily Herring Wilson.[30]

Although her fiction came only in fits and starts at the time, Welty's pithy and sometimes poignant descriptions of the garden flowed spontaneously in her letters. They reveal a depth of knowledge that she probably gleaned partly from her mother, partly from books and garden club talks. But as with most gardeners, experience was her primary teacher, as she worked in the dirt every day. "Gardening is not intellectual, you must get out and do it," she reflected later in life. "The absolute contact between the hand and the earth, the intimacy of it, that is the instinct of a gardener."[31]

CHAPTER NINE

"Flowers Are Older Than War"

It is because people are mostly layers of violence and tenderness—wrapped like bulbs, she thought soberly; I don't know what makes them onions or hyacinths.
—Eudora Welty, *Delta Wedding* (1946)[1]

Eudora Welty, reporting on the signs of spring in a 1942 letter to Russell, mentioned "the sassafras man . . . who comes in boots and cap, looking like a general this time of year with the gold roots strung on him, in bunches all up and down and across him, and on his shoulders like epaulettes. . . . He ties the roots in bundles with little strips of old inner-tubes, but when my brother bought some this year he got it untied and handed to him loose, because the sassafras man said he had to save tires."[2]

All Americans endured some degree of wartime privation, as the government started rationing certain goods and raw materials. Sugar and butter, chocolate and coffee, gasoline and rubber—these commodities and many more were scarce because they were harder to import or transport, or were commandeered for the war effort. The Weltys would have received a ration of four gallons of gas per week for the car Eudora and Chestina shared. And, as with the sassafras man, their tires were precious: vehicles that were not used to commute to work were allowed only one spare.[3]

One of Welty's flower drawings from a valentine she sent to John Robinson during the war. © Eudora Welty LLC; Euora Welty Collection, MDAH.

1943 Riverside (Jackson) Victory Garden. Courtesy of MDAH.

Above: The "sassafras man." Courtesy of Steve Colston Photography.

From *Horticulture*, January 1, 1941.

GARDEN *for* DEFENSE OF COUNTRY AND HOME

- There can be no reserve of fresh green vegetables *except in gardens*

- The interruption of the rapid transport of these foods to market next summer, may cause widespread shortage *overnight*.

- The vital importance of these protective, *vitamin rich* foods in the diet, especially of children, is well established.

- You can protect your family, and contribute to national preparedness by growing a large part of the vegetables you need in *your own back yard*.

Be Ready! PLAN AND PLANT EARLY, FOR WHAT EVER MAY COME!

Defense garden circular of the National Garden Bureau.

Rationing produced a cascade of effects that touched everyday life in less predictable ways. The shortages of gas and rubber, compounded by the lack of a reliable highway system, prompted the government to commandeer the railways to ship food to the troops. These factors combined to squeeze the civilian food supply. As in the First World War, the federal government urged Americans to grow vegetables in home and community "victory" gardens. Garden clubs and popular magazines picked up the call to action. *Horticulture* magazine, for example, pledged to dedicate more of its pages to the growing and preserving of food crops in order to encourage "the making of school gardens and community gardens on a much larger scale than has been known in recent years."[4]

The Weltys raised at least two vegetable crops a season—including beans, tomatoes, onions, corn, and strawberries—as they also may have done throughout the Depression. Eudora and her mother ate their produce fresh from the garden and also put up preserves, supplementing their crops with fruit and vegetables bought from local farmers. To Russell, Welty reported, "We have been eating corn, snapbeans and onions and butterbeans out of the backyard but our tomatoes (Mother got a special kind like they grow in her home in the mts.) were a failure. Figs are almost ripe and I wish I could send you some."[5]

"All around the rose beds we have strawberries and have daily races and fights with the birds to see who gets each berry," she wrote to Robinson. "Mother indignantly ate a little half-bowl for bkfst. this morning. . . ."[6]

In counterpoint to the home agriculture movement, J. Horace McFarland—the City Beautiful booster, national parks advocate, philanthropist, author, publisher, and rose authority, of Harrisburg, Pennsylvania—warned victory gardeners not to repeat the "pseudo-patriotic sacrifice" of World War I by "plow[ing] up good lawns to raise poor potatoes." Noting that he had served on a federal commission in 1918 to find out why "war necessities"—presumably including lawn potatoes—"were not being produced with satisfactory rapidity," McFarland said the commission discovered that "high wages, short hours and good housing were not enough. There had to be recreation, amusements, gardening. . . ." He advised

Figs, a southern summer treat. Photograph by Susan Haltom.

readers to "remember the stirring poem printed in the *Rose Annual* some years ago, 'Give Us Bread, But Give Us Roses Too.'"[7]

Later in the war, a Wayside Gardens catalogue published a similar appeal from the national chairman of the Victory Garden program: "We owe it to Johnny and Joan as they come marching home that the old home and the old home town welcome them with more flowers and greenery.... We must grow more of this food too—food for our spiritual well-being and our everyday happiness."[8] No doubt Wayside and other commercial growers were motivated partly by financial self-interest—the war was hard on the nursery business. Wayside thanked customers for "understanding the difficulties under which we are operating due to the war, and consequent shortage of man-power."[9] Because women filled many of the men's nursery jobs, work that demanded heavy lifting took longer than usual. Also, a shortage of European bulbs caused by the Nazi occupation of Holland and other export countries crimped supplies of popular plants. With a deft patriotic appeal, one magazine encouraged gardeners to turn their focus to "American-grown bulbs such as daffodils, bulbous irises, lilies, anemones, ranunculi and montbretias."[10]

Eudora Welty, 1940s.
© Eudora Welty LLC.

Welty was fortunate enough to have a private "exporter" in Europe—Robinson mailed her horticultural souvenirs from his overseas posts whenever he could. Her thank-you letters describe some of these treasures: "Nobody but you could have taken up irises in Egypt & carried them in a little paper sack to Italy & sent them home in a box & had the flowers still blue, in bud," she wrote him after receiving one choice parcel.[11]

CHANGES IN THE GARDEN

In 1943 Chestina turned sixty. In the ensuing decade her health began to decline, and Eudora took on increasing responsibility for the garden.[12] Whether or not Chestina Welty sensed her daughter's need to immerse herself in gardening, she entrusted Eudora with more planting space and creative influence, which was more horticultural than spatial. Nonetheless, Chestina retained an unchallenged role as the resident horticultural guru. (Eudora once recounted to Robinson how "a garden club lady sent over the most beautiful strange lily—very pale, silvery pink—rather frosty long slender petals—yellow stamen—seven flowers coming out of the top of a long pale green stalk. Mother took a look at it and said, 'Lycoris Squamigera.'"[13]) Both Eudora and her mother avoided the gussied-up

Eudora used these surprise lilies (*Lycoris squamigera*) to personify the character of the piano teacher in her short story "June Recital." "And Miss Eckhart pushed herself to quite another level of life for it. A blushing sensitivity sprang up in her every year at the proper time like a flower of the season, like the Surprise Lilies that came up with no leaves and overnight in Miss Nell's yard. . . ." Photograph by Susan Haltom.

new flowers that nurseries were introducing in the 1940s. "I do like the single, true, original flowers and they keep wanting to sell you extra-large double giant new hybrids," Eudora told Russell. "[W]e just had a circular from Robert Wayman of some poppies, 'Glamour Girls of the Modern Perennial Border.'" Chestina's preference for simple blooms was so well known that a local selection of "fine single dahlias" was named 'Chestina' in her honor.[14]

In the summer of 1943, Eudora sketched a curving "camellia border" in a letter to Robinson, noting the location of seven plants ('Hermé', 'Duc d'Orleans', 'Tri-Color', 'Elisabeth', 'Hermé', 'Pink Perfection', and 'Leila') with clumps of daffodils between each one, Roman hyacinths (pink, white, blue), with mixed species tulips and spring star flowers around Leila (marked on the diagram with Xs and Os) and Algerian iris behind it.[15] Although she laid out a spot to hold her growing camellia collection in the side yard, introduced more exotic bulbs, such as the Algerian iris, and dug some new beds, Welty's interest lay not in spatial design, but in

[1] [1943]

Print the complete address in plain block letters in the panel below, and your return address in the space
provided. Use typewriter, dark ink, or pencil. Write plainly. Very small writing is not suitable.

No.
158025

John F. Robinson, 2nd Lt., A.C.
(Sender's name)

Hq. Co., 3rd Bn., 180 Inf.

APO 45, c/o Postmaster

New York City, N.Y.

(CENSOR'S STAMP)

Eudora Welty
(Sender's name)
1119 Pinehurst St.
(Sender's address)
Jackson, Mississippi
~~USA~~

July 19
(Date)

Dear John--
        I just now got your little letter written c/o the Fleet Postmaster on the
boat--it went clear around the world, and came in at San Francisco. But it's a joy
to hear, it doesn't matter if it reaches back. I hope when you get ready to come you
won't take the long way and take that long.

Here it is hot. I got up early and watered a little, so I could weed a little. Mrs.
Fox sent Jake up with some figs--he came hollering "Figs, Mrs. Welty!" from down the
street. They were wonderful. I wrote a letter to Rose Russell--she had asked what
you were doing now, so I told her riding along the mountains above the sea in your
Jeep in high delight, in Africa. The yard man came and we put him in the house because
it was too hot, then we worked outdoors. I ate lunch downtown with Bessie--she'd sent
for a Western Union boy and got a poor old one nearly 90 years old--he said he'd been
sick a long time, and had trouble with his mind, and couldn't carry anything heavier
than a telegram.

We had some pretty Editor MadFarland Roses this morning. And a garden club lady sent
over the most beautiful strange lily--very pale, silvery pink--rather frosty long
slender petals--yellow stamens--seven flowers coming out of the top of a long pale
green stalk. Mother took a look at it and said, "Lycoris Squamigera." It is very
wonderful, you should see it--it smells good too. I've been thinking about bulbs.
Here's the way the camellia border will be

What do you think? Think of the color of the camellias too.
I think it will be on the abundant side, as things have all multiplied and grown.
A cardinal is singing just now. It's the middle of the afternoon. Not a breath
stirs. I practiced knitting so I can begin your sweater. I was so afraid Mother
would groan when I wanted to try to learn, but she very calmly said she thought
I could. I hope to know enough by the time you send your measurements--I go along
all right for a while, and suddenly I forget how I do it--it used to be the same
with swimming, I'd forget how. I hope for a letter soon. At the same time with
this I'm sending you some clippings, etc. by air mail, so you can see which comes
better, and let me know. I am eating a Praline and wonder what you are eating.
How is Bill? It's nice to think he is with you--tell him to stay close. I left out
the little Algerian   irises in the diagram, all of
them I transplanted   back behind the bulbs, they
make a shimmer of   V ··· MAIL   blue when all is bare, earliest

the flowers she grew. In this, she fit the description later penned by Henry Mitchell, a fellow southerner and long-running gardening columnist for the *Washington Post*: "The gardener must acquire plants, but . . . [t]he aim is to peer intensely at all of them, to enjoy the way in which they sprout up and in due season die down."[16]

A spell of intense heat and drought in the summer of 1943 may have delayed the digging of new beds. The weather sapped Welty's energy for both writing and gardening, and what vigor she had went into keeping their plants alive:

> We've had prostrating heat and have to revive things after supper every night—even the dogwood tree hangs every leaf down each day. A little rabbit ate the tops of my acidantheras—I know this rabbit, he was born here, and thinks acidantheras are just the tender things for his little teeth. He is always passing through with a little sheaf of leaves or some precious thing in his mouth, and I have to move the hose to let him by— he has got me. He is close enough to spank at all times. . . . maybe before breakfast it will be cool enough to let the brain work—I'll put a cool leaf over my head.[17]

June, the second month of drought, yielded "only one rainy afternoon, though the weather makes a phony threat every day, with stage thunder," she reported to Russell. "I begin soaking the flower beds in the morning at about 7 o'clock and am still moving the hose around when it's dark, just stopping it in the worst heat, and yet this has to be done every day or two or plants die. . . ."[18]

In late August, relief still had not come:

> It is on account of no rain here . . . that little squirrels and rabbits come up the front steps and literally press their noses against the screen door. They (squirrels only) sit in treetops now eating the seeds from green pine cones and toss down the shells with one paw just like sports [fans] in the bleachers at baseball games, and they would eat all the buds off winter

flowering shrubs if we let them, and they have eaten summer bulbs down
to the ground. It is sad. Ponds and streams are drying up too and there
is little water for anything to live on. Our town was asked today please
not to water gardens any more as the drinking supply is low, but with the
temperature at 107 as it was yesterday and must be now, things cannot
live without water. This typewriter, in a room, is a little stove to touch. It
would be worth doing without a little drinking water to save camellias—
I have had one to die, but the rest are alive. . . .[19]

Not until October did her letters mention the arrival of rain—followed by a killing frost that laid waste to the backyard bean crop.[20]

As Chestina's notebooks tapered off in the early 1940s, Eudora's letters and occasional photographs became the primary record of the garden

Chestina Welty, undated photograph. © Eudora Welty LLC; Eudora Welty Collection, MDAH.

Taken from the Weltys' sleeping porch, this photo by Eudora shows the Upper Garden and Lower Garden in the 1940s. The trellises and arbors defining the garden rooms are absent. © Eudora Welty LLC.

they shared.[21] The most striking difference is revealed in photographs: the wooden arbors and trellises that had so crisply delineated the garden rooms had grown dilapidated during the Depression, and then disappeared altogether. Likely for financial reasons, the Weltys did not replace them. Other than the addition of Eudora's camellia plot, no major design changes occurred.

Chestina stopped keeping notes of the garden club meetings in her journals, probably because she was too busy. She served another term as president of the Jackson Garden Club in 1945–1946 and as vice president the following year. Although the fuel shortage prompted at least one Jackson garden club to cut meetings from two to one a month, and then to adjourn until after the war—as did countless other garden clubs throughout the country—the clubs that stayed active focused on supporting the war effort. In Jackson, club members served refreshments to servicemen at the public auditorium on Saturday nights; sent flowers to the military hospital, the air base, and the POW camp; made bandages for the Red Cross; and danced with soldiers and sailors at the U.S.O. They promoted war (savings) bond drives to help fund military operations, and mailed vegetable seeds to ravaged Allied countries.[22]

As the war dragged on—and with her brothers, Robinson, and several friends in harm's way—Welty volunteered for similar activities to support servicemen. Her worry about her loved ones sometimes brimmed over into sadness when she met other servicemen passing through Jackson. In one letter to Robinson she mentioned an idea for "a little piece on the USO room in the station where I work Sunday nights," but her enthusiasm dimmed in the next sentence: "I get so stirred up, though—the wounded ones who are back—and the men at the prison camp, the things they say. And not being able to really help any of them."[23]

The war was virtually impossible to ignore. In addition to bond drives, victory gardens, and the constant presence of troops in the city, military training planes zoomed low over the Weltys' house. "[If] this letter sounds distracted it might be because the planes are dive-bombing *so*," she complained to Russell in January 1943. "They always pretend [Belhaven] college across the street is an objective, and our chimney is in their way." But her irritation did not keep her from befriending the young Dutch airmen performing the training runs.[24]

Eudora at work in her bedroom, probably during World War II. © Eudora Welty LLC.

In September 1943, Welty's second collection of short stories, *The Wide Net*, appeared in print. The stories were loosely connected by their settings along the Natchez Trace, an ancient Native American trail and settlers' byway rife with legend. By November, after writing little that year but book reviews for the *New York Times* and an essay for *Harper's Bazaar*, Welty sent Russell a long new story, "The Delta Cousins." She had written it for Robinson because his family history on a Delta plantation had been its inspiration, and she had sent him chapters as she finished them. Because of paper shortages, however, magazine editors had to rein in their page counts. After receiving "The Delta Cousins," Mary Lou Aswell, the fiction editor at *Harper's Bazaar*, wrote, "We have desperately little space for fiction now, so that I must warn you we may not be able to run the story until our paper allowance is increased. That means, dear Eudora, will you cut every word you feel you can eliminate."[25]

As the story made the rounds, Welty accepted another magazine assignment, this time for *Vogue*, to write a series of three short essays, each accompanying one of her photographs. The pieces, appearing under the title "Literature and the Lens," in the August 1944 issue, wove a spell that rose like smoke from a ruined plantation house, which was one of the subjects:

This photograph accompanied Welty's 1944 *Vogue* essays, one of which described this ruin where she salvaged bricks for the garden. Photograph by Eudora Welty. © Eudora Welty LLC; Eudora Welty Collection, MDAH.

> The photograph was made at my first sight of the house. A descendant of the original owner had gone looking for the place, taking me along, and we had seen the chimneys just at first dark, after following a cedar avenue that curved up out of a dark ravine where the Natchez Trace went by.
>
> It was an evening in November or December, with a wind smelling of night-rain filling the air with blowing leaves and the clouds coming over the sky. It seemed haunted and beautiful at the same time—indeed much had happened in it. . . . The bricks, baked of the red clay of the place, were of a glowing rose. . . .
>
> At last, with it all to the ground, I took some of the fiery bricks home and put them in my garden around a bed of spring bulbs.[26]

The magazine essays she wrote in 1943 and 1944 contain some of her finest nonfiction writing about place, which magazine editors seemed to

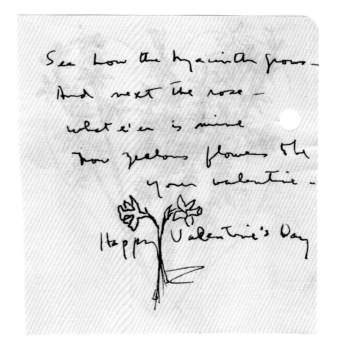

See how the hyacinth grows—
And next the rose—
what e'er is mine
now yellow flowers th
your valentine—

Happy Valentine's Day

appreciate. In the spring of 1944, Welty took on an editorial role herself, at the *Mississippi Women's War Bond News*. The newsletter went out to the women in charge of selling bonds in each county, touting their accomplishments and cheering them on. She sent Robinson part of an issue in which she addressed the readers by the names of their respective counties: "Dear Mrs. Tallahatchie, Mrs. Jones, Mrs. Jeff Davis, and the entire remainder." It is hard to imagine what her audience made of her report:

> This time the editor can only say: Ladies—you've got me. Your Fourth
> War Loan reports spread before me now, would stagger the creature who
> attempts to do any editing this month or put in any words of her own.
> For your work has said it all—and in the only way that counts. It looks
> as if all over Mississippi a perfect cyclone of ladies was moving from
> house to house.[27]

Eudora's hand-drawn valentines to John Robinson featured an assortment of flowers from the Welty yard. Here, French Roman hyacinths and daffodils. © Eudora Welty LLC; Eudora Welty Collection, MDAH.

Eudora Welty in New York City, 1940s. © Eudora Welty LLC.

Even as she seemed outwardly accepting of a routine that included working in the garden, volunteering, and working on "The Delta Cousins," the lengthy short story that eventually grew into her first novel, *Delta Wedding*, Welty was contemplating a journey that she hoped would bring her closer to Robinson. The American Academy of Arts and Letters awarded her a prize of one thousand dollars and asked her to come to New York to accept it that spring. She arrived in the city with a plan to land a job as a war correspondent with one of the city papers. But they all turned her down; such positions were highly sought after by experienced reporters. She decided to stay in the city anyway, working as a summer intern at the *New York Times Book Review*, where she edited other writers' reviews and wrote occasional ones herself under the pen name Michael Ravenna.[28]

While in New York, she relished spending time with Russell and his family, and she took in concerts and art exhibits with other friends. Through the first month she still held out hope for landing a foreign assignment. Then, in June, came D-Day. Although she stayed in the city until October, she returned to Jackson with hope that the waning war would soon bring a reunion with John. On the train home to Jackson, she wrote to him that "the Danish Underground" had bought the rights to distribute *The Wide Net*, for reasons she could not quite fathom, adding that she was "anxious to try now, the Delta Story—It might turn out to be some long book." After her sojourn in New York, she missed Mississippi: "It will be nice to see our country again—I will write you how it is looking—If only you could come soon."[29]

Back at Pinehurst Street, however, she learned that John would not be returning soon; in fact, he had volunteered to fly night missions over northern Italy.

An American Dream: The Sawada Family's Overlook Nurseries

Kosaku Sawada hybridizing a camellia. Courtesy of Lawrence G. Sawada.

The story of Kosaku Sawada and Overlook Nurseries shows how small nurseries reflect their times, linking gardens, people, and cultures through particular plants. So it has been with Sawada, his children and grandchildren, and the many thousands of camellias they have developed and sold to generations of gardeners.

Kosaku Sawada was twenty-one when he emigrated from Osaka, Japan, in 1904, fresh out of Osaka University's agriculture program. Sawada was among four young men mentored by an official representing the Japanese government at the St. Louis World's Fair, where Christian and Chestina Welty spent their honeymoon. After the fair's success, the sponsor decided that America was ripe for rice farming; he moved to the coast of Texas and recruited Sawada and the others to help start the farm. In America, "I thought I could pick up gold along the highways," Sawada later said in a 1939 interview for the Federal Writers' Project. But he soon discovered that "you get hold of money only by hard work."

Soon after starting the enterprise, the sponsor died in a tractor accident, and the four young men found themselves on their own, without contacts. After trying to make a living by selling various kinds of trees, Sawada moved to coastal Alabama, where he established a nursery offering pecan trees and citrus, including satsumas imported from Japan. Then a freeze devastated his nursery, so he decided to focus on ornamental shrubs.

In 1916 he traveled to San Francisco to marry his Japanese bride, sight unseen. Packed in her trunk were hundreds of camellia seeds. Although some had dried out during the long sea voyage, the viable seeds were soon planted, beginning the long line of Overlook introductions. By 1940, Sawada had raised about fifty thousand camellia seedlings, selling them to retailers and camellia collectors.

Unlike the detailed catalogue entries of today, Overlook Nurseries' catalogues from the early 1920s listed camellia selections simply as double- or single-flowering varieties in pink, red, or white. Sawada kept crossing and recrossing his best specimens, waiting eight years for the plants to flower or in order to see what surprise each camellia seed produced. In 1925 Mrs. Sawada's brother sent two thousand seeds from selected varieties in Japan, and from those came *C. japonica* 'K. Sawada' (pure white, very double), which first flowered at the nursery in 1933. Also from this batch came 'Mrs. K. Sawada' (palest of pinks, fully double, gardenia type, with seventy to one hundred petals; first flowered 1935). In 1931, seeds again arrived from Japan, and from this group came 'Victory White' (large blossoms with a cluster of yellow stamens within notched white petals; first flowered 1938) and 'White Empress' (large, pure-white blossoms with a golden glow from a mass of yellow stamens; first bloomed 1939). Both of these varieties were planted in the Welty garden.

Mrs. Sawada died shortly after giving birth to their fourth child, leaving Kosaku to raise his children and his plants. In his 1939 interview Sawada said that all of his children went to college, where he hoped they would acquire the business knowledge he felt he lacked. "I tell them they can see what I need here is . . . the ability to sell after I raise my nursery stock. In fact the whole country needs more commercial knowledge." He went on to explain that his nursery was labor-intensive and difficult to mechanize, so he employed twenty to twenty-five men at any given time. Because of his propagation success rate of nearly 95 percent, he was able to thrive in an industry known for its unpredictability. Despite his avowed lack of business sense, Sawada was also savvy enough to tap into commercial networks, reporting that he was connected with "all nurserymen and florists in the United States" and was a member of the Associated American Nurserymen.

Kosaku Sawada had embraced his new country from the beginning, giving his sons the most American names he could think of: Tom (for Jefferson), George (for Washington), and Ben (for Franklin). The Sawadas' positive attitude and their view of themselves as Americans protected them from some of the prejudice that other Japanese-Americans faced, especially during World War II. In 1943 Eudora told Diarmuid Russell that a white grower of camellias in Mobile had enclosed a typical diatribe with his latest mailing: "[He] is even more raging against the Japanese than ever—he has always had a rival grower there who is Japanese—this time he calls them 'insincere rats.'" (This rival was not Sawada, according to a member of the Sawada family. Japanese-Americans owned at least two of the six Mobile camellia nurseries listed in Harold Hume's 1946 *Camellias in America*.) After serving in the army during World War II, Sawada's son Tom returned to Overlook, where he oversaw the business while his father continued propagating.

Hard work, loyal customers, expertise, and the integrity of the operation kept the Sawadas' enterprise going well into the twenty-first century. In February 2009 I drove to Mobile to buy camellias to include in a plant sale to support the Welty House. I entered Overlook Nurseries through a red torii gate, which matched the logo on a business card given to me by

George Sawada, Kosaku's grandson, at Overlook Nurseries outside Mobile, Alabama,
2009. Photograph by Susan Haltom.

Camellia japonica 'Imura', one of Kosaku Sawada's hybrids, is increasingly rare. Photograph by Susan Haltom.

George Sawada, grandson of Kosaku, who runs the sixty-acre wholesale nursery. With the onset of early spring in the South, the busy season had arrived, and workers were moving cryptomeria and other landscape plants out of greenhouses.

That impression of a thriving business, however, proved deceptive. The rise of "big box," high-volume nursery centers, combined with several years of economic uncertainty, were taking a toll on small, privately owned American nurseries, including this one. These smaller nurseries cannot compete on cost, cannot risk not getting paid if a plant dies from neglect in a large retail store, and cannot wait to be paid until the plant sells.

The result is that Sawada was phasing out his business. In addition to the external stresses, the family line is at an end. "I am the last standing Sawa-da male, with no younger generation to take over the family business," he said with visible sadness.

Successors of the many camellias introduced by Kosaku Sawada live on in American gardens. In addition to *C. japonica* 'White Empress', 'Imura', 'Victory White', and 'Pink Herme', which Eudora planted in her garden, look for 'K. Sawada', 'Mrs. K. Sawada', and 'Sawada's Dream'. Sawada also introduced *C. sasanqua* 'Cleopatra' and 'Brilliancy', *C. vernalis* 'Dawn', the crepe myrtle 'Near East', and the azalea 'Gulf Pride' (also grown by the Weltys).

George Sawada remains proud of these contributions, making it clear that his decision to close had nothing to do with the worthiness of his family profession. "There is nothing negative about gardening and plants," he said.

—Susan Haltom, June 2010

CHAPTER TEN

"Happy and Thankful for Much"

Perhaps the heart always was made of different stuff and had a different life from the rest of the body. . . . It was very strange, but she had felt it. She had then known something he knew all along, it seemed then—that when you felt, touched, heard, looked at things in the world, and found their fragrances, they themselves made a sort of house within you, which filled with life to hold them, filled with knowledge all by itself, and all else, the other ways to know, seemed calculations and tyranny.

—Eudora Welty, *Delta Wedding*[1]

After spending the summer of 1944 in New York, Welty arrived home at night and checked on the camellias by match-light, finding 'Leila' to have grown prodigiously during her absence. "The apple blossom sasanquas [*Camellia sasanqua*] that smell like the earth were blooming," she told Robinson, as she prepared to leaf through the back issues of the *Market Bulletin* in search of "the hyacinthus ladies."[2] But the joy of being back home evaporated when she learned that he had chosen to go on the night raids over Italy, moved by conscience to share the risk he was assigning to younger men:

Eudora Welty, 1940s. ©
Eudora Welty LLC.

This nearly kills me—I didn't know you didn't *need* to go—what is it?
Tell me or whatever you want—only don't go in the bomb fighter—This

This dramatic ginger (*Hedychium coronarium*)—also know as butterfly lily—in the Welty garden grows to a height of six feet and blooms in late summer with an intense, luxurious fragrance. Photograph by Susan Haltom.

is with all my heart. I wish I could think of a way to ask you that would prevail, but do ask you so hard, not to go & be in all the worst danger & it not needed—O God I feel shaky & maybe am stupid in my head but it sounds wild & crazy & overworked to me & I just want you to come out of it—quick. . . . Do you remember we love you so—[3]

Welty's outburst—for which she later apologized—was uncharacteristic; but after nearly two years of relentless anxiety, she was stung by Robinson's actions, which to her may have seemed rash, even selfish. Just as he may not have understood the compounded stress of her long-term worry, she, like many American civilians, may not have fathomed the bonds of duty and comradeship among combat troops. But just eight days after her anguished letter, she was riding a surge of hope after receiving a new letter from Robinson: "that last line—maybe you'll get here to see the bulbs? O glory, I hope it happens—tell all," she wrote back.[4]

After weeks passed without a return letter, she plunged back into despair: "Mother went out to lunch a while ago & I thought now I can just *cry*, in peace and by myself, for you," she wrote. When she finally did hear from him, she realized that she had misunderstood what he had said about coming home. Although he had ceased the night missions by mid-December, Robinson would not be home in time to see the bulbs in the spring of 1945.[5]

The fact that Welty and Robinson marked time by what was in bloom is a measure of the depth and mutuality of their gardening bond. In his absence, she seems to have symbolically enshrined him in the camellia garden, where she felt a special connection to him; but she had literally implanted other potent mementos throughout the garden. "The butterfly lilies were powerful last night. One of those was what you handed me when we started to Mexico," she wrote that fall, recalling the couple's first romantic trip together in 1937. In the same letter she dreamily reported that she had picked some pomegranates "off your tree yesterday morning that dangled right down in my hand...."[6]

Prenshaw, Marrs, and other literary scholars have examined the roles of place and memory in Welty's published work. In discussing the enchanting history and natural world of the Natchez Trace portrayed in Welty's essay "The Eye of the Story," Marrs comments:

> Welty here suggests that place is a prompt to memory. But she might
> have added that the human mind grants place its significance .... Place
> may prompt the memory, but first the memory of history and legend
> must create the sense of place. More than place, it is the historian and the
> storyteller who ensure that passionate things endure....[7]

This dwarf pomegranate (*Punica granatum*), similar to a variety Chestina Welty grew, was a popular southern garden plant of the early twentieth century. Its showy, bright red flowers in summer are followed by familiar globular fruits, smaller than commercially grown varieties. Photograph by Susan Haltom.

Welty's letters to Robinson suggest that gardens, plants, and memory were similarly entwined in Welty's actual garden, and that in her life as well as her art, the garden was a place where she actively cultivated not only flowers, but memories. Marrs observes that during this same period, the early 1940s, "Welty's fiction . . . deals with the nature of memory." At times her longing for Robinson, ignited by the sensory cues of her plants, seemed charged enough to conjure him on the spot, the genie of her place: "I am just now lying in the pine needles in the side yard—it is sunny & sweet smelling—Fall butterflies . . . I wish you were here, on this day—so hard—smelling the sweet air right here in deep breaths—& your eyes on the camellias doing so well—& hear the water running over their roots, the Leila & the Herme—the way it is now. . . ."[8]

Welty's 'Leila' camellia (more commonly known as 'Catherine Cathcart') is noted for its clear pink blossoms with white marbling. This same bush, a gift from John Robinson, still stands near the corner of the porch, where Eudora planted it in the early 1940s. Photograph by Susan Haltom.

After receiving a box of gifts he had sent from Italy, which included a photo of him on a camel, in Egypt, a pair of long-cuffed gardening gloves, a piece of window glass, and some wine glasses, she set out the glasses on a table in the garden and sank into a dreamy invocation: "[T]hey seem filled with places & with times—with you—the glass from the window in the Palace in Palermo—just a circle of glass, dark & colored soft like a cloud—it seems filled with everything—I want it to, all you sent me to fill, so I will know better," she wrote.[9]

Robinson's box contained plants too, including unidentified seeds, iris rhizomes and tulip bulbs and "climbing violets" from a garden he had tended in Naples. It appears that even in wartime, he, like many other military men, had found solace in gardening. Out of her instinct to commemorate people and experiences in the garden, Welty planted his seeds on Armistice Day.[10]

That fall, while she worked on the unwieldy story that would grow into the novel *Delta Wedding*, Welty kept her connection to Robinson fresh by making forays to his family's ancestral plantation home in the Mississippi Delta. "The Delta had rosy sky halfway up to the zenith—and

reflected on the fields," she reported to Russell after one road trip. "The cotton wagons are hand-painted blue-green. The sugarcane is two shades of green and lovely like bamboo in the breeze." Bright color was in order for the home garden too. At Chestina's request, Eudora had planted two new camellias in front of the house, "a middlesized Empress and little Daikagura," both rose red.[11]

Days before Christmas, in 1944, Welty awoke to a special delivery—a handkerchief from Robinson, sent from Florence. At Christmas, her brother Walter was still on a minesweeper in the Pacific, but his wife, Mittie, and their baby, Elizabeth, helped to brighten the holiday at Pinehurst Street. Edward Welty had been medically released from combat duty in the spring of 1944, although he was still in the army.[12]

Perhaps she was feeling hopeful, but for whatever reason, Welty's writing began to flow again in 1945, her imagination sparked by trips to the Delta:

This is the photograph that Robinson enclosed in a box of Christmas gifts he sent to Welty from Europe in 1944. Robinson, fourth from left, has placed a fez on his camel's head. Courtesy Eudora Welty LLC.

'Empress', also known as 'Lady Clare', is called 'Akashi-gata' in Japan, from which it was exported in the mid-nineteenth century. From *Camellias*, Gerbing, 1943.

'Empress' still grows under Eudora's bedroom window. Photograph by Susan Haltom.

[I'm] off to the Delta! . . . I will see the house you mentioned at Sidon—we did see it, did I tell you, but in a cloud of dust that day. I remember it and used it in a way for that story, the house where the aunts lived—I subdued it, but it was that. I loved it. It's just elegant to be setting off—free—will even be taking the car I hope, will be told by the gas board in the morning if they think it is fitting or not. (Here artists get gas to go look at things but writers might not.)[13]

Reading the diaries of Nancy McDougall Robinson, John's great-grandmother, was particularly inspiring. Living in the wilderness, this pioneering forebear had chronicled her daily life in the settlement days of the Delta. "How she treasured little things—visits, rose cuttings—she could not have enough attention to give every person and thing coming her way," Welty mused to Robinson. To Russell, she wrote, "I can't tell much about my story except that it must be 100 pp. long by now. Of course I have it in the worst month of the year, September. For flowers, I mean. What there is, I've got."[14]

Captivated by the Robinson family saga and stimulated by more excursions to plantation country, Welty wove "The Delta Cousins" and a subsequent short story, "A Little Triumph," into her first novel, *Delta Wedding*.[16] Set in 1923, the book unfolds during the preparations for a wedding on a fictional plantation called Shellmound. The book is lavish in its imagery of landscape and its descriptions of women's relationship to the land. In this passage from the finished novel, the character Ellen Fairchild envisions life itself as a recurrence of seasons and patterns: "The repeating fields, the repeating cycles of season and her own life—there was something in the monotony itself that was beautiful, rewarding—perhaps to what was womanly within her. No, she had never had time—much time at all, to contemplate . . . but she knew. Well, one moment told you the great things, one moment was enough for you to know the greatest thing."[17]

That spring Welty told Robinson she had read that in Europe "astonishing wild flowers" had been "brought up to rain and sun by the bombing and were flowering and amazed people. Out of season too I think." By now, she was fully engaged in her Delta novel: "Every day I am torn—work to do inside and outside, and the days never seem long enough. . . . New leaves on the camellias are opening like fans all over them."[18]

Meanwhile, the stress of worrying about Edward and Walter had taken a toll on Chestina's health. While working upstairs at the typewriter, Eudora kept an ear tuned for "suspicious sounds" of Chestina doing chores, in defiance of her doctor. "I have to foresee everything she's going to try to do, so she won't beat me," she confided to Robinson. "The doctor told her she . . . has hypertension and should not get fatigued—simple orders but she's so indignant lying down."[19]

In describing the fictional black plantation settlement of Brunswick-town, in Delta Wedding, *Welty evoked African American gardens of the rural South during the 1920s:*

"The little houses were many and alike, all white-washed with a green door, with stovepipes crooked like elbows of hips behind, okra, princess-feathers, and false dragonhead growing around them, and China trees over them like umbrellas, with chickens beneath sitting with shut eyes in dust holes. It was shady like a creek bed. The smell of scalding water, feathers, and iron pots mixed with the smell of darkness. Here, where no grass was let grow on the flat earth that was bare like their feet.... The alleys went like tunnels under the chinaberry branches, and the pony cart rocked over their black roots. Wood smoke drifted and hung in the trees like a low and fragrant sky. In front of Partheny's house, close up to her porch, was an extra protection, a screen the same size as the house, of thick butter-bean vines, so nobody could see who might be home. The door looked around one side, like a single eye around a veil."[15]

Mound Bayou, Mississippi, 1930s.
© WPA, courtesy of MDAH.

As she divided her days between writing, housework, and gardening, Welty found inspiration for *Delta Wedding* close at hand. "I have had a hard time with the people's names [in the book]—as usual—the right one will not come to me," she said to Robinson. Then, "I was walking in a field and saw my baby's name—Bluet."

She eventually populated the story with other flower-named females, among them Primrose, Lady Clare (like the camellia), and Vi'let. Her letters of the 1940s confirm that for Welty the process of writing remained inseparable from her daily contact with nature, in the garden and beyond.[20]

Between her intense focus on the novel and "circumventing" Chestina's attempts to clean and weed, Eudora fell behind in the garden as spring came on. "The garden isn't wonderful . . . the grass so high," she told Robinson. Her discomfort with the garden's dishevelment found its way into the pages of her novel: "Of all the things she would leave undone, she hated leaving the garden untended," Welty wrote about the character Ellen Fairchild.[21]

Roosevelt's death, on April 12, 1945, prompted Welty to fret about the

Bluets (*Houstonia caerulea*). This tiny native wildflower, which grows in fields in many parts of the United States, inspired the baby's name in Welty's first novel, *Delta Wedding*. Photograph by Susan Haltom.

fate of peace, but victory in Europe arrived within a month. "How I wait for it now—for you to say you are well and it is over, truly," she wrote to Robinson on May 1, a week before V-E Day. "It seems to fill the air, the garden—but still it will feel [only] like hope, until then."[22]

Meanwhile, the war with Japan continued, and Robinson, like many American servicemen in Europe, did not know whether he would be sent home or to the Pacific.[23] Welty held out hope for his imminent return and prepared the garden for his arrival:

> I have got up early this morning planning to set petunias out while it is cool. Plants are hard to find but a lady out on the Terry road says she has some that are a little sprangley but you can panch 'em back. It is a soft cloudy morning—a dove in the woods. I have weeded some but have far to go. I feel you might walk in and I should get flowers set out in the bare places.[24]

Throughout May and June, she mailed him typed carbons of the *Delta Wedding* draft, and when summer brought no news of his return, she faithfully continued her reports on the garden. "The whole town is glowing with crape myrtles," she wrote in July. "The loveliest are the shell pinks, to me now and those big trees at the old Manship place on Fortification and West are like the flowering trees in Kubla Khan—a wonderful year this year for all flowering things. About the time the sun goes down they all fill with light (the crape myrtles) and keep it, after other things lose color and substance. . . ." When, a few weeks later, she received some royalty money in the mail, she vowed to sink some of it into bulbs and "dig up the whole border and ramify everything."[25]

In August, the dropping of the atomic bombs on Hiroshima and Nagasaki left Welty with almost as much trepidation as the first rumblings of war. "I hope this ends . . . before we drop another one," she wrote to Russell. The next day—August 14, 1945—Japan surrendered. The war was over.[26]

In early November 1945, Edward Welty arrived safely in Jackson, and

Crepe (also spelled crape) myrtles, one of the most popular flowering trees in southern landscapes, bloom prolifically in the heat of summer in white, reds, pinks, and lavenders. Welty made references to them in her fiction, as in this passage from her unpublished story "Nicotiana" or "The Last of the Figs": "Crape myrtle trees in bloom, the colors of the voile dresses that Sarahville ladies wore who were the same age as the trees—seventy-five—stood all up and down the street with the lacey light coming through them." Photograph by Susan Haltom.

the family expected Walter, who also had come through the war unharmed, to be home by Christmas. At last, Welty received the long-awaited phone call from Robinson—he would be discharged in Mississippi in mid-November. To her friend Frank Lyell she wrote, "It has been a long time." For years, Welty had been eager to begin a new life with Robinson and to join "a widening circle of friends who shared her own passion and commitment to artistic lives," Marrs writes. "She also relished being free from the familiar world of home, from the town where she and her family were so well known, from familial duties and responsibilities and restraints." But when he finally came home, Robinson was remote and, as Welty confided to Russell, "a little low in his mind."[27]

Welty tried to rekindle their bond in her garden. As she reported to Russell early in 1946, they even experimented with grafting camellias, a first for them both. Choosing two "very unattractive" specimens in the garden, she sawed off the top of one and grafted "a fine kind" onto the stout trunk. "I did that Saturday and felt so awful after sawing down a flowering tree that I couldn't sleep, and Sunday I got John to do the second one," she confessed. "When they shoot up 36 inches in a year and come out in wild magnificence, then I will write and tell you about it." The grafted trees indeed flourished, and she jokingly offered to graft Russell's trees on her next visit—"just give me a saw and tell your trees goodbye."[28]

Delta Wedding was published in the spring of 1946. Although a commercial success, the novel drew barbs from several New York critics, who marginalized Welty as a regional writer. Describing one review, she fumed, "Mr. Rosenfeld's logical steps were (a) all Southern books are regional, (b) this book deals with people as if they were like any other people, therefore (c) it fails and (d) it is escape from reality, and as a kind of extra point he adds that he doesn't see how any southerner can write anyway living in such a place."[29] The accusation in such reviews, explicit or not, was that because the novel did not make a tidy, antiracist statement, the novelist was complicit with the racial disparities of plantation life that were part of the novel's historical context. This was a charge that Welty—and many other white writers of the South—would face again and again.[30] Such reactions confirmed her sense that she "was dealing with a quality that never was and never will be understood by the North and that will always be met with suspicion and resentment up there," she confided to Russell, adding, "the North simply does not comprehend the South and for that reason will always cherish a kind of fury at it, it doesn't understand our delights and pleasures or even anything abstract about our ways."[31] In her 1965 essay "Must the Novelist Crusade?" she put the bigger issue squarely on the table. "Great fiction," she writes, "abounds in what makes for confusion . . . There is absolutely everything in great fiction but a clear answer."[32]

Regardless of this sting from the critics, Welty started writing again

with an excitement that had eluded her since before the war, telling Robinson, "I feel well—happy and thankful for much, life does seem to be opening out and once more sweet. There seems to be energy in this air and I feel I might be doing a lot of work as I never did before. Don't let me write *too* much."[33]

Robinson, meanwhile, with Welty's help and encouragement, started writing fiction, eventually publishing a few short stories in magazines. But he seemed downcast and restless, as well as distant—an emotional state that played out geographically, as he roved from Jackson to Oxford to San Francisco. Sometimes, but not always, he invited her to join him. Even as she tried to accommodate his wanderings, she did not conceal her disappointment. "How could I be all right in my heart or my mind while not knowing how you felt or doing anything or being anything that would count," she wrote during one of their times apart. "It seems a preposterous life to me. Sometimes I feel part of something I don't know all of—or its destination—sometimes left, no part. It is all right in the not knowing, but not the not being."[34]

At thirty-seven, Welty was edging past impatience into desperation, and it was not solely about Robinson's brooding reticence, or even about finding another relationship. She needed to move on—into the wider

Robinson and Welty in Florence, Italy, 1950. Photograph by Barbara Howes, used by permission of Barbara Howes estate and courtesy of Eudora Welty LLC.

world, into a cosmopolitan community of artists; away from Jim Crow Mississippi and from daily life with Chestina, whose irritability grew in proportion to her infirmity. She confessed her growing panic to Robinson: "Sometimes when I fall in bed dogtired at night I get a frantic feeling about my story and other things—where is my life? But when I can see over the things it's allright. I like the work in the yard, never get tired, and can think out there or maybe it's dreaming. . . . When I get a letter or a story from you things seem different and real."[35]

It would take the next five years for Welty to accept that the romance she had cultivated as tenderly as 'Leila' was not going to bloom. Marrs sums up the off-and-on love affair during this painful time:

During 1946 and 1947 Eudora would twice journey to San Francisco and spend several months living there near John. In 1950 John would follow Eudora to Europe, where they would share good times on the Côte d'Azure and in Florence. But there were long periods of separation between these meetings, and by the end of 1951 their relationship seemed doomed. . . . Though John may well have discussed his emotional state in postwar letters to friends, few of these letters are extant. Those he sent to Eudora—perhaps more than two hundred written between 1946 and 1951—she destroyed sometime in the 1970s so as to protect his privacy. . . . The surviving correspondence, though one-sided, clearly indicates that John was in turmoil about his future—he did not want to resume his career as an insurance adjuster, he thought longingly of permanent residence in Italy, he was moody and often depressed. . . . His alternating roles as a suitor and as a man fleeing commitment were profoundly disturbing [to Eudora].[36]

As it turned out, in addition to being overwhelmed by what has since been labeled post-traumatic stress, Robinson was wrestling with his sexual identity. Although Welty may have begun to suspect that he was homosexual—she had several male friends who were—she did not know for certain until the summer of 1951, when she observed Robinson in

New York in the company of a new friend, Enzo Rocchigiani, an Italian man twenty years his junior. The two men were constant companions, and they interacted like a couple. In the spring of 1952, Welty spent a month in New York, where she saw Robinson once and learned that he was bound for Italy soon and hoping to emigrate. They wished each other well, and exchanged letters about once a year for another five years.[37]

The slow unraveling of their relationship during the late 1940s ultimately bestowed a gift: during Robinson's frequent absences, Welty slowly began to pursue her interests and travels without him. "Not her young life with her serene mother, . . . but her middle life . . . had shown her how deep were the complexities of the everyday, of the family, what caves were in the mountains, what blocked chambers, and what crystal rivers that had not yet seen light,"[38] she had written in *Delta Wedding*. This much she already had learned largely in her home place, having traveled relatively little at that time. By the time she recognized that Robinson would not be her life's partner, "Eudora knew that she possessed the resources to lead a full life with or without the man she loved," writes Marrs. "For her . . . the independent life of a writer was a profoundly satisfying one." She traveled widely in the United States and in Europe, finding new friends, relishing new experiences and places. "She was a cosmopolitan woman still expecting to encounter and savor something new and unusual, still filled with the joy of seeing and hearing and writing."[39]

From this point on, the story of the garden—and the garden itself, twenty-five years old in 1950—began to fade, overshadowed by the richness of a life lived increasingly beyond the sheltering enclosure of camellias and pines.

PART IV

Winter—
Postwar and
Beyond

Eudora Welty, 1970s. Courtesy of Memphis *Commercial Appeal*.

CHAPTER ELEVEN

"Not a Garden Any More, but What It Is"

The roses were done for, the perennials too. But the surrounding crape-myrtle tree, the redbud, the dogwood, the Chinese tallow tree, and the pomegranate bush were bright as toys. The ailing pear tree had shed its leaves ahead of the rest. Past a falling wall of Michaelmas daisies that had not been tied up, a pair of flickers were rifling the grass. . . .

—Eudora Welty, "The Demonstrators," 1966[1]

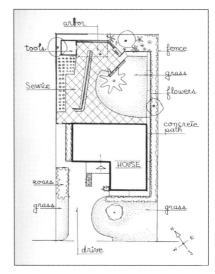

"A typical backyard" in postwar America features simplified spaces and modern amenities. The layout differs from the undulating perimeter borders around a central lawn favored in the 1930s. From *Gardens Are for People,* Thomas D. Church, 1955.

The 1950s, when Welty began to stretch her wings, were heady years for Americans. Fifty years earlier, Chestina and Christian Welty had marveled at the inventions at the St. Louis World's Fair before striking out to build a new life far from their hometowns. Their embrace of change, and Christian's belief that technology would bring about a better future, marked them as typical of their generation. A similar upwelling of change and hope, also accompanied by a belief in progress through technology, buoyed the country at midcentury. With the war over, America tapped years of pent-up energy, a reservoir of newly created income, and a new confidence born of its major role in the Allied victory.[2]

In the postwar lifestyle, a new "modern" attitude emerged: optimistic, casual, and practical. More than ever, this lifestyle depended on cars, which continued to shape the middle-class landscape. The garage, for instance, now adjoined the house, functioning as a utilitarian foyer, freeing space in the backyard and screening views from the street.[3]

195

As the pace of life sped up after the war, the era's most sought-after luxury was leisure time. Accordingly, one garden writer pronounced, Americans should create gardens of "peace and ease . . . peace to be yourself, ease in keeping it up." Influenced by California's appealing modern gardens, which melded indoor and outdoor space, Americans of the 1950s showed "an intense, abiding interest in lessening the confinements of indoor living," observed Joseph E. Howland in *The House Beautiful Book of Gardens and Outdoor Living* (1958).[4] They wanted to use their backyard as an extension of the house, and that meant making room for a furnished patio, children's play equipment, and, sometimes, a swimming pool. Plants—mostly trees and shrubs—assumed a strictly functional role: to screen views, provide shade, and enclose space. If the homeowners wanted to include ornamental plants, these had better be able to pull their weight and not add clutter. Otherwise, "to drag them in . . . is the surest way to spoil your garden," warned a 1951 article in *House Beautiful*.[5]

These postwar values and priorities spelled the end of high-maintenance perennial gardens like the Weltys'. The fate of their garden during the next few decades could serve as an example of why such gardens were often impractical in a faster-paced society in which "peace and ease" were scarce. In the case of the Weltys, Chestina's failing health and Eudora's frequent travels accounted for the garden's gradual decline. Throughout the decade, Eudora stayed home for periods of time to care for her mother and to visit her brothers, who also were experiencing grave health problems.[6] When at Pinehurst Street, she tried to keep up the garden, but Chestina's care and her own writing took priority. In the South's year-round growing season, it did not take long for rapacious insects, invading vines, and fast-multiplying perennials to gain the upper hand.

Severe weather also dealt some cruel blows in the early 1950s. A tornado "took our biggest pine tree and threw it down through the dining room roof like a javelin," Welty told Russell. To Robinson she wrote that the tree had toppled "right across the camellias but not quite on top of them," sparing 'Leila', which "stood blooming through it all." Later she reported to Russell, "We are trying to organize the bit of garden last spring's

Eudora Welty, 1950s. Photograph by Kay Bell, courtesy of Eudora Welty LLC.

'Lady Hillingdon', an old-fashioned tea rose introduced in 1910, has been replanted in the restored Welty garden. It makes a brief appearance in *Delta Wedding*. Photograph by Susan Haltom.

storm tore up, and are laying stones, steps, getting out old roots, etc. The [absence] of shade of two big pines has exposed our house and garden both to the west, very bad on us and plants—do you know any magic beanstalks?"[7]

In spite of these setbacks, the garden still brought moments of joy. Nostalgic for the old-fashioned tea roses Chestina had grown in the past, Eudora and her mother replanted old garden roses, including 'Lady Hillingdon' and 'Maman Cochet'. "Not that I'd give up a single [hybrid tea rose] we have, but I'd love to see a great, gracious, fountain-like bush again just covered with sweet-smelling flowers that felt like silk and velvet and hung their heads slightly in the dew, from the weight," she explained

'Maman Cochet', introduced in 1893, also appears in *Delta Wedding*: "Two princess baskets of pink and white Maman Cochet roses, Miss Tessie at the icehouse sent up, Dabney," said Ellen, carrying them onto the porch. "She sent them over by twins." Photograph by Susan Haltom.

Falling Back on Bulbs

"Your new garden spot will be fine," Welty wrote to Diarmuid Russell in January 1946, "but I know that burden of more and more added places, we have it too, and still keep on. What will you plant there? I've about fallen back on camellias and bulbs. . . ."

When Welty told Russell that she had "about fallen back on camellias and bulbs," she chose two iconic types of southern flowers that, if well planted, can withstand considerable neglect from the gardener. As with other plants, bulbs came in myriad varieties to research, study, and order. Old-fashioned varieties of bulbs brought back childhood memories of drawing daffodils, such as Welty re-created in *Losing Battles* and linked to her own past in *One Writer's Beginnings*:

Learning stamps you with its moments. . . . In a children's art class, we sat in a ring on kindergarten chairs and drew three daffodils that had just been picked out of the yard; and while I was drawing, my sharpened yellow pencil and the cup of the yellow daffodil gave off whiffs just alike. That the pencil doing the drawing should give off the same smell as the flower it drew seemed part of the art lesson—as shouldn't it be?

Welty mentioned to Susan Haltom that it was an old southern custom "to plant bulbs in the shape of your mother's name to commemorate her." Welty readers would recognize a reference to this in her story "The Wanderers." The main character, Virgie Rainey, is driving when a friend named Cassie pulls up beside her:

Cassie called out, driving abreast. "I want you to come see Mama's Name in the Spring, Virgie. This morning before it rained I divided all the bulbs again, and it ought to be prettier than ever!"

"Always see it when I pass your yard," Virgie called back. . . . "I guess it takes a lot of narcissus to spell Catherine," Virgie called, when Cassie still did not pass her.

"Two hundred and thirty-two bulbs! And then Miss Katie's hyacinthus all around those, and I've got it bordered in violets, you know, to tell me where it is in summer!"

Welty began to collect and try several unusual flowering bulbs in the 1940s, adding to the ones mentioned in her comic ode to the mischievous squirrel—moreas, Peruvian squills, bletilla, sparaxis, and colchicum. She found the small species tulips, such as *Tulipa clusiana* and *T. sylvestris*, were adaptable to her southern garden because they did not have to be prechilled—some Jacksonians were known to put ice cubes on the soil over their sprouting tulips—and some of her species tulips came up every spring for years. Often the nurseryman who

Welty wrote to Russell, "Did you ever buy a colchicum bulb from Woolworths and have it come out and bloom? Do it—I put it in some damp peatmoss in a bowl and it's covering itself with beautiful white-and-lavender crocus-like flowers." September 20, 1950. Photograph by Susan Haltom.

Narcissus tazetta 'Avalanche', original to the Welty garden, was called "Presbyterian sisters" by Eudora, "because they hang together." Photograph by Susan Haltom.

Clusiana tulips nodding in the restored Welty garden. "Species tulips are hard to get now but I love them best," Eudora wrote to John Robinson in July 1942. "You know, the little wild tulips that still have lightness and grace and perfume and the clear delicate colors that I guess all original flowers had. One is Clusiana, that you know, the white and red striped tulip with violet blotch. . . . They are all small and sort of bow in the wind and flare up."

sold the bulbs was as interesting as his offerings, as she recounted to Robinson after making this purchase: "Should be out putting down some tardy daffodils but it's so cold. They trailed in from Dr. Berry.

He has a nursery on the west coast and always writes long letters, very kind, a professor, only he forgets to post the daffodils on his trip to town, then confesses on a postcard. . . . He sent me many gratis, 'lovely things.' Puts dates in Roman numerals, and quantities, ix John Evelyn, sent xi–iv (1944). It's like unwrapping presents when they come—in confetti filled boxes, and each one wrapped tightly around its label, like a surprise. . . . All the prettiest ones in the yard came from him. . ." (December 4 [1944]).

One bulb also provided a notable time-release surprise in the Welty garden—Eudora planted a dozen *Amaryllis belladonna* during World War II that did not bloom in her garden until 1953.

During the restoration of the Welty garden, the tree canopy was opened up. This rose—its roots uncovered—sprang forth, as if in imitation of "Becky's Climber" in *The Optimist's Daughter*, Welty's last novel. Here, fading blossoms are intertwined with the heady fragrant blooms of Confederate jasmine (*Trachelospermum jasminoides*). Photograph by Susan Haltom.

to Russell. Her description summed up the many charms of tea roses, a type of old garden rose that grows well in the South. She added that they had uncovered a China rose—"our old little Louis Philippe that had been almost lost under some big climbers."[8]

In spring of 1954 she shared a glimpse of the rest of the garden: "Quince, jasmine, and all are blooming, also the daffodils and white hyacinths, the first blue hyacinths—bluets and onion flowers—tulip trees—the early German iris, that old blue one." Days later, she added, it "smells like cinnamon out the window—blue hyacinths."[9]

During this period Welty channeled most of her energy into traveling and writing, publishing "The Burning" (short story, 1951), "Place in Fiction" (essay, 1954), *The Ponder Heart* (novella, 1954), and *The Bride of the Innisfallen and Other Stories* (1955). While nursing Chestina after eye surgery in 1955, she started the novel *Losing Battles*, which would not be published until 1970.[10] As she spent less time at home, images of declining gardens cropped up in her fiction. The descriptions of neglected roses, her mother's greatest pride, ring with a special poignancy, as in the story "Kin": "hillocks of bushes set in hillocks of rank grass and ragged-robins, hung with roses the size of little biscuits." Perhaps Welty was picturing the gnarled old 'Silver Moon' rose climbing their garage when a character in *Losing Battles* remarks that a 'Silver Moon' rose is "about ready to pull the house down," adding that some red roses drooping on their vine have "turned as blue as bird-dog tongues."[11]

The flowers and gardens of Welty's characters express their traditions, personalities, and social backgrounds, just as gardens do in life. Distinctive plants also characterize wild places. After one spring visit to Russell, Welty returned to Jackson on the train and wrote to him about the atmospheric homeward journey: "... in the long high valley in the Chattanooga mountains there was a rain and thunder storm brushing right close to the train, with clouds with edges definite as boats and spreading like wings, dark purple. . . . The mallows were opening in the swamps (white)[,] a cucumber tree set with flowers right by the tracks."[12] Such acutely observed details of the natural landscape contributed to what Welty, in "Place in Fiction," called "a chink-proof world of appearance," exemplified in such stories as "A Worn Path," in which the character Phoenix Jackson passes through a swamp "where the moss hung as white as lace from every limb" and a forest where pine "cones dropped as light as feathers."[13]

Diarmuid Russell, undated.
© Eudora Welty LLC.

Welty's travels may have sharpened her sense that where her writing was concerned, "the home tie is the blood tie";[14] and that for her, home, garden, and the creative process were deeply connected. Following a trip to England in the early 1950s, she struggled to compose a story set there. "It was nervy of me to try it in the first place," she admitted to Russell. "Not compatible, and when real English people spoke, their words and sounds never rang in my head afterwards. I just keep looking at it, the way you do a flower-

'Lady Banks' rose cas-
cades over the trellis in the
restored Welty garden.

bed where puzzling things have started to come up, and wonder what on earth was sowed there and why."[15]

By the mid-1950s she was busy caring for her ailing mother and trying to write, and her letters to Russell contained fewer details about the garden. In August 1955, she reported, "dozens of fine roses every morning. Also weeds as high as your head."[16] The absence of comments about Chestina's once spectacular border suggests that it was succumbing to the forces of nature, but camellias and roses were still going strong. "I cut plates and plates of open camellias," she told Russell. Though her mother could no longer get out and tend the roses, Welty was keeping them vigorous. Spring of 1957 brought "the finest roses you ever saw . . . there are some 9 inches across these days. Bushes loaded." Then, a "climbing Banksia like a pale yellow waterfall."[17]

Her extant letters to Russell end in 1958, and with them, the longest and most complete record of the garden.[18] From the mid-1950s through the late 1980s, Welty also swapped garden tidbits with her editor at *The New Yorker*, Bill Maxwell, and his wife, Emmy, who were passionate rose gardeners. Perhaps for that reason, their garden discussions focused chiefly on roses. After visiting the Maxwells in 1954, she wrote, "That day was so perfect, and as they say about the right roses, it has keeping powers."[19]

The garden's decline corresponded with a series of overwhelming events in Welty's life. In the fall of 1956 Chestina and both of Eudora's brothers were hospitalized, and Russell suffered a nonfatal heart attack.[20] Three years later Walter Welty died unexpectedly of complications from rheumatoid arthritis, at age forty-three. Her friend, the writer Reynolds Price, described the troubles that beset Welty shortly after he met her, in 1951:

> Her mother, with whom she lived most of her life, became ill, and caring for her would consume Eudora's energy and stillness of mind for more than fifteen years. During that time, she could write only two short stories, a few essays, a children's book and—in scattered moments—a few more incidents for her "long story" [*Losing Battles*]. Ridden by the now eroded iron laws of family love and duty, she stayed the full and severely punishing course. I was not the only one of her friends who wondered if she'd ever work again.[21]

Amid the unfolding catastrophe, "overnight all the roses up and died," Welty said. "I never told my mother."[22] Although Chestina could no longer see out her bedroom window, which faced the backyard, Welty planted a crabapple tree in front of the rose bed to screen out the desolate scene, just in case.[23]

Chestina Welty in her rose bed, undated. © Eudora Welty LLC.

Russell, aware of the mire Welty was in, sought new opportunities for her while urging her to hire caretakers for her mother—"but without book and magazine revenue, the writer could not afford it," Kreyling reports. When Chestina and Edward died, within four days of each other, in 1966, grief again left Welty "at a loss for words" until she managed to "distill into fiction these losing battles," Marrs writes.[24]

When she finally finished *Losing Battles*, a novel drenched in the bold colors of country flower gardens, she moved on to write *The Optimist's Daughter* (1972), a "wide-ranging investigation of memory and understanding," as Marrs describes it.[25] This work—published first as a story, then revised and published as a novella—featured very different flowers, the ones dearest to Welty and her mother. Russell proclaimed the novella a masterpiece, and his judgment was affirmed the following year when it won the Pulitzer Prize. "In her story, Eudora confronted the long years of her mother's illness and the emptiness left by her death," observes Marrs. Writing the book acted as "a source of release and renewal for Eudora and helped her again to live fully in the present."[26]

It is no coincidence that flowers rich in meaning for Welty play significant roles in *The Optimist's Daughter*. The autobiographical main character, Laurel Hand, returns to her family home in Mississippi for her father's funeral. Laurel's mother, Becky, a stand-in for Chestina, has died years earlier.[27] In Becky's overgrown garden, as in Chestina's, four iconic, old-fashioned flowers have survived in spite of long neglect: irises, daffodils, camellias, and roses. They were among the mainstays of her mother's garden, and, more generally, of traditional southern gardens of Chestina's era.

These flowers also reminded Welty of specific people and places. With Russell, who favored irises, she conducted a decades-long discourse on these infinitely varied flowers, which inspired the remarkable dream about creativity she described to him in the 1940s. In *The Optimist's Daughter* Laurel kneels "among the iris that still held a ragged line along the back of the house up to the kitchen door,"[28] conjuring an image of Welty doing the same at Pinehurst Street, where the iris traced a similar course.

Welty loved 'Silver Bells' daffodils, "the nodding, gray-white kind with the square cup" that a family friend brings to the funeral in Laurel's father's house in *The Optimist's Daughter*. "You know who gave me mine—hers are blooming outside," the friend says to Laurel, alluding to Becky having shared the daffodil bulbs in typical pass-along fashion. Years after her death, Becky's gesture has circled back to comfort her daughter. Daffodils

Eudora Welty, undated, 1940s. © Eudora Welty LLC.

This tall bearded iris (*I.* × *germanica* 'Dauntless', introduced in 1929) has dramatic coloration. Photograph by Susan Haltom.

Eudora Welty sought out 'Silver Bells' daffodils (*Narcissus moschatus*) from the "*Market Bulletin*" ladies," shared them with Diarmuid Russell, and discussed them with Elizabeth Lawrence. Photograph by Susan Haltom.

'Chandleri Elegans' camellia still grows in the Welty garden. Photograph by Susan Haltom.

blooming in fields or woods throughout the South often mark the sites of bygone houses, where they traditionally lined the front walk. These flowers also may have reminded Welty of Elizabeth Lawrence, who also preferred white daffodils.[29]

With John Robinson, Welty shared a passion for camellias. In *The Optimist's Daughter* Laurel associates camellias with her father: "Laurel's eye traveled among the urns that marked the graves . . . and saw the favorite camellia of her father's, the old-fashioned 'Chandleri Elegans', that he had planted on her mother's grave—now big as a pony, saddled with unplucked bloom living and dead, standing on a carpet of its own flowers." Yet her father's crass second wife has chosen to bury him in the new part of the cemetery, where the graves are "dotted uniformly with indestructible plastic Christmas poinsettias" that hold none of the camellia's enduring meaning or beauty.[30]

Chestina had poured her heart and soul into her rose bed, and roses lie at the heart of *The Optimist's Daughter*. "'I'd give a pretty to know what exactly that rose is!' Laurel's mother would say every spring when it opened its first translucent flowers of the true rose color." Like Chestina, Becky was curious about the origins of plants, including the stout climbing rose she is admiring in this passage. "'It's an old one, with an old fragrance, and has every right to its own name. . . . All I had to do was uncover it and give it the room it asked for. Look at it! It's on its own roots, of course, utterly strong. That old root there may be a hundred years old!'" This vigorous plant, renewing itself with a power of its own, is like memory in "its ability to sustain and restore the bereaved."[31]

Clustered flowers from the rose that conjures "Becky's Climber" in the restored Welty garden. Photograph by Susan Haltom.

CONFLUENCE

In 1973 Russell was mortally ill with lung cancer, but he survived to see Welty win the Pulitzer Prize. Even more meaningful to Welty, he and his wife, Rose, traveled to Jackson for Mississippi's celebration of Eudora Welty Day, in 1973. At last he saw her garden in person. Russell died, at age seventy-one, in December. The passing of what Marrs calls "her closest friend and most trusted advisor," who had offered support and strength through all the previous losses, "left Eudora in agony."[32] Other close friends died too, and although her literary honors mounted, they failed to offset her desolation. She did not write at length again until 1983.[33]

Jackson, 1973. Courtesy of Eudora Welty LLC.

Welty's main source of comfort during this period was Ken Millar, a popular author of detective novels who wrote under the name Ross Macdonald. The two had struck up a correspondence—each was a fan of the other's work—and met by accident in 1971, in New York City. Their relationship bloomed from friendship into love, and although they conducted their romance largely through the mail—Millar lived in Santa Barbara, California—it continued until the early 1980s, when Alzheimer's disease claimed his ability to write. Because he was not a gardener, their letters contained scant news of Welty's garden.[34]

In 1980, however, Welty shared a choice piece of rosariana with the Maxwells. The Central Mississippi Rose Society had given its spring show a literary theme: "Faulkner, Welty, Williams—A Rose Show in Celebration of Three Mississippi Writers." Participants were invited to design arrangements in three categories: modern creative for Welty, traditional for Faulkner, and miniature for Williams. Subcategories matched particular books with color themes—in Welty's case, *The Ponder Heart*, in red roses; *Delta Wedding*, in pink; and *Losing Battles*, in combined colors.[35] It's unclear whether or not Welty, always alert to camp humor, thought this was funny; but Chestina, who had judged flower arrangements, surely would have been proud that her daughter had inspired these, especially in roses.

Also in 1980, it was Bill Maxwell to whom she confided the sad state of the backyard garden: "It's early in the morning, I'm having coffee by the breakfast room window looking out over the backyard (not a garden any more, but what it is)." She apparently confided her guilt about this to Elizabeth Lawrence, who wrote back, "I was sorry I wounded you by asking about your Mother's garden. It grieves me for you to feel guilty, when you have no reason to. I don't feel guilty about neglecting mine. I don't owe it to any one but myself to keep it alive. I just feel frustrated, not knowing how long I can keep it at all."[36]

That same year, Welty received an opportunity to pay tribute to her parents, when Harvard University invited her to inaugurate the William E. Massey Sr. Lectures in the History of American Civilization.[37] In April 1983, at age seventy-four, she delivered three talks that she subsequently revised and published as *One Writer's Beginnings*—a wry, poignant examination of her childhood and how it influenced her art. Throughout, she wove in affectionate memories of Christian and Chestina. The well-received lectures, delivered to packed halls, marked the final watershed of her career. Welty closed *One Writer's Beginnings* with a passage about "the wonderful word *confluence*, which of itself exists as a reality and a symbol in one":

> It is the only kind of symbol that for me as a writer has any weight, testifying to the pattern, one of the chief patterns, of human experience. . . . Of course the greatest confluence of all is that which makes up the human memory—the individual human memory. My own is the treasure most dearly regarded by me, in my life and in my work as a writer. Here time, also, is subject to confluence. The memory is a living thing—it too is in transit. But during its moment, all that is remembered joins, and lives—the old and the young, the past and the present, the living and the dead.[38]

In *The Optimist's Daughter*, Laurel voices a similar thought as she gazes at "Becky's climber":

> Sienna-bright leaves and thorns like spurts of match-flame had pierced through the severely cut-back trunk. If it didn't bloom this year, it would next: "That's how gardeners must learn to look at it," her mother would say.

Eudora and Chestina in the garden. Photograph by Rollie McKenna, courtesy of Eudora Welty LLC and Rosalie Thorne McKenna Foundation. Courtesy Center for Creative Photography, University of Arizona Foundation.

Memory returned like spring, Laurel thought. Memory had the character of spring. In some cases, it was the old wood that did the blooming.[39]

For Chestina, and then for her daughter, the garden was a lifelong place of confluence, where "all that is remembered joins, and lives." By the mid-1990s, it existed chiefly in Welty's memory. Then, unexpectedly, the longstanding pattern was reversed: instead of the memories embedded in the garden bringing renewal to Welty, she would use her memory to restore the garden.

"It Would Be Like Hell to Do"

SUSAN HALTOM

"We used to have . . ." she began. Then she stopped. "That is a sad phrase," she said. "But you all coming has given me a new outlook. I wish I could do something to help."

—Eudora Welty to Susan Haltom, October 13, 1994

During the 1980s Eudora Welty gave her home to the state of Mississippi, to be administered by the Mississippi Department of Archives and History (MDAH). She would continue to live there for the rest of her life, and after her passing it would become a literary house museum. She was a longtime friend to MDAH—indeed, former director Charlotte Capers was one of her closest friends and had facilitated the first of many gifts of Welty's papers. In a 1987 interview with Welty, Capers asked about the objects in the house as a record for the future. Between their dry quips and laughter, Capers broached the topic of the garden, saying she hoped Welty could recall some of the flowers her mother had planted in case "some ambitious soul in the future" wanted to bring them back. Welty replied, "It would be like hell to do."[1]

In the summer of 1994 I was working at MDAH at an indoor job in exhibit design. I preferred being outdoors, and I was starting to develop

Eudora Welty, 1990s. © Eudora Welty LLC.

a small business designing flower borders. So I was thrilled when Elbert Hilliard, the director of MDAH, asked me to accompany him and Hank Holmes, head of the archives library and Eudora Welty's neighbor, on a visit to Miss Welty. Apparently, she had become distressed about the condition of her garden.

Our visit was very likely prompted by a newspaper article published a few months earlier, headlined "Neighbor pitches in to clean up Welty's overgrown backyard." The Associated Press reporter noted that Miss Welty's neighbor, a Mr. Anger, "has taken over maintenance of part of her yard amid fears of snakes in the tangled weeds and bushes." More comments from Mr. Anger suggested an impossible degree of neglect: "There were snake dens . . . pools filled with dirty water."[2]

It was a typically stifling August day when we drove to Miss Welty's home on Pinehurst Street. Her longtime housekeeper ushered us into the living room where the author was waiting, sitting in a big blue chair from which she could view the shady front yard. Although the room was not air conditioned, it was cool and the light was dim—a sanctuary. Sheer curtains fluttered in the breeze, and I noticed the room was filled with letters and books—on the tables, in piles on the sofa, in towers on the floor, filling bookcases. The room smelled of books. It smelled of letters. Miss Welty welcomed us in her husky southern drawl, and I will never forget her next words: "I cannot bear to look out the window and see what has become of my mother's garden."

She explained that the infirmities of old age and the loss of her yard-man of over forty years had conspired against the landscape, and it had reached a crisis point. While Miss Welty waited indoors, we went outside and toured the yard. The grass was well maintained, although sere and parched as it is in the late Jackson summer, and in front of the house the foundation plantings—camellias and azaleas, mahonias, nandinas, and a pair of matching boxwoods flanking the front steps—looked healthy. In the backyard, no flowers were blooming, which also was typical for late summer; but, clearly, a garden had once been here. A curving border with daylily foliage marked the east side, and over many months, leaf litter had

The Welty backyard, 1994.
Photograph by Susan Haltom.

blown in and settled over the plants. Directly behind the house an oval bed contained the fans of bearded iris, more daylilies, one small, recently replanted 'Grüss an Aachen' rose, and a thalictrum, or meadow rue. Along the side of the garage was a long, narrow bed crowded with montbretia foliage, which had flopped over. An old rose climbed up out of that bed and sprawled across the garage roof.

A drift of red spider lilies blooms in the woodland garden and in various spots elsewhere. "And the spider lilies were taking everything," Welty wrote in *Delta Wedding*. Courtesy of Eudora Welty House, MDAH.

At the far back of the yard we found a wavy line of spireas, nandinas, and some camellias, silhouetted against a bamboo forest. A tangle of vines had strangled these mature shrubs, shrouding them in green. Poison ivy lurked everywhere, thorny green vines snaked above the soil from underground tubers, and invasive Japanese honeysuckle twisted and choked everything in sight. The entire backyard was shaded by mature hardwoods, the limbs of which interlaced overhead to create a dense, leafy canopy. My gardener's eye sized up the reclamation project. There were no snakes or pools of dirty water, but it might truly be hell to do.

We quickly assembled a small volunteer force: Luther Ott, a local attorney who volunteered with the soup kitchen in town, agreed to come weekly and bring two workers, Atlas Dew and Johnny Burgess, who spent endless hours grubbing out the vines in brutal heat. I met them on my days off from work. For the next five months I kept a constant case of poison ivy as we hauled off mountains of garden debris and swatted clouds of mosquitoes. When the September rains fell, the airy blossoms of red spider lilies (*Lycoris radiata*), with their long, outward-curving stamens atop bare stems, pushed their way through the deep-green ground-cover of vinca—a reminder that hidden treasures awaited their chance to spring forth.

In *A Southern Garden* Elizabeth Lawrence wrote "Frost—and the Garden Year Begins Again," referring to the southern garden's fall cleanup, which allows for renewed flowering.[3] Frost comes late to central Mississippi, usually in November, and that first fall the Welty garden was cleaned off in time for us to wait and watch. Plants such as paperwhite narcissus, camellias, and wintersweet will bloom in our "open weather"—Lawrence's term for winter's balmy days—and in many years Christmas is warm and sunny.

Each time I finished working in the garden, I would call on Miss Welty to tell her of our progress. She often invited me in and asked me to chat, and I soon discovered her love of plant lore. She loved the old garden roses 'Grüss an Aachen', because it means "greetings from Aachen" in German, and 'Rosa Mundi', which means "rose of the world." She told me that she had planted white, pink, and yellow zephyranthes—named for the Greek god of the west wind, she pointed out—at the edge of her mother's border. She liked talking about plant explorers, whom she particularly admired for risking their lives to introduce new plants.

Through the next year I visited the Welty garden merely to observe and photograph what new plants had sprouted—mysterious white daffodils, a summer snowflake (*Leucojum aestivum*), French Roman hyacinths, an oxblood lily (*Rhodophiala bifida*). But when we found montbretia corms "bulbified" and stacked five deep underground, a thinning and replanting was in order. For springtime bloom I sowed larkspur seeds and planted other over-wintering annuals—hollyhocks, pansies, snapdragons, ragged robins, Johnny jump-ups—all of which Miss Welty remembered from her mother's garden. When she reminisced about the garden in its prime, she declared, "That was a happy time, when the garden was new. We used to have . . ." Then she stopped. "That is a sad phrase," she said. "But you all coming has given me a new outlook. I wish I could do something to help."

What she did to help was to search her memory. She tantalized me by occasionally mentioning her mother's garden journal, "up in the attic somewhere—I'll go look for it someday." But Miss Welty suffered from back trouble, and that was not likely to happen. Meanwhile, at night, after working in the garden, I rediscovered her prose; the last time I had read her short stories was in high-school English class, twenty-five years earlier. With age and a new perspective, I realized how she used plants and flowers to instill a sense of place, and that many of the same plants she mentioned in her prose were still growing in her yard.

I had not yet fully studied her writing, still focused intently on discovering the story in the ground, yet the more I read, the more I became convinced of this garden's influence on her work. It was also becoming clear to me that the garden had its own story, and that its story had many layers—some connected with Miss Welty's mother, and others with Miss Welty's own life. She always referred to it as "my mother's garden," and when, with her permission, I was able to study old family photographs from the archives, I saw snapshots filled with memories: Eudora and her brothers posing in the side yard, Chestina with friends among the flowers, Christian and Chestina under a wisteria-covered arbor. When I showed her the trellis image, she exclaimed, "Oh, that was the divider between the Upper Garden and the Lower Garden. My mother planted roses there." That was an "ah-hah!" moment. Photographs of these long-gone elements sparked more of her memories and pulled the garden's spatial arrangement into clear focus for me. But before I could dream about replacing the garden architecture, my priority was to make sure Miss Welty had more and more of her favorite flowers to look at from the breakfast room window.

Meanwhile, more of the lost garden was coming to light, both in conversation and on the ground. I was convinced that I had a mission here: to ensure that when this home was eventually restored, it would be surrounded by a garden that would reflect the life and times—and favorite plants—of its gardener-author.

People in Jackson were always curious about the work I was doing, and I was happy to talk up the garden's restoration and garner support. I asked Miss Welty's permission to do that, using her family photographs, and she granted it to me. In 1995, the Southern Garden History Society invited me to present a lecture at the Tenth Conference on Restoring Southern Gardens and Landscapes in Winston-Salem, North Carolina. After that, I started lecturing to garden clubs and other groups, both locally and nationally. My talks wove in photographs of the garden with verbal images of flowers and gardens in Miss Welty's writing. Over time, as I uncovered more of the story of the garden, the story in my lecture expanded, and she gave me permission to tell that too.

As I continued to tend the flower beds, Miss Welty cautioned me, "Don't make the garden something it wasn't," and that was liberating. She did not want the garden to be pretentious, inappropriate, or filled with plants chosen for showiness. She had once looked through my copy of a gardening magazine and remarked on a story about single-color gardens. Miss Welty said she liked all colors, and asked, "Why would you have a one-color garden? To show off!" And then she continued, in a mocking falsetto, "Would you like to see my lavender garden?" It was obvious that the word "garden" was an active verb to her, not a noun. "I don't want to sightsee a garden," she said. "I don't think you could."

Yet here I was, working with the clear knowledge that visitors would one day be "sightseeing" this very garden. I was afraid that without my intervention, another layer of history would be lost, and a bland assortment of meatball-shaped shrubs would be lined up against the side of the house for the sake of low maintenance. I was discovering that historic landscape preservation was still an emerging field. When it comes to budgets, especially state budgets, buildings typically take priority. Right or wrong, this remains the case at many historic properties.

As I began to cast about for expert advice, I organized a small advisory committee for the project and then contacted the Garden Conservancy, a national organization that provides horticultural, technical, management, and financial expertise to conserve historical gardens. The Conservancy sent board members John Fitzpatrick, then the director of the Thomas Jefferson Center for Historic Plants, and James David, a landscape architect based in Austin, Texas, for a site visit. They recommended that we engage a horticulture expert from a state university to help identify existing plants; make an "as-found" site survey; and, most important, not worry about restoring every detail, but instead focus on keeping the overall sense of place. At their suggestion, the Garden Conservancy adopted our garden in an advisory capacity. Bill Noble, director of preservation, shepherded me through the process of writing a cultural landscape report, a document that records the property's history and guides preservation decisions. He also referred me to Charles Birnbaum, who was then the

A surveyor plots the location of existing plants in the Upper Garden. Photograph by Susan Haltom.

coordinator of the National Park Service's Historic Landscape Initiative. Birnbaum introduced me to the *Secretary of the Interior's Standards for the Treatment of Historic Properties with Guidelines for the Treatment of Cultural Landscapes*, an essential tool kit for anyone attempting landscape preservation.

Preparing the cultural landscape report required a new level of groundwork. A key part of the process involved determining the garden's period of significance—the years in which it most embodied the creator's vision. Because Miss Welty's letters and her mother's garden notebooks were still unavailable, I had to rely on the garden in the ground, and we had no base map of existing plants. Surveyors arrived to record the location of every plant and garden feature. I showed Miss Welty their site plan, which plotted more than three hundred points, each marking the exact position of a camellia, spirea, volunteer oak, or part of a flower border.

By this time, Miss Welty's memories and photographs had established that Chestina Welty had created the garden in the mid-1920s. This marked the beginning of the period of significance. To understand the context for the design and plantings of the period, I explored the Garden Club of America's glass slide collection at the Smithsonian Archives of American Gardens. There I found many examples of early twentieth-century gardens, including several in Mississippi. In search of popular plants of the period, I combed through old nursery catalogues at the Smithsonian, in addition to my own collection of garden books and catalogues. I determined the end point of the garden's period of significance to be 1945, which marked a watershed in American cultural life brought by World War II. After this point, not just the Welty garden but American horticulture at large went through a radical change.

Now that I knew the garden's period of significance, I could choose whether to restore it exactly to that period, or to select another option. I evaluated the preservation "treatment" that best fit our garden, based on its current condition and future use. Following the *Guidelines for the Treatment of Cultural Landscapes*, I decided on rehabilitation, which accommodates some newer adaptations, such as handrails along the garden steps. My report on the garden's history was finished in April 2001.

Miss Welty was able to remain in her home until she passed away on July 23, 2001. She lay in state in the Old Capitol rotunda, and hundreds of admirers lined up to pay their respects. For the vestibule, her family asked me to arrange a bouquet of summer flowers, gathered from her yard and mine.

Later, as her nieces went through the Welty house, they found their grandmother's garden records, including diagrams of the flower beds and more garden images. These confirmed discoveries we were making outdoors: in the Lower Garden, where Miss Welty had told us her mother planted roses, the landscape contractor and I could make out the raised form of a small, right-angled bed enclosing a smaller triangular bed. The notebook diagrams confirmed this exact layout. We also uncovered bricks buried about eight inches in the soil, edging some of the flower beds—perhaps the very bricks Miss Welty had mentioned in her 1944 article for *Vogue*—and a line of concrete rubble her mother had placed at the front of her perennial border to control erosion. With most of the cleanup done and the old garden beds revealed, it was time to re-create the garden rooms.

Susan Haltom's flower arrangement at the Old Capitol building, where Welty lay in state, July 2001. Photograph by Susan Haltom.

Scenes from the Welty garden restoration, 1994–2009. Upper right photograph by Langdon Clay. Other photographs by Susan Haltom.

Scenes from the Welty garden restoration, 1994–2009. Upper right photograph by Langdon Clay. Other photographs by Susan Haltom.

The restored Welty garden in high spring.

The re-created Welty clubhouse at the far end of the woodland garden. Photograph by Susan Haltom.

Without a doubt the most important step in the restoration of the Welty garden was the construction of the trellis and the three arbors, made possible by a generous couple, Evelyn and Michael Jefcoat. These additions immediately reinstated Chestina's original spatial design, creating a series of garden rooms where, for decades, there had been only one. Because wood rots in only a few years in our humid climate, we chose white-painted tubular steel, which was fabricated by craftsmen and welded on site according to exact measurements taken from historical photographs of the gardens. Today the original varieties of climbing roses that Chestina planted in the 1930s drape the arbors and provide a springtime bower.

Another important addition was the re-creation of the Welty boys' clubhouse. This small building, though modest in size and design provides a focal point to the farthest reach of the garden and in doing so, creates a strong sense of the middle distance.

When it came to replacing Chestina Welty's original plantings, wheth-

Nurseryman Ed Nichols custom-grows heirloom plants for the Welty garden. Photograph by Susan Haltom.

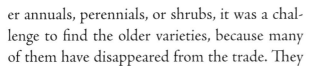

Yardman Rezell Archer uncovered the original bricks outlining the oval bed.

Landscape contractors Eric Hays and Andrew Bell have taken care of the garden since its restoration.

er annuals, perennials, or shrubs, it was a challenge to find the older varieties, because many of them have disappeared from the trade. They have been replaced by more floriferous and more compact types, which can be stacked in greater quantities in delivery trucks. The habits of these modern plants would be out of place and out of scale in the restored garden. Special heirloom seeds and plants are custom grown for our garden, and these contribute to our authentic sense of place.

Although we began our garden restoration with the lofty goal of using period tools and gardening methods, after several summertime droughts, we installed an irrigation system. It was simply impossible for the small, overworked Welty House staff to spend their days dragging water hoses

Protection for the landscape while the house was being restored. Courtesy of Eudora Welty House, MDAH.

A. P. Fatherree and Richard Carter of the Jackson Camellia Society demonstrate how to air-layer a camellia. Air-layering is a method that allows gardeners to propagate a larger plant than is possible with cuttings. Photographs by Susan Haltom.

The Cereus Weeders: Marsha Cannon, Elaine Chatham, Emily Dunbar-Smith, Leigh Eley, Mary Ann Fontaine, Darian Gibson, Julianne Summerford, and Lee Threadgill. Photographs by Susan Haltom.

The restored Eudora Welty
House in summer 2008. Photograph by Susan Haltom.

Author and gardener Susan
Haltom. Photo courtesy of
Eudora Welty House, MDAH.

around when a modern convenience might make a big difference in the plants' survival.

The public was eager to begin touring the house long before archivists and architects had completed their extensive cataloguing and work. The restoration architect, Robert Parker Adams, went out of his way to ensure the safety of mature foundation plantings as his crews repaired the cracked and shifted foundation. Because the garden rehabilitation had started much earlier, we—I was now an independent contractor to the state in charge of the garden, managing a small crew—were able to open the garden to the public in 2004, two years before the Eudora Welty House opened. In 2006, the house and garden were declared a National Historic Landmark, the highest mark of significance the federal government bestows.

Thousands of people have visited the Welty House and its garden since the property opened. Many have been visibly moved by the experience of this garden, which is interpreted as an outdoor exhibit and enhanced by related quotes from Welty writings. They may remember what certain gardens in their past have meant to them; some people like to compare our plants with those they grow at home. And, several times, readers of Miss Welty's work have commented, "I feel like I've just stepped into *The Optimist's Daughter*."

Working in the garden allowed the Welty women to take time for reflection and inspiration and gave them respite from their everyday concerns. "Weeding is good for you," Miss Welty once told me. "It's not an emergency. You must be patient and calm." For several years, a handful of women have faithfully joined me every week to tend the Welty garden. We call ourselves the Cereus Weeders, after Miss Welty's Night Blooming Cereus Club of the 1930s. When we are in need of a road trip, we become the Cereus Readers, delving into one of her books and visiting its setting.

Many people wonder if a garden is meant to live on after its creator. Of course we recognize that things can never truly stay the same, since a garden exists *in time*, with tree canopy changes and alterations in the beds

View of the garden from
the breakfast room in the
Eudora Welty House, 2010.

and borders. But meaning, in a garden, goes deeper than mere decoration or the plants themselves, and that is why I wanted to share this garden's story.

Finding meaning may also take time. As Henry Mitchell once described Miss Welty's work: "Her art, after all, appears always to have been aimed at grand simplicities, not usually found at the first flirtation with a typewriter, but not all that complicated, either. It takes years, perhaps, to learn what is simple and what is right."[4]

APPENDIX I

DECADES OF WELTY PLANTS

The plant palette of the Welty garden created an overall look that defined the garden's character at the time. The following lists are not complete, but these species were most representative of the garden in each decade, adding to the plants already growing in the garden.

1920s

Chestina planted trees and shrubs for structure, enclosure, and texture.

Trees:
Cedar (*Juniperus virginiana*)
Cherry laurel (*Prunus laurocerasus*)
Double flowering peach (*Prunus persica*)
Loblolly pine (*Pinus taeda*)
Water oak (*Quercus nigra*)

Shrubs:
Abelia (*Abelia grandiflora*)
Banana shrub (*Michelia figo*)
English dogwood (*Philadelphus coronarius*)
Forsythia (*Forsythia × intermedia*)
Gardenia (*Gardenia jasminoides*)
Nandina (*Nandina domestica*)
Pittosporum (*Pittosporum tobira*)
Privet (*Ligustrum sinense*)
Pyracantha (*Pyracantha coccinia*)
Spireas (*S. thunbergii, S. × Vanhouttei, S. prunifolia, S. cantoniensis*)
Vitex (*Vitex agnus-castus*)
Winter honeysuckle (*Lonicera fragrantissima*)
Yaupon (*Ilex vomitoria*)

Flowers and vines:
Climbing roses (*Rosa × hybrida*; see accompanying rose list)
Cornflower (a. k. a. ragged robins, *Centaurea cyanus*)
Larkspur (*Consolida ajacis*)
Morning glory (*Ipomoea tricolor*)
Sweet peas (*Lathyrus odoratus*)
Wisteria (*Wisteria sinensis*)

1930s

During this decade Chestina added lots of flowers, ensuring that something was always in bloom.

Trees:
Crape myrtle (*Lagerstroemia indica*)
Mimosa (*Albizia julibrissin*)

Shrubs:
Althea (*Hibiscus syriacus*)
Hydrangea (*Hydrangea macrophylla*)
Native azalea (*Rhododendron canescens*)
Spirea 'Anthony Waterer' (*Spirea japonica* 'Anthony Waterer')

Flowers and vines:
Blackberry lily (*Belamcanda chinensis*)
Butterfly lily (*Hedychium coronarium*)
Calla lily (*Zantedeschia aethiopica*)
Canna (*Canna × generalis*)
Chrysanthemum (*Chrysanthemum × morifolium*)
Dahlias (*Dahlia × hybrida*)
Daylilies (*Hemerocallis* sp.)
Golden Glow (*Rudbeckia laciniata* 'Hortensia')
Hardy aster (*Aster* sp.)
Hybrid tea roses (*Rosa × hybrida*)
Irises—tall bearded iris (*Iris × germanica*), Dutch iris (*I. hollandica*), Siberian iris (*I. sibirica*), and others
Lilies—tiger lily (*Lilium lancifolium*), regal lily (*L. regale*), rubrum lily (*L. rubrum*), madonna lily (*L. candidum*), Easter lily (*L. longiflorum*), Formosa lily (*L. formosanum*), and others
Lily-turf (*Liriope muscari, L. spicata*)
Marigolds (*Tagetes erecta, T. patula*)
Nasturtiums (*Tropaeolum majus*)

Night blooming cereus (*Hylocereus undatus*)
Ox-eye daisy (*Chrysanthemum leucanthemum*)
Phlox (*Phlox paniculata, P. divaricata, P. drummondii*)
Queen Anne's lace (*Daucus carota carota*)
Rain lilies (*Zephyranthes* sp.)
Rosa de Montana (*Antigonon leptopus*)
Salvia (*Salvia farinacea, S. leucantha*)
Shasta daisy (*Chrysanthemum maximum*)
Spider lilies (*Lycorus radiata*)
Stokesia (*Stokesia laevis*)
Sweet alyssum (*Lobularia maritime*)
Tuberose (*Polianthes tuberosa*)
Verbena (*Verbena* × *hybrida*)
Violets (*Viola odorata*)
Zinnias (*Zinnia elegans*)

1940s

Eudora planted camellias and unusual bulbs as she began to work more actively in the garden.

Trees:
Dogwood (*Cornus florida*)

Shrubs:
Camellias (*C. Japonica* and *C. sasanqua*)
Flowering quince (*Chaenomeles speciosa*)
Sweet olive (*Osmanthus fragrans*)

Flowers and vines:
Algerian iris (*I. unguicularis*, formerly *I. stylosa marginata*)
Confederate jasmine (*Trachelospermum jasminoides*)
Crinum (*Crinum* sp.)
Daffodils (*Narcissus* species and hybrids)
Four-o'clocks (*Mirabilis jalapa*)
French Roman hyacinths (*Hyacinthus orientalis albulus*)
Japanese iris (*Iris ensata*)
Lantana (*Lantana camera*)
Lilies—Philippine lily (*Lilium philippinense*) and species lilies (*Lilium henryi, Lilium dauricum*)
Montbretia (*Crocosmia* × *crocosmiiflora*)
Ornithogalum (*Ornithogalum umbellatum*)
Oxalis (*Oxalis rubra*)

Oxblood lily (*Rhodophiala bifida*)
Pansies (*Viola* × *wittrockiana*)
Petunias (*Petunia* × *hybrida*)
Pinks (*Dianthus plumarius*)
Species tulips (*T. clusiana* and *T. sylvestris*)
Summer snowflake (*Leucojum aestivum*)
Sunset hibiscus (*Hibiscus manihot*)
Surprise lily (*Lycorus squamigera*)

POSTWAR AND BEYOND

As time to garden became more precious, some plants began to die off, and Eudora and Chestina fell back on plants that required less work.

Trees:
Bradford pears (*Pyrus calleryana* 'Bradford', removed during restoration)
Chinese tallow or popcorn tree (*Sapium sebiferum*, removed during restoration)
Crabapple (*Malus*, removed during restoration)
Mature hardwoods—oak and elm

Shrubs:
Azalea (*Azalea indica*)
Old garden roses

Flowers and vines:
Colchicum (*Colchicum* sp.)
English ivy (*Hedera helix*)
Herbs in pots, such as apple mint (*Mentha suaveolens*) and lemon verbena (*Aloysia triphylla*)
Spanish bluebell (*Hyacinthoides hispanica*)

APPENDIX II

ORIGINAL PLANT LIST FOR 1119 PINEHURST STREET

Chestina Welty penciled the following plant names on the back of the typed list "Planting Specifications for Mr. C. W. Welty, Pinehurst, Jackson, Mississippi, January 6, 1926." These woody plants were intended to create the living structure of the garden.

10 Native yaupon (*Ilex vomitoria*)
 2 Deodar cedar (*Cedrus deodara*)
12 Cape jasmine, or gardenia (*Gardenia jasminoides*)
30 Abelia grandiflora (*Abelia × grandiflora*)
30 Spirea Van Houtte (*Spiraea × vanhouttei*)
 2 Pittosporum (*Pittosporum tobira*)
 4 *Pyracantha yuanensis, Pyracantha Fortuniana* or *P. coccinea*
 2 *Pyracantha caerulea*
10 Cherry laurel (*Prunus laurocerasus*)
 1 Mimosa (*Albizia julibrissin*)
 2 Red cedar (*Juniperus virginiana*)
10 Fragrant honeysuckle (*Lonicera fragrantissima*)
 8 Philadelphus (*Philadelphus coronarius*)
 8 Vitex (*Vitex agnus-castus*)

Several species that appear on both the specification list and Chestina's selection were popular southern garden plants of the day. These include:

Abelia (*Abelia × grandiflora*)
Banana shrub (*Michelia figo*)
Blackberries (*Rubus fruticosus*)
Camellia (*Camellia japonica* and *C. sasanqua*)
Cherry laurel (*Prunus laurocerasus*)
Chinese photinia (*Photinia serrulata*)
Crepe myrtle (*Lagerstroemia indica*)
Double flowering peach (*Prunus persica*)
Eastern red cedar (*Juniperus virginiana*)
Eleagnus (*Eleagnus pungens*)
English dogwood, or mock orange (*Philadelphus coronarius*)
Gardenia (*Gardenia jasminoides*)
Hydrangea (*Hydrangea macrophylla*)
Magnolia (*Magnolia grandiflora*)
Mahonia (*Mahonia bealei*)
Mimosa (*Albizia julibrissin*)
Nandina (*Nandina domestica*)
Pittosporum (*Pittosporum tobira*)
Privet (*Ligustrum sinense* and *L. lucidum*)
Pyracantha (*Pyracantha* sp.)
Quince (*Chaenomeles* sp.)
Roses (*Rosa* sp. and *R. hybrida*)
Spireas (*Spiraea* sp.)
Vitex (*Vitex agnus-castus*)
Winter honeysuckle (*Lonicera fragrantissima*)
Yaupon (*Ilex vomitoria*)

APPENDIX III

ANNUALS IN THE WELTY GARDEN

This partial list is compiled from Chestina's journals and Eudora's letters of the 1930s and '40s.

California poppy (*Eschscholzia californica*), orange or yellow
Castor bean (*Ricinus communis*), red
China aster (*Callistephus chinensis*), mixed colors
Columbines (*Aquilegia hybrida*), mixed colors
Cosmos (*Cosmos bipinnatus*), pink and white
Four-o'clocks (*Mirabilis jalapa*), mixed colors
Gaillardia (*Gaillardia* sp.), yellow, orange, and red
Heliotrope (*Heliotropium arborescens*), purple
Larkspur (*Consolida ajacis*), mixed colors
Marigolds (*Tagetes erecta, T. patula*), orange or yellow
Mustard (*Brassicaceae* sp.)
Nasturtium (*Tropaeolum majus*), orange or yellow

Pansy (*Viola × wittrockiana*), white or mixed colors
Petunias (*Petunia hybrida*), mixed colors
Phlox drummondii (*Phlox drummondii*), mixed colors
Queen Anne's lace (*Daucus carota carota*), white
Ragged robins (*Centaurea cyanus*), royal blue
Shirley poppies (*Papaver rhoeas*), pink
Snapdragons (*Antirrhinum majus*), mixed colors
Sweet alyssum (*Lobularia maritima*), white
Texas bluebonnets (*Lupinus subcarnosus*), blue
Verbena (*Verbena hortensis*), lavender, pink, white
Zinnia (*Zinnia elegans*), mixed colors

APPENDIX IV
ROSES IN THE WELTY GARDEN

The 1926 "Planting Specifications" for the Welty yard (Appendix II) suggested sixty *Rosa* 'Thousand Beauties' for a hedge and eighty other assorted roses. Although Chestina did not take that advice, throughout her gardening years she sampled many roses and abandoned those that proved to be too much trouble. In later life Chestina and Eudora fell back on easier-to-maintain old garden roses. These are sometimes defined as roses that were introduced before 1867 (when 'La France', the first hybrid tea rose, was introduced), but many people give the name to any rose over seventy-five years old that has fragrance, landscape value, and disease resistance. The Weltys discovered that certain roses perform better in other climates, as Eudora stated to Diarmuid Russell in the letter below.

> *Our whole southern rose problem is that down here people have obeyed without question the rules laid down by the Rose people of Harrisburg and the North in general, low pruning, grafted stock, etc., whereas Mother and some people have always held, down here we can get roses (grafted I mean, of course you don't prune tea) to be everblooming as they were in the old days by simply not pruning them severely. We can grow the roses here that I bet you did in Ireland, the old Teas, old-fashioned climbers, Chinas, Gallicas, Damasks, Noisettes etc. and they do so beautifully for us—why do we try to ape the cold climates?*
>
> *I'm ordering the old-fashioned rose catalogue from Bobbink & Atkins if they still have it, and hope to reinstate Lady Hillingdon and the Duchesse de Brabant and the Maman Cochets we've lost through the years—instead of The Doctor which is so beautiful but hard for us to grow. Have you that one?*
>
> —Eudora Welty to Diarmuid Russell, no date [1946]

The following list, compiled from Chestina's garden notes and also from Eudora's correspondence, represents the roses they most likely planted at one time or another. Although the list does not include such twentieth-century familiars as 'Radiance' and 'Red Radiance', it is possible that the Weltys also grew these and others.

'American Pillar'
'Birdie Blye'
'Charlotte'
'Climbing (cl.) American Beauty'
'Cl. Cecile Brunner'
'Cl. Charlotte Armstrong'
'Cl. Picture'
'Cl. Kaiserin Auguste Victoria'
'Cl. Killarney'
'Cl. President Herbert Hoover'
'Cl. Ruth'
'Cl. Talisman'
'Contessa de Santiago'
'Crimson Glory'
'Cynthia'
'Dainty Bess'
'Donald Prior'
'Dr. Huey'
'Dr. W. Van Fleet' (cl.)
'Duchesse de Brabant'
'Duquesa de Peñeranda'
'Edith Nellie Perkins'
'Editor McFarland'
'Etoile de Hollande'
'Fashion'
'Feu Pernet Ducher'
'Fortune's Double Yellow' (cl.)
'Frau Karl Druschki'

'Frensham'
'Gloire de Dijon'
'Good News'
'Grüss an Aachen'
'Helen Traubel'
'Joyous Cavalier'
'Lady Banks' (*Rosa banksiae* var. *luteae*) (cl.)
'Lady Hillingdon'
'Louis Philippe'
'Ma Perkins'
'Málar-Ros'
'Maman Cochet'
'Mary Wallace'
'Mermaid' (cl.)
'Mirandy'
'Mme Grégoire Staechelin' (a. k. a. 'Spanish Beauty')
'Moss Rose' (*Rosa centifolia*)
'Peace'
'Rosa Mundi'
'Safrano'
'Silver Moon' (cl.)
'Soeur Thérèse'
'Souvenir de la Malmaison'
'Sterling'
'Sutter's Gold'
'The Doctor'
'Thor'

APPENDIX V

PARTIAL LIST OF PLANTS IN WELTY PROSE

Abelia (*Abelia × grandiflora*)

Althea (*Hibiscus syriacus*)

Angel lily (probably *Crinum × powelii 'Album'*)

Angel trumpet (*Datura metel*)

Apostle lily (probably *Crinum bulbispermum*)

Banana (*Musa* spp.)

Begonia (*Begonia* spp.)

Black cherry (*Prunus serotina*)

Blackberry lily (*Belamcanda chinensis*)

Bois d'arc (*Maclura pomifera*)

Box (*Buxus sempervirens*)

Breath of spring (*Spiraea thunbergii*)

Camellia (*Camellia japonica* and *C. sasanqua*)

Candlestick lily (*Crinum scabrum*)

Canna (*Canna × generalis*)

Castor plant (*Ricinus communis*)

Cedar (*Juniperus virginiana*)

Century plant (*Agave americana*)

Cherokee rose (*Rosa laevigata*)

Chinaberry (*Melia azedarach*)

Chinese tallow (*Sapium sebiferum*)

Christmas cactus (*Schlumbergera bridgesii*)

Christmas rose (*Helleborus niger*)

Clematis (*Clematis × jackmanii*)

Cockscomb (*Celosia cristata*)

Confederate jasmine (*Trachelospermum jasminoides*)

Confederate lily (*Crinum fimbriatulum*)

Cosmos (*Cosmos sulphureus*)

Cotton (*Gossypium* spp.)

Cucumber tree (*Magnolia acuminata*)

Dahlia (*Dahlia* spp.)

Dewberries (*Rubus* spp.)

Dogwood (*Cornus florida*)

Double touch-me-not (*Impatiens balsamina*)

Elderberry (*Sambucus canadensis*)

Fairy lily, pink (*Zephyranthes rosea*)

Fairy lily, white (*Zephyranthes candida*)

False dragonhead (*Physostegia virginiana*)

Ferns (*Dryopteris* spp.)

Fig (*Ficus carica*)

Fortune grass (*Pennisetum setaceum*)

Four-o'clock (*Mirabilis jalapa*)

Geranium, speckled (*Pelargonium × hortorum*)

Gladiolus (*Gladiolus × hortulanus*)

Golden bell (*Forsythia × intermedia*)

Heliotrope (*Heliotropium arborescens*)

Hickory (*Carya* spp.)

Honeysuckle (*Lonicera* spp.)

Hyacinthus, or French Roman hyacinth (*Hyacinthus orientalis*)

Iris (*Iris* spp.)

Ironweed (*Vernonia altissima*)

Joseph's-coat (*Amaranthus tricolor*)

Lady's eardrops (*Malvaviscus arboreus* var. *drummondii*)

Lady's tresses (*Spiranthes gracilis*)

Lemon lily (*Hemerocallis lilioasphodelus*)

Live oak (*Quercus virginiana*)

Locust (*Robinia* spp.)

Magnolia (*Magnolia grandiflora*)

Maple (*Acer rubrum*)

Michaelmas daisies (*Aster novi-belgii* or *A. novi-angliae*)

Milk and wine lily (*Crinum latifolium* or *C. × herbertii*)

Mimosa (*Albizia julibrissin*)

Mistletoe (*Phoradendron serotinum*)

Montbretia (*Crocosmia × crocosmiiflora*)

Moonvine (*Ipomoea alba*)

Morning glory (*Ipomoea* spp.)

Mulberry (*Morus* spp.)

Muscadine (*Vitis rotundifolia*)

Narcissus (*Narcissus* spp.)

Nasturtium (*Tropaeolum majus*)

Night-blooming cereus (*Selenicereus grandiflorus* or *Hylocereus undatus*)

Nodding lady's tresses (*Spiranthes cernua*)

Okra (*Abelmoschus esculentus*)

Oleander (*Nerium oleander*)

Palmetto (*Sabal minor*)

Pansy (*Viola × wittrockiana*)

Passionflower, or maypop (*Passiflora* spp.)

Peach, blood-red Indian (*Prunus persica*)

Pear (*Prunus pyrifolia*)

Pecan (*Carya illinoinensis*)

Pepper grass (*Lepidium* spp.)

Persimmon (*Diospyros virginiana*)

Pheasant-eye (*Narcissus poeticus*)

Philippine lily (*Lilium formosanum* or *L. philippinense*)

Phlox (*Phlox paniculata*)

Pine (*Pinus taeda*)

Pinks (*Dianthus* spp.)

Pink Jacob's ladder (*Gladiolus byzantinus*)

Plum (*Prunus umbellata*)

Poinsettia (*Euphorbia pulcherrima*)

Pomegranate (*Punica granatum*)

Poplar (*Liriodendron tulipifera*)

Prayer plant (*Maranta leuconeura*)

Prince's feather (*Amaranthus hybridus* var. *cruentus*)

Princess feather (*Polygonom orientale*)

Privet (*Ligustrum sinense*)

Red-hot poker (*Kniphofia uvaria*)

Red salvia (*Salvia splendens* or *S. cocccinia*)

Red amaryllis (*Hippeastrum* × *johnsonii*)

Redbud (*Cercis canadensis*)

Ribbon grass (*Phalaris arundinacea* var. *picta*)

Roses—including "big white rose, little thorn rose, beauty-red sister rose, pink monthly, old-fashioned red summer rose, . . . baby rose." Also "fairy rose," and "Becky's Climber," 'Gloire de Dijon' (1853), 'Fortune's Climber' (1845), 'Safrano' (1839), 'Silver Moon' (1910), 'Mermaid' (1918), Lady Banks (by 1824), 'Maman Cochet' (1893), 'American Beauty' (1875), 'Pink Monthly' or 'Old Blush' (1752), 'Etoile de Hollande' (1919), 'Lady Hillingdon' (1910), 'Grüss an Aachen' (1909), 'Climbing Thor' (1940), 'Dainty Bess' (1925), 'Maréchal Niel' (1864)

Sage (*Salvia officinalis*)

Sassafras (*Sassafras albidum*)

Scuppernong (*Vitis rotundifolia*)

Silver bells (*Narcissus pseudonarcissus moschatus*)

Snow-on-the-mountain (*Euphorbia marginata*)

Snowball viburnum (*Viburnum macrocephalum*)

Southern blue flag (*Iris virginica*)

Southern smilax (*Smilax rotundifolia*)

Spanish moss (*Tillandsia usneoides*)

Spider lilies (*Lycoris radiata*)

Sumac (*Rhus glabra*)

Sunflower (*Helianthus annuus*)

Sweet geranium (*Pelargonium graveolens*)

Sweet gum (*Liquidambar styraciflua*)

Sweet olive (*Osmanthus fragrans*)

Sword fern (*Nephrolepis exaltata* 'Bostoniensis')

Sycamore (*Platanus occidentalis*)

"Tall vine with heart-shaped leaves"

Tiger lily (*Lilium lancifolium*)

Trumpet vine (*Campsis radicans*)

Tuberose (*Polianthes tuberosa*)

Vase palm (probably *Chamaedorea elegans*)

Verbena (*Verbena* spp.)

Vinca (*Vinca major* or *V. minor*)

Violets (*Viola odorata*)

Virgin's bower (*Clematis virginiana*)

Water hyacinths (*Eichhornia crassipes*)

Water lilies (*Nymphaea* spp.)

White flags (*Iris* × *albicans*)

White star jessamine (*Jasminum nitidum*)

Wild phlox (*Phlox divaricata*)

Willow (*Salix nigra*)

Wistaria (*Wisteria sinensis*)

Wild wistaria (*Wisteria frutescens*)

Yucca (*Yucca filamentosa*)

Zinnia (*Zinnia elegans*)

APPENDIX VI

RESOURCES FOR HISTORIC LANDSCAPE PRESERVATION

Publications

Birnbaum, Charles A. *Protecting Cultural Landscapes: Planning, Treatment and Management of Historic Landscapes*, Preservation Brief 36 (Washington, D.C.: Preservation Assistance Division, NPS, 1994).

———, with Christine Capella Peters. *The Secretary of the Interior's Standards for the Treatment of Historic Properties with Guidelines for the Treatment of Cultural Landscapes* (Washington, D.C.: U.S. Department of the Interior, NPS Cultural Resource Stewardship and Partnerships Heritage Preservation Services, Historic Landscape Initiative, 1996).

Producer of Books and Exhibitions on American Landscape History

Library of American Landscape History
Amherst, Mass.
www.lalh.org

Technical Assistance

Alliance for Historic Landscape Preservation
New York, N.Y.
www.ahlp.org

American Public Gardens Association
Kennett Square, Pa.
www.publicgardens.org

American Horticultural Society
Alexandria, Va.
www.ahs.org

American Society of Landscape Architects
Historic Preservation Professional Practice Network
Washington, D.C.
www.asla.org

The Garden Conservancy
Cold Spring, N.Y.
www.gardenconservancy.org

Research Archives

Archives of American Gardens
Smithsonian Horticultural Services Division
Washington, D.C.
www.gardens.si.edu

Environmental Design Archives
University of California, Berkeley
http://ced.berkeley.edu

James Rose Center for Landscape Architecture Research and Design
Ridgewood, N.J.
www.jamesrosecenter.org

National Park Service
Heritage Preservation Services
Historic Landscape Initiative
Washington, D.C.
www.nps.gov/hps/hli/index.htm

National Trust for Historic Preservation
Washington, D.C.
www.preservationnation.org

Society for American City and Regional Planning History
Moon Township, Pa.
www.dcp.ufl.edu/sacrph

The Cultural Landscape Foundation
Washington, D.C.
www.tclf.org

APPENDIX VII

DISCUSSION QUESTIONS FOR BOOK CLUBS

Eudora Welty created a body of modernist work, and one defining characteristic of modernist literature is that it suggests rather than declares its meaning. Another is that it rejects absolute truth and embraces individual perception, which frees both writer and reader to find personal meaning in the work. As one Welty scholar, Peggy Prenshaw, states it, "Modernists share a great skepticism about the power of generalizing words—hope, fear, love, etc.—and seek alternative imagery that communicates sensations and feelings to engage the modern reader."

This book attempts to flesh out the source of one powerful strand of imagery in Welty's fiction—flowers and gardens. One approach to discussing this book is to read it in concert with a story or a novel by Eudora Welty (for a list of her published work, visit www.eudorawelty .org/bibliography.html). Then consider the following questions:

1) How were gardens or particular plants meaningful to the characters in the story?
2) What did Welty's descriptions of certain flowers or plants tell you about the people or the place in the story?
3) How do Welty's descriptions of nature, wild or cultivated, add to the sense of place in her writing?
4) Even those of us who are not gardeners enjoy looking at gardens or arranging cut flowers in a vase. Explain why a particular garden, natural place, or flower holds special meaning for you.
5) How were garden clubs important to women during the first quarter of the twentieth century?
6) Although book groups and garden clubs include men, both are identified primarily with women. What parallels do you see between the benefits of garden clubs to women a century ago and the value of book groups for women today? What differences?
7) Both books and gardens can be personal artistic expressions. Do you believe, as some garden historians do, that a garden can be read and interpreted like a book? Why or why not?
8) Chestina Welty, Eudora's mother, viewed gardening as an educational pursuit. Today, chef and gardener Alice Waters is among those who believe that children can learn many fundamental lessons from gardening, and especially from raising their own food. What are the most valuable things you think people of any age can learn from gardening?

9) During World War II, the Pennsylvania-based rosarian and civic booster Horace J. McFarland was among those who urged Americans to raise not only food in their victory gardens, but also ornamental plants, because he believed beauty to be necessary for spiritual and emotional well-being. Explain why you agree or disagree with him.

NOTES

INTRODUCTION

1. Eudora Welty, *One Writer's Beginnings* (hereafter, *OWB*), in *Welty: Stories, Essays, & Memoir*, Richard Ford and Michael Kreyling, eds. (New York: Literary Classics of the United States, Inc., 1998, The Library of America series), 925. First published by Harvard University Press, 1984. Copyright © 1983, 1984 by Eudora Welty.

2. Welty, *OWB*, in *Welty: Stories, Essays, & Memoir*, Ford and Kreyling, eds., 900; Welty to William Maxwell, n.d. [1980], William Maxwell Papers, Rare Book and Manuscript Library, University of Illinois at Urbana–Champaign (hereafter, UIRBML).

3. Suzanne Marrs, *Eudora Welty: A Biography* (Orlando, Austin, New York, San Diego, Toronto, London: Harcourt, Inc., 2005), 33.

4. Welty, *OWB*, in *Welty: Stories, Essays, & Memoir*, Ford and Kreyling, eds., 842, 926, 935.

CHAPTER ONE

1. Welty, *OWB*, in *Welty: Stories, Essays, & Memoir*, Ford and Kreyling, eds., 896.

2. Floyd Watkins, "Notes on Eudora Welty Trip," 10–23 September 1984, typescript, 10, Floyd Watkins Papers, Manuscript, Archives, and Rare Book Library, Emory University, Atlanta, Ga.; Death Records, West Virginia Archives and History: Edward Raboteau Andrews, d. 25 March 1899.

3. Welty, *OWB*, in *Welty: Stories, Essays, & Memoir*, Ford and Kreyling, eds., 893.

4. Ibid.

5. Eudora Welty, conversation with Susan Haltom (hereafter, Welty to Haltom), 14 December 1994; Eudora Welty, "Old Mr. Marblehall," in *Welty: Stories, Essays, & Memoir*, Ford and Kreyling, eds., 114. The story was first pub-lished in *A Curtain of Green and Other Stories* by Doubleday, Doran, 1941. North American publication rights are held by Houghton Mifflin Harcourt, the publisher of the 1947 edition of *A Curtain of Green and Other Stories*.

6. Welty, *OWB*, in *Welty: Stories, Essays, & Memoir*, Ford and Kreyling, eds., 913; keepsake book belonging to Christian W. Welty, Eudora Welty House, Mississippi Department of Archives and History (MDAH), Jackson, Mississippi; Clyde S. White, "An Interview with Eudora," 1992, in *More Conversations with Eudora Welty*, Peggy Whitman Prenshaw, ed. (Jackson, Mississippi: University Press of Mississippi, 1996), 231–242; Charlotte Capers, "An Interview with Eudora Welty," typed transcript (26 October 1971), 9, Eudora Welty Collection, Mississippi Department of Archives and History (hereafter, Welty Collection, MDAH).

7. Campbell Gibson, "Rank by Population of the 100 Largest Urban Places, Listed Alphabetically by State: 1790–1990" (table), "Population of the 100 Largest Cities and Other Urban Places in the United States: 1790 to 1990," Population Division Working Paper No. 27, Population Division, U. S. Bureau of the Census, Washington, D.C.: June 1998, http://www.census.gov/population/www/documentation/twps0027/twps0027.html.

8. Welty, *OWB*, in *Welty: Stories, Essays, & Memoir*, Ford and Kreyling, eds., 904.

9. Marshall Everett, *The Book of the Fair, St. Louis, 1904* (Philadelphia: P. W. Ziegler Co., copyright 1904 by Henry Neil). Also: *1904 World's Fair, The Louisiana Purchase Exposition, St. Louis, Missouri, The Greatest of Expositions, Completely Illustrated* (St. Louis: Louisiana Purchase Exposition Press of Sam'l F. Myerson Printing Co., 1904), online edition, Washington University at St. Louis, washingtonmo.com/1904/index.htm.

10. Lee Gaskins, "At The Fair: The 1904 St. Louis World's Fair," http://atthefair.homestead.com/POH.html.

11. Dorothy Schneider and Carl J. Schneider, *American Women in the Progressive Era, 1900–1920* (New York: Facts on File, 1993), 5.

12. White, 231–242.

13. Capers (1971), 3.

14. Welty, *OWB*, in *Welty: Stories, Essays, & Memoir*, Ford and Kreyling, eds., 942.

15. Capers (1971), 9.

16. The Jaeger Company, *From Frontier Capital to Modern City: A History of Jackson, Mississippi's Built Environment, 1865–1950*, prepared for City of Jackson, Mississippi, Historic Preservation Commission, and Department of Planning and Development (Gainesville, Ga.: The Jaeger Company, 2000), 37–38, 51–58.

17. Sharon Ann Murphy, "Life Insurance in the United States through World War I," *EH.Net Encyclopedia of Economic and Business History*, Robert Whaples, ed. (N. p., Economic History Association, 2002), eh.net/encyclopedia/article/Murphy.life.insurance.us.

18. Marrs, *Eudora Welty*, 1–2.

19. Christopher Grampp, *From Yard to Garden: The Domestication of America's Home Grounds* (Chicago: Center for American Places at Columbia College Chicago, 2008), xviii.

20. The tree and boards were still present when Eudora toured the property in the early 1980s. The Junior League of Jackson, Mississippi, comp., *Jackson Landmarks* (Jackson, Miss.: 1982), 75.

21. Eudora Welty, "The Winds," in *Welty: Stories, Essays, & Memoir*, Ford and Kreyling, eds., 256. The story was first published in *A Curtain of Green and Other Stories* by Doubleday, Doran, 1941. North American publication rights are held by Houghton Mifflin Harcourt,

the publisher of the 1947 edition of *A Curtain of Green and Other Stories*.

22. Eudora Welty, "Jackson: A Neighborhood," in *Jackson Landmarks*, n. p.

23. Ibid.

24. Ibid.

25. Eudora Welty, "The Winds," in *Welty: Stories, Essays, & Memoir*, Ford and Kreyling, eds., 256.

26. Capers (1971), 4.

CHAPTER TWO

1. Welty Collection, MDAH.

2. Mary Doris Comley scrapbook, Mary Doris Comley Papers, MDAH.

3. Ibid.

4. Welty, *OWB*, in *Welty: Stories, Essays, & Memoir*, Ford and Kreyling, eds., 83; Charlotte Capers, "Eudora Welty's House: A Conversation with Charlotte Capers," typed transcript, n. d., 1987, 3, Welty Collection, MDAH; Welty to Haltom, 13 October 1994.

5. The jingle contest was sponsored by the Mackie Pine Oil Specialty Co. Eudora Welty, acceptance speech, the National Book Club Foundation's Medal for Distinguished Contribution to American Letters, National Book Awards Ceremony, 20 November 1991, http://www.nationalbook.org/nbaacceptspeech_ewelty.html. The belief that pine woods were health-giving may derive from the fact that pine resin was a common ingredient in medicinal products, such as Balmopine ointment, Thymopine cough syrup, and Pinexo disinfectant, all made in the 1920s by the Mackie Pine Oil Specialty Company in Covington, La. N. a., *Biennial Report of the Board of Curators for 1920–21*, Louisiana State Museum, New Orleans, La., January 1922. Another source says, "The chief reasons offered to explain the salubrity of the [pine] barrens rested upon a belief in the purity and elasticity of the air among the pines as contrasted with the atmosphere of the marshy and swampy sections surrounding low country homes. . . ." John H. Goff, *Place-names of Georgia: Essays of John H. Goff*, Francis Lee Utley and Marion R. Hemperley, eds. (Athens: University of Georgia Press, 1975), 86.

6. *Frontier Capital to Modern City*, 78; John R. Stilgoe, *Borderland: Origins of the American Suburb, 1820–1939* (New Haven and London: Yale University Press, 1988), 166–167.

7. *Frontier Capital to Modern City*, 68; Capers (1987), 4; Mrs. Francis (Louisa Yeomans) King, *The Little Garden* (Boston: The Atlantic Monthly Press, third impression May 1922 [first impression July 1921]), 7.

8. The architecture firm was Sanguinet, Staats, and Hedrick. Susan Haltom, conversations with Nancy Sparrow, archivist, Sanguinet, Staats, and Hedrick Papers, Alexander Architectural Archive, University of Texas, Austin, 19 February and 22 February 2008. The plans for the Lamar Life building have survived, but no plans for the Welty residence have been found. Sparrow said that a doll company in California contacted the architectural firm and wanted to buy the linen on which the drawings were done. It also was common for families to wash out linen architectural plans to make handkerchiefs or pillowcases.

9. Welty, *OWB*, in *Welty: Stories, Essays, & Memoir*, Ford and Kreyling, eds., 926.

10. Bill Ferris, "A Visit with Eudora Welty," in *Conversations with Eudora Welty*, Peggy Prenshaw, ed. (New York: A Washington Square Press Publication of Pocket Books, a division of Simon & Schuster, Inc., 1985; published by arrangement with University Press of Mississippi), 182; Eudora recalled her mother admonishing, "Never cut an oak tree," Capers (1987), 6.

11. Ibid., 7. Another northern feature of the house was a basement, unusual in a region with a high water table and unstable subsoils of Yazoo clay. Chestina and Eudora used the space as a potting shed and plant nursery. Suzanne Marrs, *One Writer's Imagination: The Fiction of Eudora Welty* (Baton Rouge: Louisiana State University Press, 2002), 6. Chestina's recipe for rose spray remains handwritten on a doorframe. Welty, *OWB*, in *Welty: Stories, Essays, & Memoir*, Ford and Kreyling, eds., 841.

12. Eudora later paid to have the porch screened, using earnings from the sale of her first short story. Capers (1987), 5–6. Hurricane Camille tore off the screening in 1969, and it has not been replaced because the house is restored to the mid-1980s.

13. Capers (1987), 10–11.

14. Welty to Haltom, 13 October 1994.

15. "The main need for foundation planting is to relieve that abrupt transition from grounds to house that the house may seem tied to, and a part of the grounds rather than like a big box in an open space." Leonidas Willing Ramsey, B.S., *Planning the Home Grounds*, Landscape Garden Series, vol. II (Davenport, Iowa: The Garden Press, 1921), 35. (Ten-volume booklet series published for the American School of Landscape Architecture and Gardening, Newark, N.Y.)

16. Deborah Nevins, "The Triumph of Flora: Women and the American Landscape, 1890–1935," *The Magazine Antiques* (April 1985): 909.

17. May Brawley Hill, *Grandmother's Garden: The Old-Fashioned American Garden 1865–1915* (New York: Harry N. Abrams, Inc., 1995), 77–78. American writer Alice Morse Earle (1851–1911) wrote more than sixteen books and thirty articles on colonial times and antiques. "Earle's passionate interest in what is now called material culture was fueled in part by a longing for continuity and status in an increasingly fluid and fragmented society. . . . Earle had probably read Jekyll's first two books . . . when she began to write her comprehensive *Old Time Gardens* (1901), for she refers to Jekyll several times."

18. Virginia Tuttle Clayton, ed., *The Once & Future Gardener: Garden Writing from the Golden Age of Magazines, 1900–1940* (Boston: David R. Godine, Publisher, 2000), xxiii.

19. Helena Rutherfurd Ely, *A Woman's Hardy Garden* (New York: The MacMillan Company, 1916 [first published 1903]), 205.

20. King, *The Little Garden*, 38.

21. A clothesline would have been a standard fixture near the house, but Eudora Welty's nieces recall that Chestina sent out the laundry.

22. King, *The Little Garden*, 11; Chestina Welty, "Scribble-in Book" [garden journal], n. d. [c. late 1930s–early 1940s], n. p., Eudora Welty LLC. The entry appears to be notes taken at a lecture or from a book, as some passages are in direct quotes.

23. Eudora Welty, "The Wanderers," in *Welty: Stories, Essays, & Memoir*, Ford and Kreyling, eds., 534–535.

24. Eudora Welty, "Kin," in *Welty: Stories, Essays, & Memoir*, Ford and Kreyling, eds., 679–680.

CHAPTER THREE

1. Helen M. Winslow, "Club Women & Club Life," *The Delineator: An Illustrated Magazine of Literature and Fashion*, vol. LXI, no. 6 (June 1903): 111. PDF.

2. The Woman's Club, *Woman's Club Yearbook, 1929–1930*, Jackson, Mississippi, MDAH.

3. Black women organized their own clubs, and the National Association of Colored Women, formed in the 1890s, grew to include fifty thousand members in more than one thousand clubs by the year 1916. Schneider and Schneider, 100.

4. Ibid, 5–6, 29–30.

5. Ibid., 30; Rita S. Saslaw, "Student Societies in Nineteenth Century Ohio: Misconceptions and Realities," *Ohio History, the Scholarly Journal of the Ohio Historical Society*, vol. 88,

no. 2 (Spring 1979): 202. Organized woman's clubs of the late nineteenth and early twentieth centuries formed out of earlier loose social networks with similar aims. Schneider and Schneider, 13–14, 95–96, n. 6; Helen M. Winslow, *The President of Quex: A Woman's Club Story* (Boston: Lothrop, Lee and Shepard, 1906), 96, 185–186, 281, 283; ibid., n. 6.

6. Grampp, 36; Clayton, xv: "[Andrew Jackson] Downing (1815–1852) . . . set himself the noble task of reforming and upgrading the standards of American gardening. For him, there was a direct correlation between the quality of landscape design and the very quality of life, but his most enduring legacy was, as observed by Neil Harris, 'his identification of aesthetic reform with a set of ethical and social ideas.' This reformist attitude, based on the premise that human character could be perfected through contact with natural beauty, was to persist in garden magazines well into the twentieth century."

7. A. T. De La Mare, ed., *Garden Guide: The Amateur Gardeners' Handbook* (New York: A. T. De La Mare Company, Inc., 1925, revised fourth edition), 8. De La Mare was among those who strongly identified a love of the outdoors with moral superiority. "The city may be a good place to work in; it undoubtedly is; but if all our homes could be in the freedom of the country we would be a superior race," he concludes (9). This attitude was born of the period's rampant nativism. Ibid., quoting Harlean James (ch. 2, n. 15: "The Baltimore Flower Market," *American City* [April 1913]: 392).

8. Different sources offer different dates and places for the founding of America's first garden club. One places it in Cambridge, Massachusetts, in 1889 (Olive Foster, "Garden Clubs and Their National Meaning," *House and Garden* [March 1936]: 36, in Grampp, ch. 2, n. 13, 233). According to the National Garden Clubs, an association of state and local garden clubs unaffiliated with the Garden

Club of America, the nation's earliest known garden club was founded in Athens, Georgia, in 1891. National Garden Clubs Web site, http://www.gardenclub.org/home.aspx.

9. Ann Gascoigne Lacey, ed., *Garden Club of America Bulletin*, Bicentennial Commemorative Issue 64 (no.2), n. d. [1976]: inside back cover (no page number); ibid., 15, quoted from president's report, *GCA Bulletin*, 1915.

10. Ibid., 3.

11. Ibid.,15.

12. Clayton, xi; *Frontier Capital to Modern City*, 58; Grampp, 30.

13. Woman's National Farm and Garden Association, Inc., Web site, http://www.nfga .org/about.htm; Thaïsa Way, *Unbounded Practice: Women and Landscape Architecture in the Early Twentieth Century* (Charlottesville & London: University of Virginia Press, 2009), 109–125.

14. Ivelisse Estrada, "The Lost Army: The Woman's Land Army of America," *Schleisinger Library Newsletter* (Cambridge, Mass.: Radcliffe Institute for Advanced Study, Harvard University, Spring 2009): 3; Elaine Weiss, *Fruits of Victory: The Woman's Land Army of America in the Great War* (Dulles, Va.: Potomac Books, 2008), 37, 39.

15. In the Deep South, not only was the Woman's Land Army's mannish clothing socially unacceptable, but women in the fields would have been working close to black men, a societal taboo. Alternatively, women in garden clubs throughout Mississippi may have created war gardens to grow food in cities and suburbs. Elaine Weiss, e-mail to Jane Roy Brown, 25 January 2010; Edith Diehl, ed., *Report of the Wellesley College Training Camp and Experiment Station for the Woman's Land Army of America* (New York: n. p., advance edition, 1918), 24.

16. Estrada, 3.

17. Schneider and Schneider, 100–102; Winslow, "Club Women & Club Life," *The*

Delineator: III. The Weltys subscribed to *The Delineator*. Eudora Welty, "Pages omitted from *A Writer's Beginnings* notes and tryouts," n.d. [summer 1983], Welty Collection, MDAH; Jacquelyn Masur McElhaney, *Pauline Periwinkle and Progressive Reform in Dallas* (College Station, Tex.: Texas A&M University Press, 1998), 36.

18. Welty, *OWB*, in *Welty: Stories, Essays, & Memoir*, Ford and Kreyling, eds., 842; Welty to Haltom, 30 August 1995; Gertrude Jekyll, *Wood and Garden: Notes and Thoughts, Practical and Critical, of a Working Amateur* (London, New York and Bombay: Longmans, Green and Co., 1904), http://www.books.google.com, 6.

19. Jackson (Miss.) *Clarion-Ledger*, 14 October 1928, n. p.

20. Ibid.

21. The Woman's Club, *Woman's Club Yearbook, 1928–1929*, n. p., Jackson, Mississippi, MDAH.

22. Ibid.

23. Welty to Haltom, (n. d.) January 1997; Jackson *Clarion-Ledger*, 14 October 1928.

24. Marrs, *One Writer's Imagination*, 4.

25. Eudora Welty, "Kin," in *Welty: Stories, Essays, & Memoir*, Ford and Kreyling, eds., 648.

26. Marrs, *Eudora Welty*, 21–25.

CHAPTER FOUR

1. Eudora Welty, "Pages omitted from *A Writer's Beginnings* notes and tryouts," n.d. [summer 1983], Welty Collection, MDAH.

2. Frederick C. Mills, "Aspects of the Price Recession of 1929–1931," *News-Bulletin*, National Bureau of Economic Research, Inc., no. 42 (23 December 1931), 1–4.

3. The basic blood types were discovered in 1901, greatly reducing the risk of fatal reactions caused by incompatibility; but the Rh factor, which can also cause lethal reactions when donors and recipients are incompatible, was not discovered until 1940. "Historical Landmarks in the Field of Study of Blood Group Systems," Blood Group Gene Antigen Database, National Center for Biotechnology Information, http://www.ncbi.nlm.nih.gov/projects/gv/mhc/xslcgi.cgi?cmd=bgmut/landmarks; Welty, *OWB*, in *Welty: Stories, Essays, & Memoir*, Ford and Kreyling, eds., 936.

4. *Jackson Daily News*, evening edition, 23 September 1931.

5. *The Clarion-Ledger*, morning edition, 25 September 1931.

6. Last Will and Testament of C. W. Welty, Hinds County Will Book 3, page 573 (1920–1932), Welty Collection, MDAH; Marrs, *Eudora Welty*, 166–167, 191, 209, 230–232.

7. Patti Carr Black, "Eudora Welty's Radio Days," *Reckon* 1, no. 1 & 2 (Premiere 1995), 140–142.

8. Ferris, "A Visit with Eudora Welty," 25 June 1994, in *Conversations*, Prenshaw, ed.

9. Welty, "Pages omitted from *A Writer's Beginnings* notes and tryouts."

10. In the 1940s Eudora also used J. W.'s remark almost verbatim in her novel *Delta Wedding*, when the yard man Howard protests: "I wish there wasn't no such thing as roses. . . . If I had my way, wouldn't be a rose in de world. Catch your shirt and stick you and prick you and grab you. Got thorns." Eudora Welty, *Delta Wedding*, in *Welty: Complete Novels*, Richard Ford and Michael Kreyling, eds. (New York: Literary Classics of the United States, The Library of America, 1998), 315. First published by Harcourt, Brace, 1946.

11. Welty, "Pages omitted from *A Writer's Beginnings* notes and tryouts."

12. Eudora Welty, "A Curtain of Green," in *Welty: Stories, Essays, & Memoir*, Ford and Kreyling, eds., 131; Marrs, *One Writer's Imagination*, 7. The story was first published in *A Curtain of Green and Other Stories* by Doubleday, Doran, 1941. North American publication rights are held by Houghton Mifflin Harcourt, the publisher of the 1947 edition of *A Curtain of Green and Other Stories*.

13. Welty, "A Curtain of Green," in *Welty: Stories, Essays, & Memoir*, Ford and Kreyling, eds., 131.

14. Marrs, *One Writer's Imagination*, 4; Welty, "A Curtain of Green," in *Welty: Stories, Essays, & Memoir*, Ford and Kreyling, eds., 130.

15. Welty, "Pages omitted from *A Writer's Beginnings* notes and tryouts."

CHAPTER FIVE

1. Effie Young Slusser, Mary Belle Williams, and Emma Burbank Beeson; Lillian McLean Waldo, ed., *Stories of Luther Burbank and His Plant School* (New York, Chicago, Boston, Atlanta, San Francisco, Dallas: Charles Scribner's Sons, 1920), 190.

2. Edith R. Fisher, *The Garden Club Manual* (New York: The MacMillan Company, 1931), 3.

3. N. a., "History of Belhaven Garden Club 1931–1962," 6 May 1957, in *Affiliated Club Histories, The Jackson Council of Garden Clubs, Inc., 1930–1960* (Jackson, Miss.: Jackson Council of Garden Clubs, 1957), n. p.; Welty to Haltom, 13 September 1994.

4. "History of Belhaven Garden Club," n. p. The organization, later renamed the Jackson Council of Garden Clubs, originally comprised six clubs, one per voting district. In May 1931, each of the members was allowed to form a club in her own neighborhood, and the number of clubs and members soared.

5. *Frontier to Capital City*, 93–94. Because garden clubs did not develop under a central organization, the number of clubs in the country at any given time is difficult to determine, but published sources of the period, including Fisher, note that the movement mushroomed during the 1920s and 1930s. Even a cursory Internet search reveals a plethora of garden clubs

in small-to-medium-size cities that record a 1930s founding date; Fisher, 1.

6. Jackson (Miss.) Council of Garden Clubs Scrapbooks, 1938–1939, 1941–1942, 1945–1946, MDAH; n. a., "About National Garden Clubs," National Garden Clubs Web site, http://www.gardenclub.org/About/ AboutNGC.aspx. The organization moved its headquarters to St. Louis, Mo., in 1958; n. a., "A Proud History of Service to America's Gardeners" ("from 2001 TGOA/MGCA information pamphlet"), The Gardeners of America Web site, http://www.tgoa-mgca.org/History .htm. The club allows women to join.

7. Fisher, 112.

8. Unidentified newspaper clipping, 1938, Friendly Diggers Club, Jackson (Miss.) Council of Garden Clubs Scrapbooks, 1938–1939, MDAH.

9. Chestina Welty, untitled typescript [History of the Jackson Garden Club], n. d. [1930s], Eudora Welty LLC; Welty to Haltom, n. d., September 1995.

10. In 1933, a Hoover administration report concluded that Americans "had become dependent on" the automobile. Kenneth T. Jackson, *Crabgrass Frontier: The Suburbanization of the United States* (New York, Oxford, Eng.: Oxford University Press, 1985), 187. In metropolitan New York City between the first and second world wars, the "average size of a building lot rose from about three thousand square feet in streetcar suburbs to about five thousand square feet in automobile suburbs," 185; Grampp, 95–96.

11. Grampp, 62. In 1912, a municipal planner observed that homeowners in Kansas City, Mo., planted the city-owned roadside strips in front of their houses of their own volition, "cheerfully, willingly, and as a matter of pride in keeping up their front lawns and premises." Chapter 2, n. 74 (239): Fred Gabelman, "Roadway and Lawn Space Widths and Maintenance of Boulevards and Streets in Kansas City, Missouri," *American City* (Oct. 1912): 352.

12. Fisher, 1.

13. Clayton, introduction, xviii–xxiii.

14. Julia Lester Dillon, *The Blossom Circle of the Year in Southern Gardens* (New York: A. T. De La Mare Company, Inc., 1922), 17.

15. Chestina Welty, *The Scribble-in Book* (unpublished clothbound diary, handwritten; hereafter, garden journal, 1937–early 1940s), garden sketch maps, n. d., n. p.

16. Eudora Welty to Diarmuid Russell, 30 December 1940, Welty Collection, MDAH.

17. Chestina Welty, garden journal, n. d., n. p.

18. Welty to Haltom, 13 September 1994.

19. Chestina Welty, spiral-bound stenographer's notebook (hereafter, garden notebook), handwritten notes, apparently for a garden-club talk, n. d. [1930s], n. p., Eudora Welty LLC.

20. Ibid.

21. Welty to Haltom, 14 December 1994.

22. This further suggests that the rest of the yard was in filtered shade; Chestina Welty, garden notebook, notes for garden-club talk, n. d., n. p., Eudora Welty LLC.

23. Marrs, *One Writer's Imagination*, 6; Welty to Haltom, 14 December 1994.

24. Chestina Welty, "The Perfect Garden," photocopy of typescript, personal collection of Suzanne Marrs.

CHAPTER SIX

1. Federal Writers' Project of the Works Progress Administration, *Mississippi: The WPA Guide to the Magnolia State* (Jackson, Miss.: University Press of Mississippi, 1988, 2009; originally published by Viking Press, 1938), "White Folkways," 13.

2. Eudora Welty, interview with Hunter Cole and Seetha Srinivasan, *Eudora Welty: Photographs* (Jackson, Miss.: University Press of Mississippi, 1989), xvii.

3. Connie Lester, "Economic Development in the 1930s: Balance Agriculture with Industry," *Mississippi History Now: An Online Publication of the Mississippi Historical Society*, http://mshistory.k12.ms.us/articles/224/ economic-development-in-the-1930s-balance-agriculture-with-industry), posted May 2004, n. p.; Bradley G. Bond, ed., *Mississippi: A Documentary History* (Jackson, Miss.: University Press of Mississippi, 2003, print-on-demand edition, http://www.books.google .com), 208; Lester, n. p.; "The Great Depression (1929–1939)," n. a. (Eleanor Roosevelt National Historic Site Web site: www.nps .gov/archive/elro/glossary/great-depression .htm, n. d.), n. p.

4. *Frontier to Capital City*, 97–98.

5. Libby Hartfield and Alan Huffman, "Fannye A. Cook, Pioneer Conservationist and Scientist, 1889–1964," *Mississippi History Now: An Online Publication of the Mississippi Historical Society*, http://mshistory.k12.ms.us/ articles/313/fannye-cook-pioneer-conservationist, posted June 2009, n. p.; "Fannye A. Cook, the force behind the creation of the Mississippi agency known as the Department of Wildlife, Fisheries and Parks, and its educational and research arm, the Mississippi Museum of Natural Science, was the first person to collect and catalog Mississippi wildlife, and to lead the effort to protect and restore the state's natural environment"; Eudora Welty, speaking in *Confluence of Memories*, Eudora Welty House visitor orientation video, n. d., Eudora Welty House, MDAH; Eudora Welty, letter to John Robinson, 22 May 1947, Welty Collection, MDAH.

6. Patti Carr Black, ed., *Early Escapades by Eudora Welty* (Jackson, Miss.: University Press of Mississippi, 2005), 30.

7. Eudora also found the business "filled with taboos," in which a bad layout or the wrong typeface could bring high-stakes consequences. "What's the use of learning fears?" she decided. Robert van Gelder, "An Interview

with Miss Eudora Welty—A Short Story Writer of Exceptional Talent Talks of Her Work," *New York Times Book Review*, photocopy, 14 June 1942, Welty Collection, MDAH; Marrs, *Eudora Welty*, 39–42.

8. As a young woman, Eudora also took lessons in drawing and painting. Welty, *OWB*, in *Welty: Stories, Essays, & Memoir*, Ford and Kreyling, eds., 924; Ford and Kreyling, Chronology, in *Welty: Stories, Essays, & Memoir*, 952.

9. Capers (1971), 13, Welty Collection, MDAH; Marrs, *One Writer's Imagination*, 8–9; Cole and Srinivasan interview, *Eudora Welty: Photographs*, xxi.

10. Marrs, *Eudora Welty*, 45–46. Two plants are called night-blooming cereus: *Selenicereus* and the *Hylocereus* genus, with *Hylocereus undatus* more common, www .arhomeandgarden.org/landscaping/SpecGar dening/night_blooming_cereus.htm. Passage from typescript, no source, author, or date, Eudora Welty LLC; Marrs, *Eudora Welty*, 45. The motto is a variation on a lyric in the 1931 popular song "Life Is Just a Bowl of Cherries" (Ray Henderson and Lew Brown), http://lyr icsplayground.com/alpha/songs/l/lifeisjust abowlofcherries.shtml.

11. The photographs, though undated, show some garden features and plants mentioned in Chestina Welty's garden notebooks, such as the bench in front of the perennial border and the trellis and arbor. The cut-flower garden is shown in both the photos and the diagram in a notebook. Welty, *OWB*, in *Welty: Stories, Essays, & Memoir*, Ford and Kreyling, eds., 928.

12. "My way to learn writing was through writing, from the start, and I did write in strict concentration." Eudora Welty, Cole and Srinivasan interview, *Eudora Welty: Photographs*, xv–xvi.

13. Eudora Welty, *One Time, One Place* (Jackson, Miss.: University Press of Mississippi, revised edition, 1996; originally published 1971),12.

14. Eudora Welty, "Place in Fiction," in *Welty: Stories, Essays, & Memoir*, Ford and Kreyling, eds., 782, 786, 793–794.

15. Ibid., 792; Reynolds Price, Foreword, *Eudora Welty: Photographs*, viii.

16. Marrs, *Eudora Welty*, 55–57. The stories were "Retreat," "A Piece of News," "Flowers for Marjorie," "Lily Daw and the Three Ladies," and "A Memory."

17. Ford and Kreyling, Chronology, in *Welty: Stories, Essays, & Memoir*, Ford and Kreyling, eds., 954.

18. Marrs, *Eudora Welty*, 55–56.

19. Ibid., 57, 61.

20. Ibid., 58.

21. Eudora Welty, "The Whistle," in *Welty: Stories, Essays, & Memoir*, Ford and Kreyling, eds., 70–71, 73. The story was first published in *A Curtain of Green and Other Stories* by Doubleday, Doran, 1941. North American publication rights are held by Houghton Mifflin Harcourt, the publisher of the 1947 edition of *A Curtain of Green and Other Stories*.

22. Eudora Welty, "Old Mr. Marblehall," ibid., 114–115.

23. Marrs, *Eudora Welty*, 245; Henry Mitchell, "Eudora Welty: Rose-Gardener, Realist, Storyteller of the South: A Writer Who Doesn't Fear the Risk of Fine Writing," *The Washington Post*, 13 August 1972, L1.

24. Eudora Welty, *Losing Battles*, in *Welty: Complete Novels*, Ford and Kreyling, eds., 431.

CHAPTER SEVEN

1. Æ (George) Russell, *The Candle of Vision* (London: MacMillan & Co., Limited, 1931, first edition 1918), 42.

2. "After my year in the city I felt like a child who wickedly stays from home through a long day, and who returns frightened and penitent at nightfall, wondering whether it will be received with forgiveness by its mother." Ibid., 1.

3. Michael Kreyling, *Author and Agent: Eu-dora Welty and Diarmuid Russell* (New York: Farrar, Straus, Giroux, 1991), 26.

4. Ibid., 13–14, 20–21. Among others, writers Katherine Anne Porter and Ford Madox Ford (a British writer and publisher of literary journals) each had recommended Welty to their respective publishing contacts.

5. Ibid., 9, 23, 30–31.

6. Ibid., 10–11; Eudora Welty to Diarmuid Russell, n. d. [reply to his letter of 30 September 1941], Welty Collection, MDAH. Eudora described the feeling of discovering his father's book as "a little like waiting on a shore and then being enveloped in a sea . . . a tender and firm and passionate experience."

7. Diarmuid Russell is credited with helping to establish the National Committee for the Wild Flowers of the United States of the New York Botanical Garden. The resulting six-volume *Wild Flowers of the United States* was sponsored by the New York Botanical Garden. Online finding aid, Harold William Rickett Papers, Archives, The LuEsther T. Mertz Library, The New York Botanical Garden, 2005; Kreyling, *Author and Agent*, 30.

8. Kreyling, *Author and Agent*, 57.

9. Welty to Russell, 18 January 1941; 23 January 1941; n. d. [winter 1940–1941], Welty Collection, MDAH.

10. Welty to Russell, 21 February 1941, Welty Collection, MDAH.

11. Russell to Welty, 20 March 1941, Welty Collection, MDAH.

12. Welty to Russell, 19 March 1941, 5 April 1941, Welty Collection, MDAH.

13. Ibid., 5 April 1941.

14. Ibid., 30 April 1941.

15. Ibid., 17 June 1941.

16. Marrs, *One Writer's Imagination*, 6; Kreyling, *Author and Agent*, 32.

17. Welty to Russell, 28 August 1941, Welty Collection, MDAH.

18. Russell to Welty, 29 August 1941, Welty Collection, MDAH; Æ Russell, *Candle*, 5–6.

19. Kreyling, *Author and Agent*, 25, 70–71; Eudora Welty, "Writing and Analyzing a Story," in *Welty: Stories, Essays, & Memoir*, Ford and Kreyling, eds.,773.

19. Eudora Welty, "A Sweet Devouring," in *Welty: Stories, Essays, Memoir*, Ford and Kreyling, eds.,798; Welty to Russell, 8 June 1942, Welty Collection, MDAH.

20. Welty to Russell, 11 August 1941, Welty Collection, MDAH.

21. Kreyling, *Author and Agent*, 78. Also, after the collection *A Curtain of Green* was published in 1941, a local reporter interviewed Welty, who seemed comfortably at home in Jackson: "Now that she has had published a volume of short stories, . . . she knows she is expected to write The Novel. She dismisses the idea with this information. 'I do not feel drawn to writing a novel now. They tell me I will later. Perhaps. But right now I want to live here and keep on writing short stories. . . .' She spends her time gardening with her family and friends and knocks out those astounding stories with this same ease." Bette Barber, "Novel Can Wait, Says Jackson Author," *Jackson Daily News*, 1 December 1941.

22. Welty to Russell, 18 August [1941], Welty Collection, MDAH. Welty's description of some of the flowers as "primal, symbolic, and imaginary" offers rich clues for literary scholars about her abundant use of flower imagery. As a reader of Greek mythology, she was aware of "flowers people have been changed into and out of," such as Hyacinthus, Narcissus, Daphne, and Crocus. Not just floral conversions, but other currents of plant mythology flow through her work. In "June Recital" (in *Welty: Stories, Essays, & Memoir*, Ford and Kreyling, eds., 337) a boy contemplates a fig tree that is glowing with a numinous radiance: "The big fig tree was many times a magic tree with golden fruit that shone in and among its branches like a cloud of lightning bugs—a tree twinkling all over, burning, on and off, off and on."

23. Russell to Welty, 21 August 1941, Welty Collection, MDAH.

24. Kreyling, *Author and Agent*, 57; Diarmuid Russell, "An Experiment with the Imagination," *Harper's Magazine*, September 1942, 428–431 (archived edition). His ideas, although expressed in psychological rather than religious language, are not so different from his father's on this topic. Æ ruminated at length on the sources of dreams, visions, and creative imagination. In his essay "Dreams," he postulated "an unsleeping consciousness within ourselves while the brain is asleep: . . . Has it a dual life as we have when waking, when half our consciousness is of an external nature and half of subjective emotions and thoughts? Are part of our dreams internal fantasy and part perceptions of an external sphere of being?" *Candle*, 83.

25. Welty to Russell, 20 September 1941, Welty Collection, MDAH.

26. Ibid., 23 December 1941.

27. Ibid.

CHAPTER EIGHT

1. Chestina Welty, "The Perfect Garden."

2. Welty to Russell, 8 December 1941, Welty Collection, MDAH.

3. Ibid., 16 January 1942.

4. Ibid., 4 February 1942.

5. *Frontier Capital to Modern City*, 105, 107; unemployment statistics: U.S. Bureau of the Census; bicentennial edition, part 2, chapter D, Labor, Series D 1-10 (note 8).

6. Ford and Kreyling, Chronology, in *Welty: Complete Novels*, Ford and Kreyling, eds., 999–1000.

7. Kreyling, *Author and Agent*, 102, 112; Marrs, *Eudora Welty*, 91; Welty to Russell, Friday, n. d., March 1942, Welty Collection, MDAH.

8. Eudora Welty, "Livvie," in *Welty: Stories, Essays, & Memoir*, Ford and Kreyling, eds., 277; Kreyling, *Author and Agent*, 90. The story was published in *The Wide Net and Other Stories* by Harcourt, Brace, 1943.

9. Welty to Russell, n. d., Easter [1942], Welty Collection, MDAH.

10. Ibid., n. d., Monday [1942].

11. Ibid., n. d., Monday [1942]. (This is not the same letter cited in note 10, but another one filed later, with the summer letters.)

12. Ibid., 19 January 1942.

13. Ibid., 4 May 1942.

14. Ibid., 20 June 1942.

15. Ibid.

16. Ibid., 22 November 1942.

17. Ibid., 25 November 1942.

18. Marrs, *Eudora Welty*, 85.

19. Welty to John Robinson, n. d., Thursday [July 1942], Welty Collection, MDAH.

20. Ibid.,14 November 1942.

21. Ibid., 4 May 1942; Welty to Russell, 3 April 1945, Welty Collection, MDAH.

22. Allen Lacy, Introduction, in Elizabeth Lawrence, *Gardening for Love: The Market Bulletins* (Durham, N.C.: Duke University Press, 1987), 18. The quote comes from a letter Lawrence wrote in response to a magazine editor; Emily Herring Wilson, *No One Gardens Alone: A Life of Elizabeth Lawrence* (Boston: Beacon Press, 2004), 256.

23. Si Corley, Commissioner, Mississippi Department of Agriculture, Jackson, Miss., *The Mississippi Market Bulletin*, Vols. 37 (N. S. Vol. 87) 1 March 1944, 1. "We desire to express our sincere appreciation to the 54,000 readers," the commissioner notes. It is not clear if this indicates subscribers or an estimate of readers reached through subscriptions, libraries, and passed-along copies. The Mississippi bulletins began publication in 1928 and are still going strong.

24. Lawrence, *Gardening for Love*, 72–73.

25. Ibid., 77; Welty to Robinson, 19 March [1945], Welty Collection, MDAH.

26. Eudora Welty, "The Wanderers," in

Welty: Stories, Essays, & Memoir, Ford and Kreyling, eds., 519–520. First published in *The Golden Apples* by Harcourt, Brace, 1949.

27. Welty to Robinson, n. d. [9 September 1944], Welty Collection, MDAH.

28. Lawrence, *Gardening for Love*, 39; Eudora Welty, "Livvie," in *Welty: Stories, Essays, & Memoir*, Ford and Kreyling, eds., 276.

29. Lawrence, *Gardening for Love*, 59, 35, 94.

30. Welty to Haltom, 14 December 1995; Wilson, 251–253.

31. Welty to Haltom, 22 August 1995.

CHAPTER NINE

1. Eudora Welty, *Delta Wedding*, in *Welty: Complete Novels*, Ford and Kreyling, eds., 130.

2. Welty to Russell, 4 February 1942, Welty Collection, MDAH.

3. "World War II Rationing," online exhibit, Ames (Iowa) Historical Society, http://www.ameshistoricalsociety.org/exhibits/events/rationing.htm (n. d.), 1–2. "Some statements included from *V for Victory, America's Home Front During World War II*, 1991 by Stan Cohen; and *America at War, 1941–1945 The Home Front*, 1990 by Clark Reynolds," 4.

4. N. a., "Defense Gardens in 1941," *Horticulture* (1 January 1941): 4.

5. Welty to Russell, 8 July 1943, Welty Collection, MDAH.

6. Welty to Robinson, 17 April [1944], Welty Collection, MDAH.

7. J. Horace McFarland, "Mr. McFarland's War Views," *Horticulture* (15 October 1940): 408.

8. H. W. Hockbaum, Chairman, Victory Garden Committee, U. S. Department of Agriculture, "What—No Flowers?" Wayside Gardens catalogue, 1944, n. p. [back cover, "By courtesy of *House & Garden*"].

9. N. a., Wayside Gardens catalogue (N. p. d.: Wayside Gardens Co., 1944), n. p. [inside front cover].

10. N. a., "Summing Up the Present Bulb Situation," *Horticulture* (1 July 1940): 296.

11. Welty to Robinson, Monday 13 November [1944], Welty Collection, MDAH.

12. Marrs, *Eudora Welty*, 247, 252, 258–59, 261, 263, 265.

13. Welty to Robinson, 19 July 1943, Welty Collection, MDAH.

14. Welty to Russell, n. d., 1940; Welty to Robinson, Friday, 17–21 September [1943], Welty Collection, MDAH.

15. Welty to Robinson, 19 July [1943], Eudora Welty Collection, MDAH.

16. Henry Mitchell, "The Dawn Lies in Wait," in *The Essential Earthman: Henry Mitchell on Gardening* (Boston, New York: Houghton Mifflin Company, 1981; exp. paperback edition, 1993), xii.

17. Welty to Russell, 9 June 1943, Welty Collection, MDAH.

18. Ibid., 23 June 1943.

19. Ibid., 28 August 1943.

20. Ibid., 18 October [1943].

21. In a letter to Robinson (26 November 1943, quoted in Marrs, *Eudora Welty*, 105), Welty thanked him for his Christmas gift of a leather-bound portfolio and said she planned to use it as a garden journal. It has not come to light.

22. N. a., *Affiliated Club Histories, The Jackson Council of Garden Clubs*, vol. I, n. p.

23. Marrs, *Eudora Welty*, 98; Welty to Robinson, 20 January [1945], Welty Collection, MDAH.

24. Welty to Russell, 24 January 1943, Welty Collection, MDAH; Marrs, *Eudora Welty*, 98. Four of the Dutch fliers who were among those dive-bombing the Weltys' chimney formed a string quartet and performed one evening at the Jackson residence in which they were housed.

25. Mary Lou Aswell to Welty, 16 December 1943, in Kreyling, *Author and Agent*, 104.

26. Eudora Welty, "Literature and the Lens," photocopy, *Vogue*, 1 August 1944, n. p.

27. Welty to Robinson, 9 March [1944], Welty Collection, MDAH.

28. Marrs, *Eudora Welty*, 108–111; Pearl Amelia McHaney, ed., *A Writer's Eye: Collected Book Reviews* by Eudora Welty (Jackson, Miss.: University Press of Mississippi, 1994), xix–xx. Welty's friend and fellow writer Nash K. Burger shared this pseudonym for some of his reviews published in the *New York Times Book Review*. It was the publication's policy to publish staff-written reviews under pseudonyms.

29. Marrs, *Eudora Welty*, 114–118; Welty to Robinson, 10 October 1944, Welty Collection, MDAH.

CHAPTER TEN

1. Eudora Welty, *Delta Wedding*, in *Welty: Complete Novels*, Ford and Kreyling, eds., 121–122.

2. Welty to Robinson, 16 October [1944], Jackson, Welty Collection, MDAH; Marrs, *Eudora Welty*, 119.

3. Welty to Robinson, n. d. [20 October 1944], Welty Collection, MDAH.

4. Marrs, *Eudora Welty*, 119 (n. 36: Welty to Robinson, 9 November 1944); Welty to Robinson, 28 October [1944], Welty Collection, MDAH.

5. Welty to Robinson, 16 November [1944], Welty Collection, MDAH.

6. Marrs, *Eudora Welty*, 56; Welty to Robinson, 16 October [1944], Welty Collection, MDAH.

7. Marrs, *One Writer's Imagination*, 47.

8. Ibid., 55. Here Marrs is identifying Welty's emphasis on memory as a survival mechanism in the face of Hitler. "Welty [as opposed to Hitler] suggests that the past must be constantly reexamined and reinterpreted in the view of new situations and insights." Other scholars have written about the importance of

memory in Welty's work, but literary analysis lies beyond the scope of and research for this book; Welty to Robinson, 18 October [1944], Welty Collection, MDAH.

9. Welty to Robinson, 9 November [1944], Welty Collection, MDAH.

10. See Kenneth I. Helphand, *Defiant Gardens: Making Gardens in Wartime* (Hartford, Conn.: Trinity University Press; annotated edition, 2006); Welty to Robinson, Monday 13 November [1944], Welty Collection, MDAH.

11. Welty to Robinson, n. d. [fall 1945], 4 December 1944, Welty Collection, MDAH. *C. japonica* 'Empress' still thrives in front of the Welty house, underneath Eudora's bedroom window.

12. Marrs, *Eudora Welty*, 107, 120–124.

13. Ibid., 127–129; Welty to Robinson, 10 February [1945].

14. Welty to Robinson, Saturday 24 March [1945]; Welty to Russell, 19 March [1945], Welty Collection, MDAH.

15. Eudora Welty, *Delta Wedding*, in *Welty: Complete Novels*, Ford and Kreyling, eds., 216–217.

16. Between "The Delta Cousins" and *Delta Wedding*, Welty wrote a story for Robinson that helped her bridge the two, called "A Little Triumph" (1944). Marrs, *Eudora Welty*, 120–121.

17. Eudora Welty, *Delta Wedding*, in *Welty: Complete Novels*, Ford and Kreyling, eds., 329.

18. Welty to Robinson, 19 March [1945].

19. Ibid., 24 March [1945].

20. Ibid. In a later letter Eudora writes of her own process in supporting John's effort to develop a creative regimen: "I think to write a story and then walk in the woods is good, and one thing is working and one is celebrating, but maybe there, of all places, they could be more side by side, two flowers from one stalk in the hand—do you think?" Welty to Robinson, n. d. [19 March, 1948], Welty Collection, MDAH.

21. Ibid., 31 March [1945]; Eudora Welty, *Delta Wedding*, in *Welty: Complete Novels*, Ford and Kreyling, eds., 315.

22. Marrs, *Eudora Welty*, 132; Welty to Robinson, 1 May [1945], Welty Collection, MDAH.

23. Marrs, *Eudora Welty*, 132.

24. Welty to Robinson, Monday 14 May [1945], Welty Collection, MDAH.

25. Ibid., 9 July [1945]; ibid., n. d. [23 July 1945].

26. Welty to Russell, 13 August [1945], Welty Collection, MDAH.

27. Marrs, *Eudora Welty*, 139 (quoting Welty to Frank Lyell, 11 November [1945], Welty Collection, MDAH), 209; Welty to Russell, n. d. [January 1946?], Welty Collection, MDAH.

28. Welty to Russell, 26 January 1946, 31 March [1946], Welty Collection, MDAH.

29. Ibid., 16 May 1946.

30. Eudora Welty, "Must the Novelist Crusade?" in *Welty: Stories, Essays, & Memoir*, Ford and Kreyling, eds., 804.

31. Welty to Russell, 23 April 1946, Welty Collection, MDAH.

32. Eudora Welty, "Must the Novelist Crusade?" in *Welty: Stories, Essays, & Memoir*, Ford and Kreyling, eds., 806.

33. Welty to Robinson, Sunday morning [29 September? 1946].

34. Kreyling, *Author and Agent*, 120–123; Marrs, *Eudora Welty*, 188; Welty to Robinson, 17 August [1946], Welty Collection, MDAH.

35. Welty to Robinson, n. d., Monday [16 September 1946], Welty Collection, MDAH.

36. Marrs, *Eudora Welty*, 138–140, 156.

37. Ibid., 202–203, 218–219.

38. Eudora Welty, *Delta Wedding*, in *Welty: Complete Novels*, Ford and Kreyling, eds., 246.

39. Marrs, *Eudora Welty*, 209–210.

1. Eudora Welty, "The Demonstrators," in *Welty: Stories, Essays, & Memoir*, Ford and Kreyling, eds., 749. Published by permission of Russell & Volkening, New York.

2. "America now sees itself as having effected social changes, . . . so that architecture and building, transportation and communication, all bear toward each other new, evolving relationships, created by, and affecting, the individual." Joseph E. Howland, *The House Beautiful Book of Gardens and Outdoor Living* (N. p.: Doubleday & Company Inc., 1958), 6. See also Clayton, xii.

3. Landscape architect Thomas Church (1902–1978) distinguished between late twentieth-century modernism and the excesses of 1930s modernism, which resulted in "modern" degenerating "into a style and, finally, into a nasty word." "'Modern' can be revived as an honest word when we realize that modernism is not a goal but a broad highway." Thomas D. Church, *Gardens Are for People* (New York: Reinhold Publishing Corporation, 1955), 35; Howland, 6.

4. Howland prefaced this statement by commenting, "Today all America builds not with the goal of making pretty pictures but with the intention of creating handsome, useful outdoor living space." The language exudes more than a whiff of masculine bias and suggests that "pretty" and "useful" are opposing qualities. The subject of gender roles and influence on the domestic landscape of the 1950s, a topic ripe for scholarly exploration, lies beyond the scope of this book. Howland, 6.

5. Elizabeth Gordon, "A Garden Is American Style," *House Beautiful* (February 1951): 58, in Grampp, 162.

6. Marrs, *Eudora Welty*, 263.

7. Welty to Russell, 26 March [1953], 20 September [1950]; Welty to Robinson, n. d. [April 1950], Welty Collection, MDAH. In the

1950s she no longer wrote as often to Robinson, and the chief record of the garden is her correspondence with Russell.

8. Welty to Russell, 3 November [1953], Welty Collection, MDAH.

9. Ibid., 10 February, 23 February [1954].

10. Ford and Kreyling, Chronology, in *Welty: Stories, Essays, & Memoir*, Ford and Kreyling, eds., 956–957.

11. Eudora Welty, *Losing Battles*, in *Welty: Complete Novels*, Ford and Kreyling, eds., 683. First published by Random House, 1970.

12. Welty to Russell, Thursday [12 June 1952], Welty Collection, MDAH.

13. Eudora Welty, "A Worn Path," in *Welty: Stories, Essays, & Memoir*, Ford and Kreyling, eds., 171, 174.

14. Welty, *OWB*, in *Welty: Stories, Essays, & Memoir*, Ford and Kreyling, eds.,794.

15. Welty to Russell, n. d., May 1953, Welty Collection, MDAH.

16. Ibid., n. d., Thursday [August 1955].

17. Ibid., n. d., Wednesday [February 1957 is noted in archive, but these roses would bloom at least two months later.—S. H.]; Wednesday, n. d. 1957; 4 March 1957.

18. In 1973 Russell ostensibly returned all of her letters to him (Kreyling, *Author and Agent*, 210; Marrs, *Eudora Welty*, 389). As of this writing, however, the Welty Collection at MDAH contains Welty's letters to Russell from 1940 through 1958, comprising all of the letters bequeathed by Welty's estate.

19. Welty to Maxwell, 29 June [1954 or 1955], Maxwell Papers, UIRBML.

20. Marrs, *Eudora Welty*, 263; Kreyling, *Author and Agent*, 183.

21. Reynolds Price, "One Writer's Place in Fiction" (Cambridge, Mass.: WGBH Public Broadcasting Station), www.pbs.org/wgbh/masterpiece/americancollection/ponder/place.html). This essay was originally published in *The New York Times*, 27 July 2001.

22. An expert diagnosed an incurable virus and warned her never to plant roses there again. Welty to Haltom, 3 November 1994.

23. Mitchell, *The Washington Post*, 13 August 1972.

24. Kreyling, *Author and Agent*, 192; Marrs, *Eudora Welty*, 320.

25. Marrs, *Eudora Welty*, 331–332.

26. Ibid., 331.

27. Ibid.

28 Eudora Welty, *The Optimist's Daughter*, in *Welty: Complete Novels*, Ford and Kreyling, eds., 946. First published by Random House, 1972. *The Optimist's Daughter* originally appeared in *The New Yorker* magazine in 1969 and was subsequently revised and expanded before being published as a book; Marrs, *Eudora Welty*, Appendix 1, 576.

29. Ibid., 917–918; Elizabeth Lawrence, *A Southern Garden* (Chapel Hill, N.C.: University of North Carolina Press, 1942; 1991 paperback edition reproducing the text of a 1991 special anniverary edition), 30.

30. Eudora Welty, *The Optimist's Daughter*, in *Welty: Complete Novels*, Ford and Kreyling, eds., 937–938.

31. Ibid., 952; Marrs, *Eudora Welty*, 332.

32. Marrs, *Eudora Welty*, 394, 396–397.

33. Between the publication of *The Optimist's Daughter* in book form, in 1972, and *One Writer's Beginnings*, in 1984, Eudora published only a collection of her essays and reviews, *The Eye of the Story*, in 1978. Marrs, *Eudora Welty*, Appendix I, 576–577. The honors included thirty-nine honorary degrees (1954–1998), the Howells Medal from the American Academy of Arts and Letters (1955), the Gold Medal for Fiction from the National Institute of Arts and Letters (for *The Optimist's Daughter*, 1972), the National Medal of Literature and the Medal of Freedom (1981), the National Medal of the Arts (1986), and the French Legion of Honor (1996), Marrs, *Eudora Welty*, Appendix 2, 578–579.

34. Ibid., 359, 462–464, 489.

35. 1980 Spring Rose Show schedule, Central Mississippi Rose Society. Enclosed with cover letter to Welty from chairman, 4 December 1979, Maxwell Papers, UIRBML.

36. Welty to Maxwell, 13 June 1980, Maxwell Papers, UIRBML; Lawrence to Welty, 6 April 1982, Welty Collection, MDAH.

37. Letter to Welty from David Herbert Donald, Harvard University, 24 March 1982, Welty Collection, MDAH.

38. Welty, *OWB*, in *Welty: Stories, Essays, & Memoir*, Ford and Kreyling, eds., 947–948.

39. Eudora Welty, *The Optimist's Daughter*, in *Welty: Complete Novels*, Ford and Kreyling, eds., 952.

EPILOGUE

1. Capers (1987), 54, MDAH.

2. Gina Holland, "Neighbor Pitches in to Clean Up Welty's Overgrown Backyard," Associated Press. Photocopy, unidentified newspaper clipping, n. d. [9 May 1994, clipping service date stamp].

3. Lawrence, *A Southern Garden*, 173.

4. Mitchell, in *More Conversations with Eudora Welty*, Prenshaw, ed.; "Eudora Welty's Garden of Triumphant Simplicities," *The Washington Post*, 10 June 1980, Sec. B, 1, 11.

BIBLIOGRAPHY

Bailey, Liberty H., and Ethel Z. Bailey. *Hortus Third*. Rev. and exp. ed. New York: Macmillan, 1976.

Baird, Bessie Mary. *Roses for Southern Gardens*. Chapel Hill, N.C.: The University of North Carolina Press, 1948.

Ballard, Ernesta D. "Horticultural and Gardening Organizations." *The American Horticultural Magazine* 45, No. 3 (July 1966): 347–350.

Batson, F. S., and R. O. Monosmith. *An Illustrated Guide to the Care of Ornamental Trees and Shrubs*. Extension Service of Mississippi State College, *Extension Bulletin No. 117*. Reprint. N. p. [Mississippi State, Miss.], Oct. 1942.

Battles, Marjorie Gibbon, and Catherine Colt Dickey. *Fifty Blooming Years, 1913–1963: The Garden Club of America*. New York: The John B. Watkins Company, 1963.

Bennett, Ida D. *The Flower Garden: A Handbook of Practical Garden Lore*. New York: McClure, Phillips and Company, 1903.

Biles, Roy E. *The Complete Book of Garden Magic*. 1935. Garden City, N.Y.: Garden City Books, 1947.

Birnbaum, Charles A., ed., with Christine Capella Peters. *The Secretary of the Interior's Standards for the Treatment of Historic Properties with Guidelines for the Treatment of Cultural Landscapes*. Washington, D.C.: U. S. Department of the Interior, National Park Service, Cultural Resources Stewardship and Partnership, Heritage Preservation Services, Historic Landscape Initiative, 1995.

Black, Patti Carr, ed., comp. *Eudora*. Catalogue for exhibition at the Mississippi State Historical Museum, a division of the Mississippi Department of Archives and History (MDAH), with an introduction by Patti Carr Black. Jackson, Miss.: MDAH, 1984.

———. "Eudora Welty's Radio Days." *Reckon* 1, Nos. 1 and 2 (1995): n. p.

———. "History and Significance of the Welty House, 1119 Pinehurst Street, Jackson, Miss." Photocopy. Typescript. N. d.

———, ed. *Early Escapades* by Eudora Welty. Jackson, Miss.: University Press of Mississippi, 2005.

Blood Group Gene Antigen Database. "Historical Landmarks in the Field of Study of Blood Group Systems." National Center for Biotechnology Information, U. S. Library of Medicine, National Institutes of Health, Bethesda, Md. http://www.ncbi.nlm.nih.gov/projects/gv/mhc/xslcgi.cgi?cmd=bgmut/landmarks.

Bush-Brown, Louise, and James Bush-Brown. *America's Garden Book*. 1939. New York: Charles Scribner's Sons, 1949.

Capers, Charlotte. "Eudora Welty's House: A Conversation with Charlotte Capers." Photocopy. Typed transcript of interview. MDAH, Jackson, Miss., 1987.

———. "An Interview with Eudora Welty by Charlotte Capers." Photocopy. Typed transcript of interview. Oral History Program, MDAH, Jackson, Miss., 26 October 1971.

City of Jackson, Miss., Historic Preservation Commission, Application for Jackson Historic District Designation, 21 June 199–[after 1996].

Clayton, Virginia Tuttle, ed. *The Once & Future Gardener: Garden Writing from the Golden Age of Magazines, 1900–1940*. Boston: David R. Godine, Publisher, 2000.

Comley, Mary Doris. Scrapbook, Mary Doris Comley Papers, MDAH, Jackson, Miss.

Cridland, Robert B. *Practical Landscape Gardening*. New York, N.Y.: A. T. De La Mare Printing and Publishing Co. Ltd., 1916.

De La Mare, A. T., ed. *Garden Guide: The Amateur Gardeners' Handbook*. Rev. 4th ed. New York: A. T. De La Mare Company, Inc., 1925.

Dillon, Julia Lester. *The Blossom Circle of the Year in Southern Gardens*. New York: A. T. De La Mare Company, Inc., 1922.

Dirr, Michael A. *Manual of Woody Landscape Plants: Their Identification, Ornamental Characteristics, Culture, Propagation and Uses*. Rev. 4th ed. Champaign, Ill.: Stipes Publishing Co., 1990.

Earle, Alice Morse. *Old Time Gardens: A Book of the Sweet O' the Year*. New York: The Macmillan Company, 1901.

Ely, Helena Rutherfurd. *A Woman's Hardy Garden*. New York: The Macmillan Company, 1916.

Estrada, Ivelisse. "The Lost Army: The Woman's Land Army of America," *Schleisinger Library Newsletter*. Cambridge, Mass.: Radcliffe Institute for Advanced Study, Harvard University, Spring 2009.

Everett, Marshall. *The Book of the Fair, St. Louis, 1904*. Philadelphia: P. W. Ziegler Co., copyright 1904 by Henry Neil.

Feathers, David L., ed., and Milton H. Brown, assoc. ed. *The Camellia: Its History, Culture, Genetics, and a Look into Its Future Development*. Columbia, S.C.: printed by the R. L. Bryan Company, copyright 1978 by the American Camellia Society.

Federal Writers' Project of the Works Progress Administration, comp. *Mississippi: The WPA Guide to the Magnolia State*. 1938. Reprint, Jackson, Miss.: University Press of Mississippi, 2009.

Ferris, Bill. "A Visit with Eudora Welty." (Summer 1975 and 1976.) In *Conversations with Eudora Welty*, Peggy Prenshaw, ed. Jackson, Miss.: University Press of Mississippi,

1984. Reprint, New York: Washington Square Press (Pocket Books), 1985.

Findlay, Hugh. *Garden Making and Keeping*. 1925. Reprint, Garden City, N.Y.: Doubleday, Doran & Company, Inc., 1934.

Fisher, Edith R. *The Garden Club Manual*. New York: The MacMillan Company, 1931.

Ford, Richard, and Michael Kreyling, eds. *Welty: Stories, Essays, & Memoir*. New York: Literary Classics of the United States, Inc., The Library of America, 1998.

———, eds. *Welty: Complete Novels*. New York: Literary Classics of the United States, The Library of America, 1998.

Garden Club of America. *Bulletin* 64, No. 2 (1976). N.a., n.p.d.

The Garden of a Commuter's Wife. N.a. New York: The Macmillan Company, 1905.

Gaskins, Lee. "At The Fair: The 1904 St. Louis World's Fair." http://atthefair.homestead .com/POH.html.

Gerbing, G. G. *Camellias*. Fernandina, Fla.: G. G. Gerbing; completely produced by J. Horace McFarland Company, Mount Pleasant Press, Harrisburg, Pa., 1943.

Gibson, Campbell. "Rank by Population of the 100 Largest Urban Places, Listed Alphabetically by State: 1790–1990" (table) in "Population of the 100 Largest Cities and Other Urban Places in the United States: 1790 to 1990." Population Division Working Paper No. 27, Population Division, U. S. Bureau of the Census, Washington, D.C., June 1998. http://www.census .gov/population/www/documentation/ twps0027/twps0027.html.

Goff, John H. *Placenames of Georgia: Essays of John H. Goff*. Francis Lee Utley and Marion R. Hemperley, eds. Athens, Ga.: University of Georgia Press, 1975. http://books .google.com.

Goodman, Ernestine Abercrombie. *The Garden Club of America: History, 1913–1938*. Philadelphia: Edward Stern & Co., Inc., 1938.

Grampp, Christopher. *From Yard to Garden: The Domestication of America's Home Grounds*. Chicago: Center for American Places at Columbia College Chicago, 2008.

Helphand, Kenneth I. *Defiant Gardens: Making Gardens in Wartime*. Annotated edition. Hartford, Conn.: Trinity University Press, 2006.

Hill, May Brawley. *Grandmother's Garden: The Old-Fashioned American Garden, 1865–1915*. New York: Harry N. Abrams, Inc., 1995.

Hofstadter, Richard. *The Age of Reform*. New York: Vintage Books, a Division of Random House, 1955.

Hogg, Charlotte. *From the Garden Club: Rural Women Writing Community*. Lincoln, Neb.: University of Nebraska Press, 2006.

Holland, Gina. "Neighbor Pitches in to Clean Up Welty's Overgrown Backyard." Associated Press. Photocopy. Unidentified newspaper clipping, n. d. [9 May 1994, clipping service date stamp].

Hottes, Alfred Carl, ed. *My Better Homes and Gardens Garden Helper: What to Do Each Month and How to Do It*. Des Moines, Iowa: Meredith Publishing Company, n. d. [c. mid-1920s to mid-1930s].

Howland, Joseph E. *The House Beautiful Book of Gardens and Outdoor Living*. N. p.: Doubleday & Company Inc., 1958.

Hume, H. Harold. *Camellias in America*. Harrisburg, Pa.: J. Horace McFarland Company, Mount Pleasant Press, 1946.

Humphreys, Phebe Westcott. *The Practical Book of Garden Architecture*. Philadelphia and London: J. B. Lippincott Company, 1914.

Jackson, Kenneth T. *Crabgrass Frontier: The Suburbanization of the United States*. New York, Oxford, Eng.: Oxford University Press, 1985.

Jackson (Miss.) *Clarion-Ledger*. Sunday, 14 October 1928; 25 September 1931, morning edition.

Jackson (Miss.) *Daily News*. 23 September 1931, evening edition.

Jackson Council of Garden Clubs. *Affiliated Club Histories: The Jackson Council of Garden Clubs, Inc.* Vol. I. Jackson, Miss.: 1930–1960.

The Jaeger Company, for the City of Jackson, Mississippi, Historic Preservation Commission, and Department of Planning and Development. *From Frontier Capital to Modern City: A History of Jackson, Mississippi's Built Environment, 1865–1950*. Gainesville, Ga.: The Jaeger Company, 2000.

Jekyll, Gertrude. *Wood and Garden: Notes and Thoughts, Practical and Critical, of a Working Amateur*. London, New York and Bombay: Longmans, Green and Co., 1904. Online edition: http://www.books.google .com.

———. *Colour Schemes for the Flower Garden*. 1908. Introduced and revised by Graham Stuart Thomas. Salem, N.H.: The Ayer Company, 1983.

———, and Lawrence Weaver. *Arts and Crafts Gardens*. 1912. Rev. ed. N. p.: Garden Art Press, 1997.

Junior League of Jackson, Mississippi, comp. *Jackson Landmarks*. Jackson, Miss.: 1982.

Kift, Jane Leslie. *The Woman's Flower Garden: Indoor and Outdoor*. New York: A. T. De La Mare Company, Inc., 1927.

King, Mrs. Francis. *The Little Garden*. Boston: The Atlantic Monthly Press, 1921. Third impression, 1922.

———. *The Beginner's Garden*. New York: Charles Scribner's Sons, 1927.

Kirby, A. M. *Daffodils, Narcissus, and How to Grow Them*. New York: Doubleday, Page & Company, 1907.

Kreyling, Michael. *Author and Agent: Eudora Welty and Diarmuid Russell*. New York: Farrar, Straus, Giroux, 1991.

Lacey, Ann Gascoigne, ed. *Garden Club of*

America Bulletin, Bicentennial Commemorative Issue 64, No.2, n. d. [1976].

Lanman, Susan W. "Colour in the Garden: 'Malignant Magenta.'" *Garden History* 28, No. 2 (Winter 2000): 209–221.

Lawrence, Elizabeth. *A Southern Garden*. 1942. Chapel Hill, N.C.: The University of North Carolina Press, 1991 paperback edition reproducing the text of a 1991 special anniversary edition.

———. *Gardening for Love: The Market Bulletins*. Allan Lacy, ed. Durham, N.C.: Duke University Press, 1987.

Louisiana State Museum. *Biennial Report of the Board of Curators for 1920–21*. New Orleans, La., January 1922.

McFarland, J. Horace, and Robert Pyle. *How to Grow Roses*. 18th ed. New York: The Macmillan Company, 1937.

———. *Modern Roses III*. Harrisburg, Pa.: J. Horace McFarland Company, 1947.

———, R. Marion Hatten, and Daniel J. Foley. *Garden Bulbs in Color*. New York: The Macmillan Company, 1938.

McGuire, Diane Kostial, ed. *American Garden Design: An Anthology of Ideas that Shaped Our Landscape*. New York: A Horticulture Book, Macmillan U.S.A., 1994.

Marrs, Suzanne. *One Writer's Imagination: The Fiction of Eudora Welty*. Baton Rouge: Louisiana State University Press, 2002.

———. *Eudora Welty: A Biography*. Orlando, Austin, New York, San Diego, Toronto, London: Harcourt, Inc., 2005.

———. "A Mother–Daughter Garden." *Garden & Gun*, March/April 2008,71.

Mills, Frederick C. "Aspects of the Price Recession of 1929–1931." *News-Bulletin*, National Bureau of Economic Research, Inc., no. 42 (23 December 1931).

Mitchell, Henry. *The Essential Earthman*. 1981. Boston: Houghton Mifflin Company, 1993.

Mobley, Jane, and Nancy Whitnell Harris. *A City Within a Park: One Hundred Years of Parks and Boulevards in Kansas City, Missouri*. N. p.: The American Society of Landscape Architects, 1991.

Mulford, Furman Lloyd. *Herbaceous Perennials*. U.S.D.A. Farmers' Bulletin No. 1381. 1924. Washington, D.C. [U. S. Department of Agriculture], 1929.

Murphy, Sharon Ann. "Life Insurance in the United States through World War I." *EH.Net Encyclopedia of Economic and Business History*. Robert Whaples, ed. N. p.: Economic History Association, 2002. http://eh.net/encyclopedia/article/Murphy.life.insurance.us.

Nevins, Deborah. "The Triumph of Flora: Women and the American Landscape, 1890–1935." *The Magazine Antiques* (April 1985): 904–922.

1904 World's Fair, The Louisiana Purchase Exposition, St. Louis, Missouri, The Greatest of Expositions, Completely Illustrated. St. Louis: Louisiana Purchase Exposition Press of Sam'l F. Myerson Printing Co., 1904. Washington University at St. Louis, Mo. washingtonmo.com/1904/index.htm.

Pack, Charles Lathrop. *The War Garden Victorious*. Philadelphia: J. B. Lippincott Company, 1919.

Prenshaw, Peggy Whitman, ed. *Conversations with Eudora Welty*. New York: Washington Square Press [Pocket Books],1985.

———. *More Conversations with Eudora Welty*. Jackson, Miss.: University Press of Mississippi, 1996.

Price, Reynolds. "One Writer's Place in Fiction." *The New York Times*, 27 July 2001. Radio version. Cambridge, Mass.: WGBH Public Broadcasting Station, www.pbs.org/wgbh/masterpiece/americancollection/ponder/place.html.

Pyle, Robert. *How to Grow Roses*. 14th ed. West Grove, Pa.: The Conard & Jones Company, 1923.

———, J. Horace McFarland, and G. A. Stevens. *How to Grow Roses*. 17th ed., enlarged and entirely rewritten. New York: The Macmillan Company, 1930.

Ramsey, Leonidas Willing. *Planning the Home Grounds*. Vol. II of the ten-volume Landscape Garden Series. Ralph Rodney Root, series ed. Davenport, Ia.: The Garden Press, 1921. Published for the American School of Landscape Architecture and Gardening, Newark, N.Y., 1921.

Rogers, Elizabeth Barlow. *Landscape Design: A Cultural and Architectural History*. New York: Harry N. Abrams, Inc., 2001.

Russell, Æ (George). *The Candle of Vision*. 1918. New York: The Macmillan Company, 1931. PDF, Google Books.

Russell, Diarmuid. "An Experiment with the Imagination." *Harper's Magazine*, Sept. 1942 (bound): 428–431.

Sanguinet, Staats and Hedrick Collection. Drawings, photographs, and archival records, 1910–1969, 1991, Texas. Alexander Architectural Archive, University of Texas Libraries, University of Texas at Austin.

Sansing, David G. "Mississippi: 1900–1904." *Mississippi History Now*. Posted January 2004. http://mshistory.k12.ms.us/articles/265/index.php?s=extra&id=136.

Saslaw, Rita S. "Student Societies in Nineteenth Century Ohio: Misconceptions and Realities." *Ohio History: The Scholarly Journal of the Ohio Historical Society* 88, No. 2 (Spring 1979).

Savige, Thomas J., International Registrar, comp. *International Camellia Register*. N. p.: International Camellia Society, 1993.

Schneider, Dorothy, and Carl J. Schneider. *American Women in the Progressive Era, 1900–1920*. New York: Facts on File, 1993.

Seymour, E. L. D., ed. *The New Garden Encyclopedia*. New York: Wm. H. Wise & Co., Inc., 1946 ed., originally published 1936.

Shull, Carol D., supervis. *National Register Bulletin: Historic Residential Suburbs, Guide-*

lines for Evaluation and Documentation for the National Register of Historic Places. "Trends in Subdivision Design." Washington, D.C.: U.S. Department of the Interior, National Park Service, 2002. http://www .nps.gov/history/nr/publications/bulle tins/suburbs/text1.htm.

Slusser, Effie Young, Mary Belle Williams, and Emma Burbank Beeson. Lillian McLean Waldo, ed. *Stories of Luther Burbank and His Plant School.* New York: Charles Scribner's Sons, 1920.

Southern Pine Association. *Beautifying the Home Grounds.* New Orleans: n. d. [1920s].

Steele, Fletcher. *The House Beautiful Gardening Manual.* Boston: The Atlantic Monthly Company, 1926.

Stilgoe, John R. *Borderland: Origins of the American Suburb, 1820–1939.* New Haven and London: Yale University Press, 1988.

Stout, A. B. *Daylilies: The Wild Species and Garden Clones, Both Old and New, of the Genus Hemerocallis.* New York: The Macmillan Company, 1934.

Tabor, Grace. *Making the Grounds Attractive with Shrubbery.* New York: McBride, Nast & Company, 1912.

———. *The Old-Fashioned Garden: A History and a Reconstruction.* New York: McBride, Nast & Company, 1913.

Tankard, Judith B. "An American Perspective on Gertrude Jekyll's Legacy." *Journal of the New England Garden History Society,* 6 (Fall 1998): 42–51.

———. *Gardens of the Arts and Crafts Movement: Reality and Imagination.* New York: Harry N. Abrams. Inc., n. d. [2004].

Taylor, Albert D. *The Complete Garden.* Garden City, N.Y.: Garden City Publishing Co., Inc., 1921.

Watkins, Floyd. "Notes on Eudora Welty Trip." Unpublished typescript, 10–23 September 1984. Floyd Watkins Papers. Manuscript, Archives, and Rare Book Library, Emory University, Atlanta, Ga.

Waugh, Frank A. *Rural Improvement.* New York: Orange Judd Company, 1917, originally 1914.

———. *Landscape Gardening.* New York: John Wiley & Sons, Inc., 1922.

Way, Thaïsa. *Unbounded Practice: Women and Landscape Architecture in the Early Twentieth Century.* Charlottesville, Va., and London: University of Virginia Press, 2009.

Weiss, Elaine F. *Fruits of Victory: The Woman's Land Army of America in the Great War.* Washington, D.C.: Potomac Books, Inc., 2008.

Welch, William C., and Greg Grant. *The Southern Heirloom Garden.* Dallas: Taylor Publishing Company, 1995.

Welty, Chestina. The Scribble-in Book. Clothbound diary ("garden journal"). N. d. [late 1930s–1940s] © Eudora Welty LLC.

———. Spiral-bound stenographer's notebook ("garden notebook"). N. d. [1930s]. © Eudora Welty LLC.

———. "The Perfect Garden." Photocopy. Typescript, n. d. Collection of Suzanne Marrs.

Welty, Christian W. Last Will and Testament of C. W. Welty. Hinds County Will Book 3, p. 573 (1920–1932), Eudora Welty Collection, MDAH.

Welty, Eudora A. "Jackson: A Neighborhood." In *Jackson Landmarks.* Jackson, Miss.: The Junior League of Jackson, Miss., 1982.

———. Acceptance speech, the National Book Foundation's Medal for Distinguished Contribution to American Letters. The National Book Awards Ceremony, 20 November 1991. http://www.nationalbook .org/nbaacceptspeech_ewelty.html.

———. Letters to Diarmuid Russell. 1940–1958. Eudora Welty Collection, MDAH.

———. Letters to John Robinson. 1942–1950. Eudora Welty Collection, MDAH.

———. "Literature and the Lens." Photocopy. *Vogue* (1 August 1944), 102–103.

———. *One Time, One Place: Mississippi in the Depression / A Snapshot Album.* New York: Random House, 1971.

———. *One Writer's Beginnings.* The William E. Massey Sr. Lectures in the History of American Civilization, 1983. Cambridge, Mass: Harvard University Press, 1984.

———. "Pages omitted from *A Writer's Beginnings,* notes and tryouts." Eudora Welty Collection, MDAH.

———. *Eudora Welty: Photographs.* Foreword, "The Only News," by Reynolds Price. Introduction, "Eudora Welty and Photography: An Interview," by Hunter Cole and Seetha Srinivasan. Jackson, Miss.: University Press of Mississippi, 1989.

Westling, Louise. *Sacred Groves and Ravaged Gardens: The Fiction of Eudora Welty, Carson McCullers, and Flannery O'Connor.* Athens, Ga.: University of Georgia Press, 1985.

White, Clyde S. "An Interview with Eudora" (1992). In *More Conversations with Eudora Welty,* ed. Peggy Whitman Prenshaw. Jackson, Miss.: University Press of Mississippi, 1996.

Wilson, Emily Herring. *No One Gardens Alone: A Life of Elizabeth Lawrence.* Boston: Beacon Press, 2004.

Winslow, Helen M. "Club Women & Club Life." *The Delineator: An Illustrated Magazine of Literature and Fashion* LXI, No. 6 (June 1903).

———. *The President of Quex: A Woman's Club Story.* Boston: Lothrop, Lee and Shepard, 1906.

Wister, John C. *Bulbs for American Gardens.* Boston: The Stratford Company, 1930.

———, ed. *Woman's Home Companion Garden Book.* New York: P. F. Collier & Son Corporation, 1947.

Wright, Mary, and Russell Wright. *Guide to Easier Living.* New York: Simon and Schuster, 1950. Salt Lake City: Gibbs Smith, Publisher, Design Classic Reprint, introduction by Massimo Vignelli, foreword by Ann Wright, 2003.

Wright, Richardson. *House & Garden's Book of Gardens*. New York: Condé Nast & Company, 1921.

Yerkes, Guy E. *Propagation of Trees and Shrubs*. U.S.D.A. Farmers' Bulletin No. 1567. 1929. Washington, D.C.: [U. S. Department of Agriculture], 1932.

Popular Magazines and Ephemera Consulted for Background

Better Homes and Gardens 5, No. 2 (Oct. 1926); 8, No. 2 (Oct. 1929).

Burpee's Annual Garden Book. Catalog. W. Atlee Burpee Co. Seedgrowers, Philadelphia, Pa. 1932; 1935.

Burpee's Bulbs for Fall Planting. Catalog. W. Atlee Burpee Co., Philadelphia, Pa. 1934.

The Garden Magazine, 37, No. 3 (May 1923). Garden City, N.Y.: Doubleday, Page & Company.

The Garden Magazine: Southern Number 38, No. 3 (Nov. 1923). Garden City, N.Y.: Doubleday, Page & Company.

The Garden Magazine: Pacific Coast Annual 38, No. 4 (Dec. 1923). Garden City, N.Y.: Doubleday, Page & Company.

Hardy Plants by Wayside Gardens. Catalog. Mentor, Ohio, 1934.

Holland's: The Magazine of the South 49, No. 11 (Nov. 1930).

Horticulture, Vol. 18 (1940), No. 1 (Jan. 1); No. 3 (Feb. 1); No. 5 (March 1); No. 6 (March 15); No. 8 (April 15); No. 9 (May 1); No. 10 (May 15); No. 11 (June 1); No. 13 (July 1); No. 14 (July 15); No. 15 (Aug. 1); No. 17 (Sept. 1); No. 18 (Sept. 15); No. 19 (Oct. 1); No. 20 (Oct. 15); No. 21 (Nov. 1).

Horticulture, Vol. 19 (1941): No. 1 (Jan. 1); No. 5 (March 1); No. 6 (March 15); No. 8 (April 15); No. 9 (May 1); No. 10 (May 15); No. 11 (June 1); No. 14 (July 15); No. 16 (Aug. 15); No. 18 (Sept. 15); No. 19 (Oct. 1); No. 21 (Nov. 1); No. 22 (Nov. 15).

Wayside Gardens. Catalog, Mentor, Ohio, 1944.

CREDITS

Excerpts from the following are © Eudora Welty, LLC; Eudora Welty Collection—Mississippi Department of Archives and History:

Series 17, *One Writer's Beginnings*, Typescript, Part III, Eudora Welty, "Pages omitted from A Writer's Beginnings notes and tryouts," [Summer 1983], Eudora Welty Collection, MDAH.

Series 29a, Eudora Welty letters to John Robinson, Eudora Welty Collection, MDAH.

Series 29a, Eudora Welty letters to Diarmuid Russell, Eudora Welty Collection, MDAH.

The following selections reprinted by the permission of Russell & Volkening as agents for the author:

Eudora Welty, *One Writer's Beginnings*, The William E. Massey Sr. Lectures in the History of American Civilization, 1983 (Cambridge, Mass: Harvard University Press, 1984), 5, 52, 54, 55, 60, 82, 83, 84–85, 93, 97–98, 102, 104.

Eudora Welty, *Welty: Stories, Essays, & Memoir* (New York: Literary Classics of the United States, Inc., 1998; The Library of America), 70, 71, 73, 114, 131, 256, 276, 519–20, 534–35, 648, 658, 679–80, 749, 773, 782, 786, 792, 793–94, 806.

Eudora Welty, *One Time, One Place* (Jackson, Miss.: University Press of Mississippi, revised edition, 1996; originally published 1971), 12.

Eudora Welty, *Welty: Complete Novels* (New York: Literary Classics of the United States, The Library of America, 1998). *Delta Wedding*: 122, 130, 246, 315, 329; *Losing Battles*: 431, 683; *The Optimist's Daughter*: 917, 937–38, 946, 952.

Eudora Welty, "Literature and the Lens," *Vogue*, 1 August 1944.

Eudora Welty, "Jackson: A Neighborhood," The Junior League of Jackson, Mississippi, comp., *Jackson Landmarks* (Jackson, Miss.: 1982), 1, 3, 5

William Ferris, "An Interview with Eudora Welty" (25 June 1994), *Reckon* (Vol. I, No. 1, 1995): 140–42.

Clyde S. White, "An Interview with Eudora," 1992, in *More Conversations with Eudora Welty*, Peggy Whitman Prenshaw, ed. (Jackson, Mississippi: University Press of Mississippi, 1996), 232.

Hunter Cole and Seetha Srinivasan, Introduction, "Eudora Welty and Photography: an Interview," *Photographs* by Eudora Welty (Jackson, Miss.: University Press of Mississippi, 1989), xvii, xxi.

Robert van Gelder, "An Interview with Miss Eudora Welty—A Short Story Writer of Exceptional Talent Talks of Her Work," *New York Times Book Review* (photocopy), 14 June 1942, Welty Collection, MDAH.

Excerpts reprinted by permission of the publisher from *One Writer's Beginnings* by Eudora Welty, pp. 5, 52, 54, 55, 60, 82, 83, 84–85, 93, 97–98, 102, 104, Cambridge, Mass: Harvard University Press, Copyright © 1983, 1984 by Eudora Welty.

INDEX

Page numbers in **bold** indicate illustrations.

Abelia (*Abelia grandiflora*), 235, 237, 242

Abelmoschus esculentus (okra), 242

Acer rubrum (red maple), 242

Acidanthera (*Acidanthera bicolor*), 162

Agave americana (century plant), 242

Air-layering (camellias), **226**. *See also* Camellias

'Alba Plena' camellia (*Camellia japonica* 'Alba Plena'), 135. *See also* Camellias

Albizia julibrissin (mimosa), 235, 237, 242

Algerian iris (*Iris unguicularis*), 160, 236. *See also* Irises

All-America Selections program, 98

Aloysia triphylla (lemon verbena), 236

Althea (*Hibiscus syriacus*), 110, 113, 150, 235, 242

Amaranthus hybridus var. *cruentus* (prince's feather), 243

Amaranthus tricolor (Joseph's-coat), 242

Amaryllis belladonna (belladonna lily), 199

'Amaryllis' daylily (*Hemerocallis* 'Amaryllis'), 73. *See also* Daylilies

Ambler, Pennsylvania, 48

American Academy of Arts and Letters, 168

American Camellia Society, 137

Andrews, Eudora Carden, xix, 3

Andrews, Ned, 3, 4

Anemones, 158

Angel lily (*Crinum* × *powellii* 'Album'), 242

Angel trumpet (*Datura metel*), 242

Annuals, 89, 90, 98–99, 109, 112, 217, 225

Antigonon leptopus (Rosa de Montana), 236

Antirrhinum majus (snapdragon), 217

Apostle lily (*Crinum bulbispermum*), 242

'Apple Blossom' camellia (*Camellia sasanqua* 'Apple Blossom'), 173. *See also* Camellias

Appendices: Appendix I, Decades of Welty Plants, 235–36; Appendix II, Original Plant List for 1119 Pinehurst Street, 237; Appendix III, Annuals in the Welty Garden, 238; Appendix IV, Roses in the Welty Garden, 240–41; Appendix V, Partial List of Plants in Welty Prose, 242–43; Appendix VI, Resources for Historic Landscape Preservation, 244; Appendix VII, Discussion Questions for Book Clubs, 245

Apple mint (*Mentha suaveolens*), 236

Aquilegia hybrida (columbine), 238

Arbor, **28**, 29, **31**, 32, 33, **33**, **36**, 37, 82, 95, 107, 164, **164**, 218, 224

Aster (*Aster* sp.), 90; China (*Callistephus chinensis*), 98, 238; hardy, 235

Aster novi-belgii or *A. novi-angliae* (Michaelmas daisy), 242

Aswell, Mary Lou, 166

Atlantic, The, 125–26, 142

Atlantic Monthly, 124

Author and Agent, xii, 124

Auto vase, 54, **54**

Automobiles, 6, 23, 44, 46, 54, 77, 81, 82, 195, 250

Avery Gardens (Louisiana), 137

Ayres, Eudora, xix

Azalea, 87, 89, 137, 214, 236; Florida flame (*Rhododendron austrinum*), **87**; 'Gulf Pride' (*R. indicum*), 87, 171; indica (*R. indicum*), **87**, 236; pink native (*R. canescens*), **94**, 95

Bachelor buttons (cornflower or ragged robins) (*Centaurea cyanus*), 99

Backyard, 12, 14, **14**, 16, 24, 28, 55, 82, **87**, 127, 157, 163, 195, **195**, 196, 203, 208, 214, **215**, 216

Ball Seed Company, 98

Baltimore, Maryland, 3, 4, 5, 76

Baltimore Women's Civic League, 45

Bamboo, 216

Banana (*Musa* spp.), 242

Banana shrub (*Michelia figo* or *Magnolia fuscata*), 41, 90, 128, 235, 237

Beauty Lovers Circle (Jackson garden club), 76. *See also* Garden clubs

Begonia (*Begonia* spp.), 242

Belamcanda chinensis (blackberry lily), 235, 242

Belhaven College, 23, 27, 165

Belhaven Garden Club (Jackson), 53, 75, 249. *See also* Garden clubs

Belhaven suburb, **16**, 23–24, 45, 81

Belladonna lily (*Amaryllis belladonna*), 199

Bellingrath Gardens (Alabama), 137

Bennett, Ida B., 18

Better Homes and Gardens, **44**

Black, Patti Carr, xii, 103

Black cherry (*Prunus serotina*), 242

Blackberry (*Rubus fruticosus*), 237

Blackberry lily (*Belamcanda chinensis*), 235, 242

Blue wonder lily (*Scilla hyacinthoides*), 150

Bluebonnets, Texas (*Lupinus subcarnosus*), 88, 89

Bluet (*Houstonia caerulea*), 181, **181**, 200

Bogue Chitto, Mississippi, 151

Bois d'arc (*Maclura pomifera*), 242

Bordeaux mixture, 97

Bottle trees, 142, 152, **152**

Bowles, E. A., 40

Box (or boxwood) (*Buxus sempervirens*), 214, 242

Bradford pear (*Pyrus calleryana*), 236

Brassicaceae sp. (mustard), 238

Breath of spring (*Spirea thunbergii*), 87, 242

Bridal wreath (*Spirea* × *vanhouttei* and also *S. prunifolia*), 87, 235

Brown, Jane Roy, xi

Buddleia davidii (butterfly bush), **40**

Bulbs, 8, 51, 84, **84**, 93, 145–47, 148, 149, 150, 151, 155, 158, 160, 163, 166, 175, 176, 182, 198–99, **199**

Burbank, Luther, 75

Burger, Nash, 104, 253

Burpee, W. Atlee, & Co., 98, 99, 126

Butter and eggs jonquil (*Narcissus* 'Aurantius Plenus'), 88

Butterfly bush (*Buddleia davidii*), **40**

Butterfly lily (*Hedychium coronarium*), 132, **174**, 175, 235

Buxus sempervirens (box or boxwood), 242

California poppy (*Eschscholzia californica*), 238

Calla lily (*Zantedeschia aethiopica*), 235

Callistephus chinensis (China aster), 98, 238

'Calypso' daylily (*Hemerocallis* 'Calypso'), 73. *See also* Daylilies

Cambridge School of Architecture and Landscape Architecture for Women, 48

Camellia, 72, 85, 87, 89, 107, 127, 133–34, **134**, 135–37, **136**, 148, **148**, 160, 163, 164, **169**, 169–71, 173, 175, 176, 177, 179, 187, 196, 198, 202, 204, 206, 214, 216, 217, 220, 236, 237, 242; air-layering, **226**; border, 160, **161**; grafting, 184; hybridizing, 170

    Varieties (*Camellia japonica*): 'Akashigata' ('Empress', 'Lady Clare'), 177, **178**, 254; 'Alba Plena', 135; 'Berenice Boddy', 137; 'Catherine Cathcart', 147, **147**, **176** (*see also* 'Leila'); 'Daikagura', 177; 'Dr. Tinsley', 137; 'Duc d'Orleans', 160; 'Elegans' (or 'Chandleri Elegans'), 89, 137, 206, **206**; 'Elisabeth', 160; 'Empress', 177, **178**; 'Gloire de Nantes', 89; 'Herme', 127, 137, 160, 176; 'Imura', 137, 171, **171**; 'K. Sawada', 170, 171; 'Lady Clare', 137, **178**; 'Leila', 147, **147**, 148, 160, 173, 176, **176**, 197; 'Magnoliaeflora', 137; 'Mathotiana', 137; 'Mrs. K. Sawada', 170, 171; 'Pink Herme', 171; 'Pink Perfection', 160; 'Sawada's Dream', 171; 'Tricolor', 137, 160; 'Victory White', 170, 171; 'White Empress', 137, 170, 171

Camellia japonica, 87, 127, 135, 137, 170, **171**, 177, **178**, 236, 237, 242, 254

Camellia sasanqua, 135, 171, 236, 237, 242

Varieties: 'Apple Blossom', 173; 'Brilliancy', 171; 'Cleopatra', 171

Camellia sinensis, 135

Camellia Trail, 137

Camellia vernalis 'Dawn', 171

Camellias (Gerbing), 135, **147**, **178**

Camellias in America (Hume), 170

Campernelle (*Narcissus* × *odorus*), 88

Campsis radicans (trumpet vine), 243

Candlestick lily (*Crinum scabrum*), 242

Canna (*Canna* × *generalis*), **14**, 110, 112, 150, 235, 242; pink, 90, **94**; 'Mrs. Pierre S. du Pont', **94**

Cape jasmine (*Gardenia jasminoides*), 88, 237. *See also* Gardenia

Capers, Charlotte, 213

Carolina jessamine (*Gelsemium sempervirens*), 90, **91**

Carya illinoinensis (pecan), 243

Carya spp. (hickory), 242

Castor bean (*Ricinus communis*), 238, 242

'Catherine Cathcart' (or 'Leila') camellia (*C. japonica* 'Catherine Cathcart'), 147, **147**, 148, 160, 173, 176, **176**. *See also* Camellias

Cedrus deodara (deodar cedar), 237

Celosia cristata (cockscomb), 242

Cemetery whites (*Iris albicans*), 37. *See also* Irises

Centaurea cyanus (bachelor buttons, cornflower, or ragged robins), 37, 99, 201, 217, 235, 238

Central Mississippi Rose Society, 208

Century plant (*Agave americana*), 242

Cercis canadensis (redbud), 243

Cereus Weeders, **227**, 229

Chaenomeles speciosa (quince), 200, 236

Chamaedorea elegans (vase palm), 243

'Chandleri Elegans' camellia (*C. japonica* 'Elegans'), 89, 206, **206**. *See also* Camellias

Cherokee rose (*Rosa laevigata*), 242. *See also* Roses

Cherry laurel (*Prunus laurocerasus*), 41, 235, 237

Chesapeake and Ohio Railroad, xix

Chestina dahlia (*Dahlia variabilis*), 160

Chicago, Illinois, 47, 123

China aster (*Callistephus chinensis*), 98

China rose, 'Louis Philippe', 200. *See also* Roses

Chinaberry (*Melia azedarach*), 235, 242

Chinese photinia (*Photinia serrulata*), 237

Chinese tallow tree (*Sapium sebiferum*), 236, 242

Christmas cactus (*Schlumbergera bridgesii*), 242

Christmas rose (*Helleborus niger*), 242

Chrysanthemum (*Chrysanthemum* × *morifolium*), 90, **92**, 148, 235

Chrysanthemum leucanthemum (ox-eye daisy), 236

Church, Thomas D., *Gardens Are for People*, **195**, 254

City Beautiful movement, 47, **47**, 55, 157

Civil War, 9, 11, 49, 55, 137

Clay, Langdon, 114

Clayton, Virginia Tuttle, 32; *The Once and Future Gardener: Garden Writing from the Golden Age of Magazines, 1900–1940*, xii, 248

Clematis (*Clematis* × *jackmanii*), 242

Clematis virginiana (virgin's bower), 243

Climbing rose (*Rosa* × *hybrida*), 12, 68, **86**, 87, 97, 201, 202, 206, 224, 235, 240. *See also* Roses

Climbing violet, 176

Clubhouse (Welty), 37, 224, **224**

Clusiana tulips (*Tulipa clusiana*), 198, **199**

Cockscomb (*Celosia cristata*), 242

Colchicum (*Colchicum* sp.), 198, **199**, 236

Colour in My Garden (Wilder), 40

"Colour in the Garden: 'Malignant Magenta,'" (Lanman, *Garden History Society Journal*), 40

Columbia University, 52–53, 63, 72, 103

Columbines (*Aquilegia hybrida*), 238

Compost, 37, 84

Confederate jasmine (*Trachelospermum jasminoides*), 52, **200**, 236, 242

Confederate lily (*Crinum fimbriatulum*), 242

Confluence, 209, 210

Consolida ajacis (larkspur), 37, 51, **51**, 90, 99, 217, 235, 238

Cook, Frances A. (Fannye), 102–3, 250

Cornflower (or bachelor buttons, ragged robins) (*Centaurea cyanus*), 90, 99, 217, 235; 'Jubilee Gem', **91**

Cornus florida (flowering dogwood), 87, 90, 95, 162, 195, 236, 242

Cosmos (*Cosmos bipinnatus* or *C. sulphureus*), **14**, 98, 238, 242

Cotton (*Gossypium* sp.), 242

Cottonseed meal, 148

Council for Roadside Improvement, 77

Crabapple tree (*Malus* sp.), 203, 236

Crape (or crepe) myrtle (*Lagerstroemia indica*), 50, 77, 151, 152, 182, **183**, 195, 235, 237; 'Near East', 171; pink, **78**

Creekmore, Hubert, 104–5

Crepe (or crape) myrtle (*Lagerstroemia indica*), 50, 77, 151, 152, 182, **183**, 195, 235, 237; 'Near East', 171; pink, **78**

Crinum sp. (milk and wine lily), **111**

Crocosmia × crocosmiiflora (montbretia), 110, 112, 215; bulbs, 145, **145**, 158, 217, 236, 242

Crocus, 144, 146

Cryptomeria, 171

Cucumber tree (*Magnolia acuminata*), 242

Cut-flower garden, **36**, 37, 38, 64–65, 85, 91, 98, 251; diagram, **85**

Daffodil, 158, 160, **167**, 198, 199, 200, 204, 236; pink-cupped (*Narcisssus* 'Mrs. R. O. Backhouse'), **146**; 'Silver Bells' (*Narcisssus moschatus* 'Silver Bells'), 204, **205**; white, 206, 217. *See also* Narcissus

Dahlia (*Dahlia variabilis*), single, 160, **160**, 235; *D. hybrida*, 242

'Dainty Bess' rose, **96**. *See also* Roses

Daisy, 89; Michaelmas (*Aster novi-belgii* or *A. novi-angliae*), 242; ox-eye (*Chrysanthemum leucanthemum*), 236; Shasta (*Chrysanthemum maximum*), 236

Datura metel (angel trumpet), 242

Daucus carota carota (Queen Anne's lace), 236, 238

Daylily (*Hemerocallis*), **67**, 88, 89, 90, **92**, 93, 114, 214, 235; *H. aurantica*, 73; *H. citrina*, 73; *H. fulva*, 73; Lemon lily (*H. lilioasphodelus*), 73, 242

Varieties: 'Amaryllis', 'Apricot', 'Calypso', 'Cressida', 'Dr. Regel', 'Florham', 'The Gem', 'George Yeld', 'Hyperion', 'J. A. Crawford', 'Mandarin', 'Modesty', 'Mrs. W. H. Wyman', 'Ophir', 'Sovereign', 'Wau-bun', 73

D-Day, 168

De La Mare, A., *Garden Guide: The Amateur Gardeners' Handbook*, 248

Delineator: An Illustrated Magazine of Literature and Fashion, The, 43, 248, 249

Delphinium (*Delphinium elatum*), 127, 128, **129**

Deodar cedar (*Cedrus deodara*), 237

Dewberry (*Rubus* spp.), 242

Dianthus plumariusi (pinks), 236

Dickens, Charles, xix, 49

Diligent Diggers (Jackson garden club), 76. *See also* Garden clubs

Dillon, Julia Lester, xii

Diospyros virginiana (persimmon), 243

Dogwood (*Cornus florida*), 87, 90, 95, 162, 195, 236, 242

Double touch-me-not (*Impatiens balsamina*), 242

Doubleday, Doran publishing company, 124, 126

Double-flowering peach (*Prunus persica*), **41**, 235, 237, 243

Downing, Andrew Jackson, 248

'Dr. W. Van Fleet' rose, **86**, 87, 241. *See also* Roses

Dream, 132–33, 134, 142

Drummond phlox (*Phlox drummondii*), 91, 98, 238

Dryopteris spp. (ferns), 242

Dublin, Ireland, 124

'Duchesse de Brabant' rose, 97, 240. *See also* Roses

Dutch iris (*Iris hollandica*), 235. *See also* Irises

Dwarf pomegranate (*Punica granatum*), **175**

Earle, Alice Morse, *Old Time Gardens*, 247

Easter lily (*Lilium longiflorum*), 235. *See also* Lilies

Eastern red cedar (*Juniperus virginiana*), 32, 41, 235, 237, 242

Eichhornia crassipes (water hyacinths), 243

1893 Columbian Exposition (Chicago World's Fair), 47

Elderberry (*Sambucus canadensis*), 242

Eleagnus (*Eleagnus pungens*), 41, 150

1119 Pinehurst Street (Welty residence): house and garden, ix, xix, 16, 23, **23**, **24**, 24–25, **26**, 27, 45, 51, 68, 97, 168, 177, 196, 204, 214; funeral, 64–65; side yard, **26**, 27–28, 29, 32, **33**, 85, 160, 176, 218. *See also* Welty garden

Ely, Helena Rutherford, xii, 29; *A Woman's Hardy Garden*, 18, 247

Engel, Lehman, 104

England, 40, 46, 201

English dogwood (mock orange) (*Philadelphus coronarius*), 235, 237

English ivy (*Hedera helix*), 236

Eschscholzia californica (California poppy), 238

'Etoile de Hollande' rose, v., **96**, 241. *See also* Roses

Eudora Welty: A Biography (Marrs), xix

Eudora Welty Day (1973), 207

Eudora Welty House (1119 Pinehurst Street), **228**, 229

Euphorbia marginata (snow-on-the-mountain), 243

Euphorbia pulcherrima (poinsettia), 243

Eustylis purpurea (Pinewood lily or purple pleat-leaf), 145

Evans, Mrs. U. B., 151

Fair Labor Standards Act, 49

Fairy lily: pink (*Zephyranthes rosea*), 242; white (*Z. candida*), 242

False dragonhead (*Physostegia virginiana*), 242

Farm women, x, 112, 149

Farmerettes, 48. *See also* Woman's Land Army

Faulkner, William, 208

Federal Writers' Project, 169, 250

Federated Garden Clubs, 77. *See also* Garden clubs

Federated Women's Clubs, 77. *See also* Woman's clubs

Ferns (*Dryopteris* spp.), 242

Ferry-Morse (seed company), 98

'Festiva Maxima' peony (*Paeonia lactiflora*), 150

Fig (*Ficus carica*), 157, **157**, 242; tree, 252

Fisher, Edith, 77, 82; *The Garden Club Manual*, 76, 249

Fleur-de-lys (lily flower), 142

Florida flame azalea (*Rhododendron austrinum*), **87**. *See also* Azalea

Flower Lovers (Jackson), 76. *See also* Garden clubs

Flower show, 77, **78**, 79, **79**

Ford, Ford Madox, 251

Ford Model T, 54

Forsythia (*Forsythia × intermedia*), 235; 'Golden Bell', 242

Fortune grass (*Pennisetum setaceum*), 242

Foundation planting, 29

Four o'clocks (*Mirabilis jalapa*), 16, 38, 101, 150, 236, 238, 242

Fragrant honeysuckle (or winter honeysuckle) (*Lonicera fragrantissima*), 237

France, 142

French Roman hyacinth (*Hyacinthus orientalis*), **151**, 160, **167**, 217, 236, 242. *See also* Hyacinthus

Friendly Diggers (Jackson), 76, 250. *See also* Garden clubs

From Yard to Garden: The Domestication of America's Home Grounds (Grampp), xii, 55

Front yard, 12, 17, 27, **29**, 47, **47**, 55, 82, 101, 214

Fruitlands Nursery (Augusta, Georgia), 135

Funeral flowers, 37–38, 64, 204

G. P. Putnam publishing company, 123, 125

Gaillardia (*Gaillardia* sp.), 238

Garage, 24, **24**, 195

Garden Bulbs in Color (Hatten and Foley), **94**

Garden Club Manual, The (Fisher), 75, 76, 249

Garden Club of America, 46, 47, 76, 220, 248. *See also* Garden clubs

Garden Club of Philadelphia, 45–46. *See also* Garden clubs

Garden clubs, x, 43, 44–47, 75, 76–77, 98, 157, 164–65, 249–50; Beauty Lovers Circle (Jackson), 76; Belhaven Garden Club (Jackson), 53, 75, 249; Diligent Diggers (Jackson), 76; Federated Garden Clubs, 77; Flower Lovers (Jackson), 76; Friendly Diggers (Jackson), 76, 250; Garden Club of America, 46, 47, 76, 220, 248; Garden Club of Philadelphia, 45–46; Gardeners of America (or Men's Garden Clubs of America), 76; Glad Circle (Jackson), 76; Jackson Council of Garden Clubs, 53, 75, 249; Jackson Council of Garden Clubs, scrapbook of, **76**, **82**, **83**, 250; Men's Garden Clubs of America, 76; National Council of State Garden Clubs, 76; National Garden Clubs, 76, 248; Sunnywild Circle (Jackson), 76; Woman's National Farm and Garden Association, 47, 76, 248

Garden Conservancy, The, 219, 220

Garden design, 21, 29, 32, 37, 73, 82

Garden Guide (De La Mare, ed.), 55

Garden History Society Journal, 40

Garden Lovers Group, of Jackson Woman's Club, 43, 50–51, 53, 77, 123. *See also* Garden clubs; Woman's clubs

Garden Magazine, The, advertisements, **45**, **47**, 77

Garden rehabilitation, xi–xii, 221, 225, 229

Garden rooms, 32, 37, **50**, 82, **82**, 84, 164, **164**, 221, 224. *See also* Outdoor rooms

Garden tools, 18, **19**; advertisement, **45**

Garden writers, xii, 24, 29, 32, 40, 55, 85, 196

Gardeners of America (or Men's Garden Clubs of America), 76

Gardenia or cape jasmine (*Gardenia jasminoides*), 41, **88**, 235, 237

Gardening for Love: The Market Bulletins (Lawrence), 151, 252

Gardens Are for People (Church), **195**, 254

Gelsemium sempervirens (Carolina jessamine or yellow jasmine), 90

Geranium, speckled (*Pelargonium × hortorum*), 242; sweet (*P. graveolens*), 243

Gerbing, G. G., *Camellias*, 135, **147**, **178**

German (or tall bearded) iris (*Iris × germanica*), 200. *See also* Irises

Ginger (*Hedychium coronarium*), 132, **174**, 175

Glad Circle (Jackson), 76. *See also* Garden clubs

Gladiolus (*Gladiolus × hortulanus*), 242

Gladiolus byzantinus (pink Jacob's ladder), 243

'Gloire de Nantes' camellia, 89. *See also* Camellias

'Golden Bell' forsythia (*Forsythia × intermedia* 'Golden Bell'), 242

Golden glow (*Rudbeckia laciniata*), **111**, 235

Gossypium sp. (cotton), 242

Grampp, Christopher, *From Yard to Garden: The Domestication of America's Home Grounds*, xii, 55

Great Depression, 63, 65, 76, 82, 101–2, **102**, 104, 106, 109, 123, 141, 157, 164, 250

'Grüss an Aachen' rose, 215, 217, 240. *See also* Roses

'Gulf Pride' azalea (*Rhododendrum indicum* 'Gulf Pride'), **87**, 171. *See also* Azalea

Halifax, Nova Scotia, 10

Haltom, Susan, ix, x–xi, 73, 198, 213, **228**

Hardy aster (*Aster* sp.), 235

Harper's Bazaar, 166

Harper's Magazine, 124, 133

Harris Seeds, 98

Harrisburg, Pennsylvania, 157

Harvard University, 209

Hedera helix (English ivy), 236

Hedge, **29**, 37, 55, 69, 82

Hedrick, Wyatt C., 25

Hedychium coronarium (ginger or butterfly lily), 132, **174**, 175, 235

Helianthus annuus (sunflower), 243

Heliotrope (*Heliotropium arborescens*), 38, 238, 242

Helleborus niger (Christmas rose), 242

Hemerocallis. See Daylilies

Herbs, 236

'Herme' camellia (*Camellia japonica* 'Herme'), 127, 137, 160, 176. See also Camellias

Hibiscus manihot (sunset hibiscus), 236

Hibiscus syriacus (althea), 110, 113, 150, 235

Hickory (*Carya* spp.), 242

Hilliard, Elbert, 214

Hippeastrum × johnsonii (red amaryllis), 243

Historic Iris Preservation Society, **86**

Hollyhock (*Alcea rosea*), 217

Holmes, Hank, 214

Honeysuckle (*Lonicera* spp.), 16, 242; Japanese, 216; winter (*Lonicera fragrantissima*), 41, 235

Horticulture magazine, 156–57

Horticulture programs for women, 48; advertisement, **47**

House Beautiful Book of Gardens and Outdoor Living (Howland), 196, 254

Houstonia caerulea (bluet), 181, **181**, 200

Howland, Joseph E., *The House Beautiful Book of Gardens and Outdoor Living*, 196, 254

Hume, Harold, *Camellias in America*, 170

Hurricane Camille, 247

Hyacinth, French Roman or Roman. See Hyacinthus

Hyacinthoides hispanica (Spanish bluebell), 90, 236

Hyacinthus (*Hyacinthus orientalis*), 144, 151, **151**, 155, 160, **167**, 173, 198, 200, 217, 236, 242

Hybrid tea rose (*Rosa × hybrida*), **96**, 97, 197, **197**, 200, 235; 'La France', 240. See also Roses

Hydrangea (*Hydrangea macrophylla*), 235, 237

Hylocereus undatus (night blooming cereus), 104–5, **105**, 236, 242, 251

Ilex vomitoria (yaupon), 41, 235, 237

Illustrated Guide to Landscaping Mississippi Homes, An (Extension Service Bulletin), **83**

Impatiens balsamina (double touch-me-nots), 242

Indian pink (*Spigelia marilandica*), 93, **94**

Indica azalea (*Azalea indica*), **87**. See also Azalea

International Camellia Register, 137

International Camellia Society, 137

Ipomoea alba (moonvine), 242

Ipomoea tricolor (morning glory), 110, **111**, 112, 235, 242

Ireland, 123

Irises (*Iris*), **33**, 89, 90, 114, 127, 128, 142, 144, **153**, 158, 176, 204, 242; *I. albicans* (white flag iris), 37, 243; Algerian iris (*I. unguicularis*), 160; *I. × germanica* 'Dauntless', 205; Dutch (*I. hollandica*), 235; German or tall bearded (*Iris × germanica*), 85, **86**, 87, 200, **205**, 215, 235; Japanese (*I. ensata*), 89, 236; Siberian (*I. sibirica*), 235; *I. stylosa marginata* (see Algerian iris); Southern blue flag (*I. virginica*), 243

Irish Literary Revival, 124

Ironweed (*Vernonia altissima*), 242

J. W. (yard boy), 67–68, 107, 249

Jackson, Mississippi, ix, xix, 6, 9, **9**, **10**, **11**, 11–12, 15, 16, **16**, 21, **23**, 23–24, 40, 51, 87, 182, 207, 246; first skyscraper, 25, **25**, 27; friends in, 63, 103, 104, 108, 185; front yard display, **81**; garden clubs, 43, 45, 47, 49–50, 53, 75–76, 77, **78**, 79, 123, 164–65; garden room, **82**; Great Depression in, 102, **102**; Eudora Welty Day, 207, **207**; victory garden, **156**; washwoman, **107**; Welty in, 15–16, 52, 65, 72, 104, 105, 168, 201, 252; World War II in, 165; World War II military parade, **141**

Jackson Army Air Base, 141

Jackson Camellia Society, **226**

Jackson Council of Garden Clubs, 53, 75, 249;

Scrapbook of, The, **76**, **82**, **83**, 250. See also Garden clubs

Jackson Daily News, 53, 64, 99

Jackson Garden Club, 164, 250

Japanese honeysuckle (*Lonicera japonica*), 216

Japanese iris (*Iris ensata*), 89. See also Irises

Jasminum nitidum (white star jessamine), 243

Jefcoat, Evelyn and Michael, v, 224

Jekyll, Gertrude, 29, 40, 46, 49, 247, 249

Johnny jump-ups (*Viola cornuta*), 217

Johns Hopkins hospital, 4

Jonquil, butter and eggs (*Narcissus* 'Aurantius Plenus'), 88

Jonquilla simplex (Sweeties), 93

Joseph's-coat (*Amaranthus tricolor*), 242

Joyce, James, 124

'Jubilee Gem' cornflower (*Centaurea cyanus* 'Jubilee Gem'), **91**

Juniperus virginiana (Eastern red cedar), 32, 41, 235, 237, 242

Katonah, New York, **123**, 125, **125**

King, Louisa Yeomans (Mrs. Francis), xii, 24, 29, 32, 37, 40, 47

Kniphofia uvaria (red-hot poker), 243

Kreyling, Michael, 129, 132, 203; *Author and Agent*, xii, 124

'Lady Banks' rose (*Rosa banksia lutea*), **86**, 87, 202, **202**. See also Roses

'Lady Hillingdon' rose, 97, 197, **197**. See also Roses

Lady's eardrops (*Malvaviscus arboreus* var. *Drummondii*), 242

Lady's tresses (*Spiranthes gracilis*), 242

Lagerstroemia indica (crape or crepe myrtle), 50, 77, **78**, 151, 152, 171, 182, **183**, 195, 235, 237

Lamar Life Insurance, 12, 64; headquarters building, 25, 65

Lamar Life Radio News, The, 65

Landscape Garden Series, 55

Lanman, Susan, "Colour in the Garden: 'Malignant Magenta,'" 40

Lantana (*Lantana camera*), 236

Larkspur (*Consolida ajacis*), 37, 51, **51**, 90, 99, 217, 235, 238

Lathyrus odoratus (sweet pea), 98, 235

Lawrence, Elizabeth, xii, 149, **149**, 150, 151, **153**, **205**, 206, 208–9; *A Southern Garden*, 149, 153, 217; *Gardening for Love: The Market Bulletins*, 151, 252

'Leila' camellia (*Camellia japonica* 'Catherine Cathcart'), 147, **147**, 148, 160, 173, 176, **176**. *See also* Camellias

Lemon lily (*Hemerocallis lilioasphodelus*), 73, 242. *See also* Daylilies

Lemon verbena (*Aloysia triphylla*), 236

Lepidium spp. (pepper grass), 243

Leucojum (summer snowflake), **84**, 146; *L. aestivum*, 217, 236

Life magazine, 107–8

Ligustrum lucidum (glossy privet), 237

Ligustrum sinense (Chinese privet), 29, 41, 59, 88, 235, 243

Lilies (*Lilium*): *L. candidum* (Madonna lily), 235; *L. dauricum*, 236; Easter (*L. longiflorum*), 235; flower, 142; *L. formosanum* (Formosa lily), 235; *L. henryi* (Henry's lily), 236; *L. lancifolium* (tiger lily), 235; *L. longiflorum* (Easter lily), 235; *L. philippinense* (Philippine lily), 236, 243; *L. regale* (regal lily), 235; *L. rubrum* (rubrum lily), 235; Madonna (*Lilium candidum*), 235. *See also* Daylilies

Lily-turf (*Liriope muscari, L. spicata*), 235

Liquidambar styraciflua (sweet gum), 243

Liriodendron tulipifera (poplar), 243

Liriope muscari, L. spicata (lily-turf), 235

Live oak (*Quercus virginiana*), 242

Livingston Park (Jackson), rose plantings, **78**

Loblolly pine tree (*Pinus taeda*), 135, 235

Lobularia maritime (sweet alyssum), 90, 236, 238

Locust (*Robinia* spp.), 242

Lonicera fragrantissima (fragrant or winter honeysuckle), 41, 237

'Louis Philippe' rose, 97, 200. *See also* Roses

Lower Garden (Welty), **31**, **36**, 37, **38**, **164**, 218, 221. *See also* Welty garden

Lowthorpe School of Landscape Architecture for Women, 48

Lupinus subcarnosus (Texas bluebonnets), 88, 89, 238

Lycoris radiata (spider lily), 216–17, 236, 243

Lycoris squamigera (surprise lily) 159, **159**, 236

Lyell, Frank, 104, 149, 183

Maclura pomifera (bois d'arc), 242

Madonna lily (*Lilium candidum*), 235. *See also* Lilies (*Lilium*)

Magenta, 40

Magnolia (*Magnolia grandiflora*), 237, 242

Magnolia acuminata (cucumber tree), 242

Magnolia fuscata (banana shrub), 128. *See also* *Michelia figo*

Magnolia Gardens (South Carolina), 137

Magnolia grandiflora (magnolia), 237, 242

Mahonia (*Mahonia bealei*), 214, 237

Malus sp. (crabapple), 203, 236

Malvaviscus arboreus var. *Drummondii* (Lady's eardrops), 242

'Maman Cochet' rose, 97, 197, **197**. *See also* Roses

Manuscript magazine, 106

Maple, red (*Acer rubrum*), 242

Maranta leuconeura (prayer plant), 243

Marigold (*Tagetes patula, T. erecta*), 90, 98, 99, 235, 238

Marigold Garden Circle (Jackson garden club), **76**

Marrs, Suzanne, xii, 52, 95, 108, 175, 183, 187, 203, 204, 207; *Eudora Welty: A Biography*, xix; *One Writer's Imagination*, 4, 6, 7, 8–9, 47

Marshall College, 4

Massachusetts, 48

Maxwell, Emmy, 202, 208

Maxwell, William (Bill), xix, 202, 208

Maypop (or passionflower) (*Passiflora* spp.), 243

Maysel, West Virginia, 3

McFarland, J. Horace, 157–58, 241; 'Editor McFarland' rose, 245

Meadow rue (thalictrum), 215

Melia azedarach (chinaberry), 235, 242

Memory, 113, 130, 175–76, 204, 206, 209–10, 217, 253–54

Memphis *Commercial Appeal*, 103

Men's Garden Clubs of America, 76. *See also* Garden clubs

Michaelmas daisy (*Aster novi-belgii* or *A. novi-angliae*), 242

Michelia figo (banana shrub), 41, 90, 128, 235, 237

Michell seed company, 98

Milk and wine lily (*Crinum* sp.), **111**, 242

Millar, Ken (Ross McDonald), 207

Mimosa (*Albizia julibrissin*), 235, 237

Mirabilis jalapa (four o'clock), 16, 38, 101, 150, 236, 238, 242

Mississippi, xi, 9, 106; native plants, 97; poverty in, 101; seasons of central, xiii

Mississippi: The WPA Guide to the Magnolia State, 101, 108, 250

Mississippi Delta, 101, **101**, 176–79

Mississippi Department of Archives and History (MDAH), xi, 213, 214

Mississippi Market Bulletin, x, 149–51, **149**, 173, **205**, 252–53

Mississippi State Fair, flower shows, 77, 79

Mississippi Women's War Bond News, 167

Mistletoe (*Phoradendron serotinum*), 242

Mitchell, Henry, ix, 162, 230, 253

Mobile, Alabama, 135, 137, 169, 170

Mock orange (or English dogwood) (*Philadelphus coronarius* or *Philadelphus* × *virginalis*), xx, 87, 150, 237

Montbretia (*Crocosmia* × *crocosmiiflora*), 110, 112, 215; bulbs, 145, **145**, 158, 217, 236, 242

Moonvine (*Ipomoea alba*), 242

More Conversations with Eudora Welty (Prenshaw, ed.), 72, 245

Morning glory (*Ipomoea tricolor*), 110, **111**, 112, 235, 242

Morus spp. (mulberry), 242

Mound Bayou, Mississippi, **180**
Mulberry (*Morus* spp.), 242
Muscadine (*Vitis rotundifolia*), 242
Mustard (*Brassicaceae* sp.), 238

Nandina (*Nandina domestica*), 214, 215, 235, 237
Narcissus (*Narcissus*), 198, 242; 'Avalanche', **84**, **199**; 'Mrs. R. O. Backhouse', 146, **146**; paperwhite, 217; *N. pseudonarcissus moschatus* ('Silver Bells' daffodil), 204, **205**, 243; *N. tazetta* (paperwhite), **199**
Nasturtium (*Tropaeolum majus*), 98, 99, 235, 238, 242
Natchez Trace, 151, 165–66, 175
National Association of Colored Women, 248. *See also* Woman's clubs
National Committee for the Wild Flowers of the United States, 251
National Council of State Garden Clubs, 76. *See also* Garden clubs
National Garden Clubs, 76, 248. *See also* Garden clubs
National Geographic magazine, 103
National Park Service Historic Landscape Initiative, 220
Nazi Party, 65
'Near East' crepe myrtle (*Lagerstroemia indica* 'Near East'), 171
'New Dawn' rose, **86**. *See also* Roses
New Garden Encyclopedia, The, 79
New Orleans, Louisiana, 137
New York Botanical Garden, 251
New York City, 63, 65, 76, 103–4, **104**, 107, 123, 168, **168**, 173, 187, 207, 250
New York Times, 166
New York Times Book Review, 168, 253
New Yorker, The, xix, 103, 202
Nephrolepis exaltata 'Bostoniensis' (sword fern), 243
Niagara Falls, 10
Night-blooming cereus (*Selenicereus grandiflorus* or *Hylocereus undatus*), 104–5, **105**, 236, 242, 251

Night-Blooming Cereus Club, 104, 229
1904 World's Fair, 5, 6–7, 8, **8**, 169, 195, 246
1929 stock market crash, 81
Nodding lady's tresses (*Spiranthes cernua*), 242
North Carolina State College, 149
Nosegays, 38
Nymphaea spp. (water lily), 243

Oak (*Quercus* spp.), 220, 235, 236
Oakhurst Gardens (California), 145
Ohio, xix, 5
Old Capitol (Jackson), 221
Old garden roses, 197, **197**, 200. *See also* Roses
Old maids (or zinnias) (*Zinnia elegans*), 101
Oleander (*Nerium oleander*), 242
Okra (*Abelmoschus esculentus*), 242
One Writer's Imagination (Marrs), 4, 6, 7, 8–9, 47
Onion flowers (*Allium* sp.), 200
Ornithogalum (*Ornithogalum umbellatum*), 236
Osaka, Japan, 169
Osaka University, 169
Osmanthus fragrans (sweet olive), 236, 243
Ott, Luther, 216
Outdoor rooms, 32, **50**, 82–83. *See also* Garden rooms
Overlook Nurseries (Mobile, Alabama), 135, 169–70
Oxalis (*Oxalis rubra*), 236
Oxblood lily (*Rhodophilia bifida*), 217
Ox-eye daisy (*Chrysanthemum leucanthemum*), 236

Paeonia lactiflora 'Festiva Maxima' (peony), 150
Palmetto (*Sabal minor*), 242
Panic of 1907, 63
Pansy (*Viola × wittrockiana*), 98, 107, 217, 238, 242
Paperwhite narcissus, 217. *See also* Narcissus
Papaver rhoeas (Shirley poppy), 51, 90, 98, 238
Paradise Lost, 67
Park Seed Company, 98
Pass-along plants, 111, 112, 204
Passionflower (or maypop) (*Passiflora* spp.), 243

Paus, Herbert Andrew, poster, **47**
Peach, double-flowering (*Prunus persica*), **41**, 235, 237, 243
Pear: common (*Pyrus communis*), 243; Bradford (*P. calleryana*), 236
Pearl Harbor, 133, 139, 141
Pecan (*Carya illinoinensis*), 243
Pelargonium graveolens (sweet geranium), 243
Pelargonium × hortorum (speckled geranium), 242
Pennisetum setaceum (fortune grass), 242
Pepper grass (*Lepidium* spp.), 243
Perennials, 29, 89, 90, 93, 98, 112, 225
Perkins, Maxwell, 125
Persimmon (*Diospyros virginiana*), 243
Petunia (*Petunia × hybrida*), 99, 182, 236, 238
Phalaris arundinacea var. *picta* (ribbon grass), 243
Philadelphia, Pennsylvania, 135
Philadelphus (mock orange or English dogwood) (*Philadelphus coronarius*), 41, 87, 235, 237
Phlox, annual and perennial, 90, 98, 101, 107, 236
Phlox divaricata (wild phlox), 236, 243
Phlox drummondii (annual phlox), **91**, 98, 238
Phlox paniculata (summer phlox), 236, 243
Phlox subulata (thrift), 40
Phoradendron serotinum (mistletoe), 242
Photinia serrulata (Chinese photinia), 237
Photography, Eudora Welty, xi, 64, 104, 105–6, 107, **107**, 114, **114**, 124, 152, 163, 166, 219, 220
Physostegia virginiana (false dragonhead), 242
Pine, health benefits of, 247
Pinehurst Street, 16, 21
Pink (*Dianthus plumariusi*), 236, 243
Pink Jacob's ladder (*Gladiolus byzantinus*), 243
Pinus taeda (loblolly pine), 135, 235, 243
Pittosporum (*Pittosporum tobira*), 235, 237
Platanus occidentalis (sycamore), 243
Plum (*Prunus americana*), 243
Poinsettia (*Euphorbia pulcherrima*), 243
Poison ivy (*Toxicodendron radicans*), 216

Polianthes tuberosa (tuberose), 236, 243

Polygonom orientale (princess feather), 243

Pomegranate (*Punica granatum*), 175, 243

Popcorn tree (*Sapium sebiferum*), 236

Poplar (*Liriodendron tulipifera*), 243

Poppy, 160; Shirley (*Papaver rhoeas*), 51, 90, 98

Porch, **26**, 27, 82

Porter, Katherine Anne, 251

Portulacas, 98

Prayer plant (*Maranta leuconeura*), 243

Prenshaw, Peggy, xii, 175, 245; *More Conversations with Eudora Welty*, 72

Price, Reynolds, 203; *One Writer's Place in Fiction*, 255

Prince's feather (*Amaranthus hybridus* var. *cruentus*), 243

Princess feather (*Polygonom orientale*), 243

Privet (*Ligustrum sinense* and *L. lucidum*), 29, 41, 59, 88, 235, 237, 243

Progressive era, ix, 5, 11, 38, 45, 49

Prunus: *Prunus americana* (plum), 243; *P. laurocerasus* (cherry laurel), 41, 235, 237; *P. persica* (double-flowering peach), **41**, 235, 237, 243; *P. serotina* (black cherry), 242

Pulitzer Prize, xx, 204, 207

Punica granatum (pomegranate), **175**, 243

Pyracantha (*Pyracantha coccinia*), 235, 237

Pyracantha caerulea, 237

Pyracantha coccinia (Scarlet firethorn), 235, 237

Pyracantha fortuniana (archaic; now *P. fortuneana* or *P. coccinea*) (Chinese firethorn), 237

Pyracantha yuanensis (or *P. fortuniana*, both archaic; now *P. fortuneana* or *P. coccinea*), 237

Pyrus calleryana (Bradford pear), 236; *P. communis* (common pear), 243

Queen Anne's lace (*Daucus carota carota*), 236, 238

Quercus nigra (water oak), 235

Quercus virginiana (live oak), 242

Questions for book clubs, 245

Quince, flowering (*Chaenomeles speciosa*), 200, 236, 237

Ragged robins (or cornflower or bachelor buttons) (*Centaurea cyanus*), 37, 99, 201, 217, 235, 238

Rain lily (*Zephyranthes* sp.), 143–44, 236

Raleigh, North Carolina, 149

Ranunculi, bulbs, 158

Rationing (World War II), 155, 157, 158, 164, 166, 253

Ravenna, Michael (pen name), 168

Red amaryllis (*Hippeastrum × johnsonii*), 243

Red salvia (*Salvia splendens* or *S. coccinia*), 243

Redbud (*Cercis canadensis*), 243

Red-hot poker (*Kniphofia uvaria*), 243

Regal lily (*Lilium regale*), 235. *See also* Lilies

Rhododendron austrinum (Florida flame azalea), 87. *See also* Azalea

Rhododendron canescens (Piedmont azalea or pinxter azalea), 95, 235. *See also* Azalea

Rhododendron indicum, **87**. *See also* Azalea

Rhodophiala bifida (oxblood lily), 217

Rhus glabra (smooth sumac), 243

Ribbon grass (*Phalaris arundinacea* var. *picta*), 243

Ricinus communis (castor bean plant), 238, 242

Riverside Victory Garden, **156**

Robinia spp. (locust), 242

Robinson, John, xi–xii, 108, **108**, 113, 133, 135, 147–48, **147**, 158, 159, 165, 166, 167, 168, 174–75, **176**, **177**, 178, 182, 183, 185, 186–87, **186**, 206; correspondence with Welty, 148, 150, 151, **155**, 157, 160, **161**, 165, **167**, 173–75, 176, 177, 178–79, 181, 182, 185, 186, 187, 196, **199**

Robinson, Nancy McDougall (John's great-grandmother), 178–79

Robinson, William, 46

Rodale publishing company, 153

Roosevelt, President Franklin D., 101, 105, 181

Rosa banksiae var. *lutea* ('Lady Banks' rose), **86**, 87, 202, **202**. *See also* Roses

Rosa de Montana (*Antigonon leptopus*), 236

Rosa laevigata (Cherokee rose), 242. *See also* Roses

'Rosa Mundi' rose, 217. *See also* Roses

Rosa × hybrida (climbing rose), 12, 68, **86**, 87, 97, 201, 202, 206, 224, 235, 237. *See also* Roses

Roses, **96**, 202, 206, 217, 221, 237, 240, 243

Rosa spp.: 'Lady Banks', **86**, **202**, 241; 'Moss Rose', 241

Varieties: 'American Pillar', 'Birdie Blye', 'Charlotte', 'Climbing (cl.) American Beauty', 'Cl. Cecile Brunner', 'Cl. Charlotte Armstrong', 'Cl. Picture', 'Cl. Kaiserin Auguste Victoria', 'Cl. Killarney', 'Cl. President Herbert Hoover', 'Cl. Ruth', 'Cl. Talisman', 241; 'Contessa de Santiago', 'Crimson Glory', 'Cynthia', 241; 'Dainty Bess', **96**, 241; 'The Doctor', 240, 241; 'Donald Prior', 'Dr. Huey', 241; 'Dr. W. Van Fleet', 87, 241; 'Duchesse de Brabant', 97, 240, 241; 'Duquesa de Peñeranda', 'Edith Nellie Perkins', 'Editor McFarland', 241; 'Etoile de Hollande', v., **96**, 241; 'Fashion', 'Feu Pernet Ducher', 'Fortune's Double Yellow', 'Frau Karl Druschki', 'Frensham', 'Gloire de Dijon', 'Good News', 241; 'Grüss an Aachen', 215, 217, 241; 'Helen Traubel', 'Joyous Cavalier', 241; 'Lady Hillingdon', 97, 197, **197**, 240, 241; 'Louis Philippe', 97, 241; 'Ma Perkins', 241; 'Málar-Ros', 241; 'Maman Cochet', 97, 240, 241; 'Mary Wallace', 241; 'Mermaid', 87, 241; 'Mirandy', 'Mme Grégoire Staechelin', 241; 'Paul's Scarlet', 77; 'Peace', 241; polyantha, 90; 'Radiance', **96**, 240; 'Red Radiance', **96**, 240; 'Rosa Mundi', 217, 241; 'Safrano', 241; 'Silver Moon', 68, **84**, 201, 241; 'Soeur Thérèse', 'Souvenir de la Malmaison', 'Spanish Beauty', 'Sterling', 'Sutter's Gold', 'Thor', 241; 'Thousand Beauties', 240

Rubus fruticosus (blackberry), 237

Rubus spp. (dewberry), 242

Rudbeckia laciniata (golden glow), **111**, 235

Russell, Æ (George William), 123–24, **123**, 129; *The Candle of Vision*, 124, 125, 251, 252; "Dreams," 252

Russell, Diarmuid (agent), xi, **122**, 123, 124, 125, **125**, 126, 127, **127**, 129, 130, 133, 141, 142, 149, 166, 168, 201, **201**, 203, 204, **205**, 207; correspondence with Welty, 73, 87, 99, 114, 126, 127–30, 132–34, 135, 137, 139, 141, 142, 143–45, 148, 155, 157, 160, 162–63, 165, 170, 176–77, 179, 182, 183, 184, 196–97, 198, 199, 200, 201–2, 203, **205**, 240, 250, 255

Russell, Rose, 123, **125**, 207

Russell & Volkening literary agency, 125

Sackville-West, Vita, 153

Sage (*Salvia officinalis*), 243

Salix nigra (black willow), 243

Salvia coccinia (Texas sage), 243

Salvia farinacea (Mealy cup sage), 236

Salvia leucantha (Mexican bush sage), 236

Salvia officinalis (sage), 243

Salvia splendens (scarlet sage), 243

Sambucus canadensis (elderberry), 242

Sapium sebiferum (Chinese tallow or popcorn tree), 236, 242

Saratoga Springs, New York, 128, 132

Sassafras (*Sassafras albidum*), 243

Sassafras man, 15, 155, **156**

Satsumas, 169

Sawada, George, 170, 171, **171**

Sawada, Kosaku, **169**, 169–70, 171

Schlumbergera bridgesii (Christmas cactus), 242

School of Horticulture for Women, 48

Scott, Frank, 55

Scuppernong (*Vitis rotundifolia*), 243

Secretary of the Interior's Standards for the Treatment of Historic Properties with Guidelines for the Treatment of Cultural Landscapes, 220, 221

Selenicereus grandiflorus (night blooming cereus), 104–5, **105**, 242, 251

741 North Congress Street, **11**, 12, 14, 15, 16, 45

Shasta daisy (*Chrysanthemum maximum*), 236

Shirley poppy (*Papaver rhoeas*), 51, 90, 98

'Silver Bells' daffodil (*Narcissus pseudonarcissus moschatus*), 204, **205**, 243. See also Narcissus

'Silver Moon' rose, 67–68, **84**, 107, 201. See also Roses

Smilax rotundifolia (Southern smilax), 243

Smithsonian Archives of American Gardens, 220–21

Snapdragon (*Antirrhinum majus*), 217, 238

Snowball viburnum (*Viburnum plicatum*), 243

Snow-on-the-mountain (*Euphorbia marginata*), 243

Solomon's Seal (*Polygonatum commutatum*), 132, 133

Southern blue flag iris (*Iris virginica*), 243. See also Irises

Southern Garden, A (Lawrence), 149, 153, 217

Southern Garden History Society, 219

Southern Seedsmen's Association, 98

Southern smilax (*Smilax rotundifolia*), 243

Spanish bluebell (*Hyacinthoides hispanica*), 90, 236

Spanish moss (*Tillandsia usneoides*), 243

Spider lily (*Lycoris radiata*), 145, 216, **216**, 236, 243

Spigelia marilandica (Indian pink), 93, **94**

Spiranthes cernua (nodding lady's tresses), 242

Spiranthes gracilis (lady's tresses), 242

Spirea, 33, 41, **84**, 85, 87, **91**, 216, 220, 237; 'Anthony Waterer', 235; white, 87

Spirea cantoniensis (Reeves spirea), 235

Spirea japonica 'Anthony Waterer' (Anthony Waterer spirea), 235

Spirea prunifolia (bridal wreath spirea), 235

Spirea thunbergii (breath of spring), 87, 235, 242

Spirea × vanhouttei (Van Houtte's spirea, sometimes also called bridal wreath spirea), 87, 235, 237

St. Elmo (Evans), 97

St. Louis, Missouri, 5, 6

St. Louis World's Fair (1904), 5–8, 169, 195, 246

State Fair. *See* Mississippi State Fair

Stokesia (*Stokesia laevis*), 236

Suburb, **16**, 23, 55, 81

Suburban Gardens (Tabor), 55

Sumac (*Rhus glabra*), 243

Summer snowflake (*Leucojum aestivum*), 217, 236

Sunbonnets, 18, **19**

Sunflower (*Helianthus annuus*), 243

Sunnywild Circle (Jackson), 76. See also Garden clubs

Sunset hibiscus (*Hibiscus manihot*), 236

Surprise lily (*Lycoris squamigera*), **159**, 236

Sweet alyssum (*Lobularia maritima*), 90, 236, 238

Sweet geranium (*Pelargonium graveolens*), 243

Sweet gum (*Liquidambar styraciflua*), 243

Sweet olive (*Osmanthus fragrans*), 236, 243

Sweet pea (*Lathyrus odoratus*), 98, 235

Swept yard, 142, 180

Sword fern (*Nephrolepis exaltata* 'Bostoniensis'), 243

Sycamore (*Platanus occidentalis*), 243

Tabor, Grace, *Suburban Gardens*, 55

Tagetes erecta (African marigold), *T. patula* (French marigold), 98, 235, 238

Tall bearded (or German) iris (*Iris × germanica*), 85, **86**, **205**, 215. See also Irises

Tea rose, hybrid, **96**, 97, 197, **197**, 200, 235. See also Roses

Texas, 25, 41, 88, 89, **91**, 151, 169

Texas bluebonnets (*Lupinus subcarnosus*), 88, 89, 238

Thalictrum (meadow rue), 215

Thomas Jefferson Center for Historic Plants, 219–20

Thousand Islands region, New York, 9, 10, **10**

Thrift (*Phlox subulata*), 40

Tiger lily (*Lilium lancifolium*), 235, 243. See also Lilies

Tillandsia usneoides (Spanish moss), 243

Tishomingo County, Mississippi, 106, 109

Toxicodendron radicans (poison ivy), 216

Trachelospermum jasminoides (Confederate jasmine), **200**, 236, 242

Trellis, 17, 29, 30, **31**, 32, 33, **35–36**, 37, **38–39**, 82, 87, **94**, 97, 107, 164, **164**, 202, 218, 224, 251
Tropaeolum majus (nasturtium), 98, 235, 238, 242
Trousers for women, 18
Trumpet vine (*Campsis radicans*), 243
Tuberose (*Polianthes tuberosa*), 236, 243
Tulip, 160, 198, 236; clusiana, 198, **199**, 236; sylvestris, 198, 236; trees, 200
Tulipa clusiana (clusiana tulip), 198, **199**, 236
Tulipa sylvestris, 198, 236

University of Wisconsin, 52, 123
Upper Garden (Welty), **28**, **31**, 33, **33**, **36**, 37, 38, **49**, **53**, **84**, **85**, 87, **91**, **92**, 164, 218, **220**. *See also* Welty garden
Utica, Mississippi, 108

Vanity Fair, 104
Varley, Elsie, 18
Vase palm (*Chamaedorea elegans*), 243
Verbena (*Verbena* spp.), 243
Verbena × *hybrida* or *Verbena hortensis* (garden verbena), 38, 101, 110, 113, 236, 238
Vernonia altissima (ironweed), 242
Viburnum macrocephalum (snowball viburnum), 243
Victorian carpet bedding, 8, **8**
Victory Garden program, 158
Victory gardens, 12, **156**, 157, 158, 165, 248
View of gardens from house, 28, **28**, 37, 84
Village Improvement Societies, 46–47
Vinca (*Vinca major* or *V. minor*), 217, 243
Viola cornuta (Johnny jump-ups), 217
Viola × *wittrockiana* (pansy), 98, 107, 217, 236, 238, 242
Violets (*Viola odorata*), 236, 243
Virgin's bower (*Clematis virginiana*), 243
Vitex (*Vitex agnus-castus*), 41, 235, 237
Vitis rotundifolia (muscadine or scuppernong), 242, 243
Vogue, 166, **166**, 221
Volkening, Henry, 125, 127, **127**

Washington Post, ix, 162
Water hyacinths (*Eichhornia crassipes*), 243
Water lily (*Nymphaea* spp.), 243
Water oak (*Quercus nigra*), 235
Wayside Gardens catalogue, **41**, **92**, 158, 253
Weigela florida (weigela), 150
Wellesley College Training Camp, Woman's Land Army, 48. *See also* Woman's Land Army
Welty, Chestina Carden Andrews, ix, xii, xix, 3–6, **4**, **5**, **8**, 9, **10**, **11**, 12, 14, **14**, **15**, 16, **20**, 23, 24, 25, **26**, 28, 29, **29**, **31**, 32–33, **33**, **36**, 37, 38, 40, 45, **49**, **62**, 63–64, 65, **69**, **74**, **92**, **93**, **97**, **127**, **129**, 153, **164**, 179, **203**, **210**; brothers, 6; club involvement, 49–50, 52, 53, 69, 75, 88, 164; garden journal, xi, 21, 37, **38**, **85**, 88–89, 99, 104, 164, 218, 221, 238, 248, 250; garden notebook, 52, 163, 220, 221, 250, 251; love of botany, xix, 4, 8, 49; love of reading, xx, 49; marriage, 5–6; original plant list, 41; "The Perfect Garden," 139; roses, **15**, 84, 89, **93**, 95, 97, **97**, 114, 197, 201, 202, 203, 204, 206, 208, 218, 221, 224
Welty, Christian, Jr., 12
Welty, Christian Webb, xix, **4**, 5, **5**, 6, 8, 9, **10**, 10–11, **11**, 12, **21**, 23, 24, 25, **25**, **29**, **62**, **64**, 169, 195, 209, 218; death, 64; funeral, 64–65; leukemia, 53, 63; photography, 6, 12, 64; reading preferences, xx
Welty, Edward, 12, **15**, **37**, 102, 139, **140**, 177, 179, 182, 203
Welty, Elizabeth, 177, **208**, 221
Welty, Eudora: childhood, **12**, **14**, 15–16, **15**, **17**, **22**, **25**, **29**, **36**, **52**, **64**, **106**, **108**, **112**, **124**, **126**, **129**, **144**, 209; death, x, 221; drawings, **154**, **167**; dreams, 132–33, 142, **143**, 144, 204; photography, xi, 64, 104, 105–6, 107, 114, 124, 152, 163, 166, 219, 220
   Works: "At the Landing," 144; "The Bride of Innisfallen and Other Stories," 200; "The Burning," 200; "A Curtain of Green," 68, 108, 109, 249; *A Curtain of Green*, 141, 249; "Death of a Traveling Salesman," 107; "The Delta Cousins," 166, 168, 179, 254; *Delta Wedding*, 54, **96**, 141, 155, 168, 173, 176, 179, 180, 181, 182, 184, 187, **197**, 208, **216**, 249, 254; "The Demonstrators," 195; "The Eye of the Story," 175, 255; "Flowers for Marjorie," 104; "The Golden Apples," 141; "June Recital," **159**; "Kin," 37, 52; "The Last of the Figs," **183**; "Lily Daw and the Three Ladies," 108; "Literature and the Lens," 166; "A Little Triumph," 179, 254; "Livvie," 141–42, 144, 151, 152; *Losing Battles*, **96**, 108–9, 198, 200–201, 203, 204, 208; "Magic," 107; "Moon Lake," **96**; "Must the Novelist Crusade?," 184; "Nicotiana," **183**; "Old Mr. Marblehall," 5, 108, 109; *One Time, One Place*, 106; *One Writer's Beginnings*, xix, xx, 6, 23, 106, 152, 198, 209, 246; *The Optimist's Daughter*, **200**, 204, 206, 209–10, 229, 255; "Place in Fiction," x, 200, 201; *The Ponder Heart*, 200, 208; "Powerhouse," 125; *The Robber Bridegroom*, 141; "Shower of Gold," 107; "A Still Moment," 144; "The Wanderers," 37–38, 150, 198; "The Whistle," 108–9; "Why I Live at the P. O.," 98; *The Wide Net*, 141, 165–66, 168; "The Winds," 14–15, 16, 144, 246; "A Worn Path," 201
Welty, Jefferson, **14**
Welty, Mary Alice, **208**, 221
Welty, Walter, 12, **37**, **140**, 177, 179, 183, 203, **208**
Welty garden: Chestina Welty's diagram, **85**; decline of, 196, 202, 203, 208–9; Lower Garden, **31**, **36**, 37, **38**, **164**, 218, 221; original plant list, 41, 237; schematic layout, **30**; Upper Garden, **28**, **31**, 33, **33**, **36**, 37, 38, **49**, **53**, **84**, **85**, 87, **91**, **92**, 164, 218, **220**. *See also* Maxwell, William (Bill); Russell, Diarmuid: correspondence with Welty
Welty house, **22**, 25, **26**, 27
West Virginia, xix, 3, 4, 5, 9, 97; mountains of, 6, 9; in *The Optimist's Daughter*, 255
White, E. B., 54

White flag iris (*Iris albicans*), 37, 243. *See also* Irises

White star jessamine (*Jasminum nitidum*), 243

Wild phlox (*Phlox divaricata*), 243

Wild wisteria (*Wisteria frutescens*), 243

Wilder, Louise Beebe, *Colour in My Garden*, 40

Wildflowers of the United States (Rickett), 251

William E. Massey Sr. Lectures in the History of American Civilization, 209

Williams, Tennessee, 208

Willow, black (*Salix nigra*), 243

Wilson, Emily Herring, 153

Winslow, Helen M., *The Delineator: An Illustrated Magazine of Literature and Fashion*, 43, 248

Winston-Salem, North Carolina, 219

Winter honeysuckle (*Lonicera fragrantissima*), 41, 235, 237

Wintersweet (*Chimonanthus praecox*), 217

Wisconsin Literary Magazine, 52

Wistaria (or wisteria) (*Wisteria sinensis*), 52, 89, 218, 235, 243

Wisteria frutescens (wild wisteria), 243

Wisteria sinensis (wisteria or wistaria), 52, 89, 218, 235, 243

WJDX (Jackson radio station), **64**, 65

Woman's Club, The, 43, 49, 249; in Jackson, 50, 248

Woman's clubs, 44–45, 49, 248; Federated Women's Clubs, 77; Garden Lovers Group (of Jackson Woman's Club), 43, 50–51, 53, 77, 123; National Association of Colored Women, 248. *See also* Garden clubs

Woman's Land Army, 48, 248; poster, **48**

Woman's National Farm and Garden Association, 47, 76, 248. *See also* Garden clubs, Woman's Land Army

Women's Christian Temperance Union, 99

Woodburn, John, 124, 125

Works Progress Administration, 101, 105–6, **106**, 109, 123, 152

World War I, 12, 23, 44, 48, 98, 157

World War II, xx, 45, 133, 134, **140**, 144, 164–65, **165**, 170, 182, 199, 221; rationing, 155, 157, 164, 166

Yaddo artists' community, 128, **129**

Yardman (yardmen), x, 67, **80**, 107, **107**, 214

Yaupon (*Ilex vomitoria*), 41, 235, 237

Yucca (*Yucca filamentosa*), 243

Zantedeschia aethiopica (calla lily), 235

Zephyranthes (rain lily), 146, 217, 236

Zephyranthes candida (white fairy lily), 242

Zephyranthes rosea (pink fairy lily), 242

Zinnia (*Zinnia elegans*), 37, 90, 98, 99, 101, 109, **110**, 236, 238, 243